The True Story of a Secret Agent's Escape from the IRA and MI5

Dead Man Running

MARTIN McGARTLAND

Best-selling author of
Fifty Dead Men Walking

Hastings House Publishers
9 Mott Ave.
Norwalk, CT 06850

Originally published: Great Britain
MAINSTREAM PUBLISHING, LTD., 1998.

ISBN: 0-8038-2005-4

Printed in the United States of America

Acknowledgments

I would like to thank Sam Cushnahan of FAIT – Families Against Intimidation and Terror – who has not only given me help and guidance in preparing this book but who has worked tirelessly to bring peace to Northern Ireland. Thanks also to Jack McKee, a highly valued community worker, and MP Robert McCartney whose advice I freely sought.

I wish to thank certain members of the Press who have supported and assisted me, including Chris Thornton of the *Belfast Telegraph*, John Cassidy of the *News of the World*, Liam Clarke of the *Sunday Times*, and the writer Kathy Johnston. I want also to thank my hard-working solicitor, Nigel Dodds, and my barrister, Glenn Gatland, two men who gave me the courage to fight the authorities.

There are others, in the Security Services and on both sides of the sectarian divide, whom I also thank but whose identities I can never reveal. And, of course, there is Mike, whose honesty began my search for the truth.

Most importantly, a big thank you to my best friend and partner, Jo, who has supported me during these difficult times when striving for the truth and justice has sapped my strength and my patience. To her I owe a deep sense of gratitude.

Martin McGartland, 1998

CHAPTER ONE

Summer 1998

I awoke with a start in the cold, soft dawn that was Ireland in an autumn mist. The events of the previous night came rushing to my mind and I lay still, not daring to move, listening to the rustling of the grass and straining to hear whether army foot patrols were on the move. But all seemed silent. I lay under the hawthorn hedge giving my mind time to think through what I must do that day, to plan my movements carefully and to avoid any of the traps which I felt sure were waiting for me. I could hear my heart thumping and feel my hands sweat. My whole body shivered like jelly, for the night had been cold and damp and I was wearing nothing save for my everyday clothes; a light zipped jacket, sweatshirt, a pair of jeans and a baseball cap. I shut my mouth to make sure my teeth wouldn't chatter and wrapped my arms around my body in a vain attempt to keep warm.

It was too early to move, just minutes after five o'clock. I knew I had to wait for an hour or two until there were more people about, more activity, more travelers giving me protection in numbers as they headed towards the ferry which would be my sanctuary. Only when I was safely aboard and the ferry had slipped its lines and was heading for Stranraer would I begin to relax. I guessed I was only a mile or so from the docks at Larne, a place I knew well, but also a place which I knew was under twenty-four hour surveillance by the RUC. As I lay in the damp grass I kept making plans for the final lap of my escape, trying to forget the pangs of hunger in my stomach, and wondering what the future would hold. The meadow where I had sought cover that night seemed strangely silent and before me I could see the myriad of colorful flowers so beautiful, innocent and peaceful. And then I saw the poppies, somewhat taller than the other flowers, their pale red petals grabbing my attention. They seemed to mesmerize me. I watched them waving gently in the early morning mist and thoughts of death filled my mind.

I looked at them, almost hypnotized, thinking of the funerals I had attended. The poppies I had seen, always so beautiful and fragile, recalled the most horrible and tragic deaths. Every time my eyes were drawn back to these flowers my mind filled again with images of death and horror, of tears and sadness. I thought of the shootings, the bombings and the mayhem that I had witnessed and my mind recalled the times that I had seen the shocked and scarred children, all but lost amid the funereal black dresses, coats and suits, placing posies of poppies on their daddies' graves.

Buttercups and daisies, hawkbit, harebell, ball-flower, knapweed, St. John's wort and a host of other meadow flowers, whose names I didn't know, I saw that morning as I tried to take my mind off the cold and the fear of what possibly lay ahead. It had been my supervisor in the Youth Training Program, a gentle, kind Orangeman, who had taught me the names of the wild flowers during the time I was training to become a gardener. With others, we would take walks together across Black Mountain, the wild and beautiful hills at the edge of the Ballymurphy estate, the heart of Republican West Belfast. And I had never forgotten them.

That morning the time moved so slowly I thought 6:30 would never arrive. I tried not to look at my watch and deliberately hid it under the sleeve of my sweatshirt. But every time I treated myself to a peek the hands on the watch seemed barely to have moved. At one point I even put the watch to my ear, checking whether it was working. Then I smiled, realizing my battery watch made no noise. To pass the time I dreamed of bacon and eggs, hot sausages and buttered toast all washed down with cups of hot tea and promised myself if I ever made the ferry I would treat myself to the biggest fry-up of my life. But every time I came to my senses I would squeeze back against the prickly hawthorn hedge, making sure the soft rain couldn't reach me and trying to make myself as inconspicuous as a sparrow. More importantly, I scanned that field every few minutes in case, just in case, an RUC or an army foot patrol was out and about.

I wondered whether to try and hitch a lift in a passing car but realized that would be a stupid idea. I probably looked more like a scarecrow than a respectable young man on his way to catch a ferry. And then, of course, I hadn't even taken into consideration the fact that early in the morning many of the people driving to the Larne ferry would have been peelers driving to work or, worse still, plainclothes Special Branch men. 'Fuck,' I thought to myself sternly, 'get a grip of yourself and start thinking straight.'

Every plan I thought of seemed hopeless. Somehow I had to make my way from this God-forsaken sodden meadow along the open road to the ferry without being noticed by any peelers or Special Branch men. It seemed ironic, however, for now I was desperately trying to escape the law having spent most of my adult life desperately trying to keep one step ahead of the IRA who had sworn to kill me on sight. I had, according to the IRA, betrayed the cause and there was only one penalty for traitors – a bullet in the back of the head.

Shortly before 6:30, when the day was light and the rain had stopped, I hit on a plan. I knew it was useless to try and walk the mile to the ferry, not only because of the way I must have looked after a night sleeping in the rough but also because I had to presume that the RUC, and maybe even the British Army, were looking for me.

In my youth on the Ballymurphy estate I had learned the art of hijacking cars. By the age of fourteen I had learned how to get into a locked car without damaging the lock and 'black box' the vehicle – starting the car by by-passing the ignition – within a minute. In those carefree early days when our great sport was baiting the British troops we would have competitions among ourselves, seeing how quickly we could open and start a car as a dare. As a teenager I loved cars. My ambition was to own a really fast car but not some high-speed expensive vehicle, just an ordinary car with a powerful engine. After I turned seventeen and had passed my test, I loved doing spectacular spins, screeching the tires on the asphalt road while kids from the estate roared and cheered their appreciation. And now, I decided, those tricks that I had learned in my teenage years would be put to good use.

Carefully I stood up, my whole body aching from the night beneath the hedge, and peeked through the hawthorn, checking the lay of the land and seeing if many vehicles were about. Over the past hour or more I had heard increasing numbers of cars and lorries heading towards the ferry and knew that the world was awake and about its business. I watched as seven or eight vehicles, mostly cars, roared past my hiding place at about forty to fifty miles an hour. I knew they would be slowing shortly as they approached the docks but those few hundred yards would be too dangerous to risk. I thought of walking alongside the hedge but that was impossible for the hedge soon became a wall; a low, three-foot-high, dry-stone wall which would offer little or no protection. Worse still, if someone did indeed see me creeping along a wall towards the docks, the peelers would be alerted and, within minutes, I would be in a police station answering questions I did not want to hear.

So I decided to nick a car instead.

On the way to my strange refuge beneath the stars that night I had seen a number of houses only a couple of hundred yards from my hiding place and decided to 'borrow' a car from one of them for the run to the ferry. Technically, I knew this was stealing, but I had no intention of actually permanently removing the car, just borrowing it for a matter of minutes. I felt in my pocket, found a ten pound note, and vowed to leave that on the driver's seat as payment for the petrol and use of the car. I hoped that the owner wouldn't be too angry and I felt convinced that he wouldn't mind at all if he realized the pickle I had landed in.

Before venturing out I inspected myself, straightening my jacket, checking that my jeans were passable, pulling out bits and pieces of grass and shrub and wishing that I had a mirror to check my hair and face. For all I knew my hair, naturally unruly, was sticking up and my face could have been smudged with mud from the ground where I had slept. I rubbed my face as though I was washing it and looked at my hands. Clean. That was something. The rest I would trust to luck. I walked gingerly down the side of the hedge to the five-barred gate and, when there was no traffic passing, nipped over.

As I landed on the other side I checked again. Still no traffic. So I quickly ran across the road and began to walk away from the ferry, back towards Belfast. I tried to appear nonchalant, as though I walked along this stretch of road each and every morning on my way to work. A car went by and suddenly I didn't know whether I should wave or not. My training had always emphasized that I should aim to melt into the background on all occasions, never draw attention to myself or whatever I was doing; act naturally and, above all else, stay calm. That morning I consciously thanked my handlers and remembered all they had taught me. I put my head down and pretended not to notice anyone driving along the road. I felt sure that's what they would have advised. And that gave me another idea. I decided to think of their advice before I did anything risky that morning. I pretended I was on an exercise, a training exercise given on occasions by my Special Branch handlers in which they would ask me how I would react or behave in certain circumstances and I would give the answers. These particular tests taught me a lot because, in the beginning, most of the answers I gave were wrong. But this would be one of my biggest tests. And I had to succeed. It was no exaggeration that at that moment I was convinced my life depended on it.

As I walked along the rain-soaked footpath I kept looking surreptitiously hither and thither, hoping to see a car parked in a drive or the roadway. I wanted something ordinary, like a Ford or a Vauxhall, something that I knew would be easy to open and start, and a car which no one would notice or remember. I saw a Rover 800 and decided against that. I saw a couple of small trucks but thought they might be more difficult to start because I had only concentrated on cars. Then, in a driveway on the right, I saw a dirty blue Vauxhall which looked about five or six years old. I looked up and down the road and saw no one about. I glanced at the windows and saw the curtains drawn which, I hoped, meant the people living there were still in bed and, hopefully, sleeping peacefully. There was another great plus. The drive was on a slight gradient, which meant that I could open the car, get inside, let slip the brake and roll out of the drive and perhaps a few yards down the road before needing to start the engine.

I crossed over the road and checked for people and vehicles as I approached the drive. Nothing coming. I took a deep breath, wished myself luck and took a few steps up the short drive which was not much longer than the car. I took another look at the window and to my astonishment, realized the curtains were now open. At the same time I realized the front door was opening and I stood stock still, half in panic, half in fright, as I wondered what the hell I should do.

'Good morning,' I said to the man who looked somewhat astonished to find a total stranger standing in his drive shortly after 6:30 in the morning. 'How are you today?' I continued, not realizing what I was saying, having not thought through my plans for such an eventuality. I cursed myself, realizing that I had not planned well enough. 'Idiot,' I thought. Somehow, my brain had come to my rescue, gone into automatic and the right words were coming out of my mouth. But what to do next?

'Good morning,' said the large, middle-aged man as he tried to come to terms with my presence in his drive. I guessed he was a Protestant, a true Ulsterman, and I decided to slightly alter my accent so that he would think I was a God-fearing young Protestant and not a young nationalist tear-away from West Belfast.

'Are you going towards the ferry?' I asked, trying to sound as if I was asking for the time of day.

'Aye,' he said, looking at me in a strange way. 'Why?'

'Could you give me a lift?' I asked.

'Sure I could,' he said. 'What's the matter? Has your car broken down?'

'Aye,' I lied. 'I couldn't get the damn thing to start this morning. Must have been the damp. I have to be at the docks for 6:30 and it's late now.'

'Get in,' said the man as he opened the door to let me clamber into the front seat beside him.

For a minute I wondered whether he was playing with me. If he suspected that I was an IRA man he only had to drive to the nearest RUC station and I would be done for. I must have looked a sight - scruffy, unshaven, my hair a mess and my clothes dirty. I just prayed that he didn't suspect that I was on the run, still I must have shown all the signs of a young man up to no good. I looked at him more closely as he walked across the front of the car towards the driver's door. He didn't look like a peeler or even a Special Branch man but I knew from experience that SB men can adopt the most extraordinary appearances. I looked at his jacket to see whether I could detect a bulge at his shoulder but could see no sign. I examined his clothes – a pair of dark brown trousers, white shirt, plain tie and brown leather jacket – and thought that he might even have worked at the docks.

'Where are you heading?' he asked, casually enough.

'I'm catching the ferry,' I said. 'Seeing some relatives in Scotland.'

'Well, by the looks of things you shouldn't have too rough a crossing. There's not too much wind about this morning.'

'Fingers crossed,' I replied.

'Are you a good sailor?' he inquired.

'Not bad,' I replied, hoping that the inquisition wouldn't go on much longer.

'Where's your suitcase?' he asked. 'Did you forget it?' and he laughed.

I didn't know what to reply. I searched my mind not knowing how to answer. So I decided to say nothing, to change the subject, pretend I didn't hear the question. 'We're nearly there,' I said as the docks loomed ahead of us out of the early morning mist.

'Where do you want to be dropped?' he asked.

'At the passenger terminal if that's not out of your way,' I replied. 'That would be grand.'

'Not at all,' he replied. 'It's a pleasure.'

As he drew up at the passenger terminal I clambered out, wondering if I was in a daydream. I could not believe that this man had been the genuine article, straight and honest and ready enough to believe my preposterous story. 'That's very kind of you,' I said as I stood on the road by the side of the car. 'Thanks a million.'

'Think nothing of it,' he said. 'See you around.'

'Aye. Look after yourself and good luck,' I replied and slammed shut the door. I walked quickly into the terminal and turned as if to wave but he had gone. I went back to the door to check that he was in fact driving away and not searching out some peeler to tell of the scruffy young man he had found in his driveway acting suspiciously. I watched as he drove his car away to the other side of the docks and I lost him.

'Don't worry,' I said to myself, 'remember you're a lucky bastard. You've been in worse scrapes than this and you've always come up smelling of roses.'

I was dying for a hot cup of tea and, before checking in, went to the cafeteria. I could smell the hot food; the sizzling bacon, the hot toast but I had this nagging suspicion that if I ate now, rather than on the boat, I would tempt fate and never make my escape. So I sat in a corner with my back to the wall, watching the entrance to the café, checking in case the peelers had been alerted and were searching for me. I sat there for fifteen minutes, drinking the sweet, hot tea slowly, relishing every sip. Every minute that ticked by gave me confidence. I checked everyone coming into the café and reckoned that no one looked suspicious. After ten minutes I guessed that the coast was clear for if I had been reported as a suspicious character the authorities would have been there with their guns in minutes. I was clean, carrying no weapon, and if they had come for me I could have done nothing but gone quietly. A smile crossed my lips as I finished my tea, gaining in confidence every second, knowing that my luck had held. If luck had gone against me I knew that I would now be in police custody replying to questions I had no wish to answer. I checked through my pockets, searching every one, pulling out the linings to make sure that I had no incriminating evidence on me; nothing bearing my old name, address, driving license or credit card. All I had was an English driving license bearing my alias, Martin Ashe. Throughout the forty-eight hours I was in Northern Ireland I kept the Ashe driving license hidden in my waistband. If I had been stopped and taken in for questioning by the peelers I had no wish for them to discover my alias. I was clean. I just had £50 in notes on me and nothing else. It was time to go.

Forty-five minutes later I stood in the shadow of the ship's funnel and looked back at the Larne docks as the ferry moved out into clear water. As I gazed at the seabirds squawking overhead, a wonderful relief, a sense of freedom, surged through my heart. I went down to the café and ordered the meal I had dreamed of in the early hours of that morning as I lay beneath the hedge. Every mouthful tasted like heaven. As I drank my second cup of hot, sweet tea that morning, however, I became more serious, more somber, as I realized with near certainty that an attempt had been made by British Intelligence to have me kidnapped and murdered by the IRA.

CHAPTER TWO

Only a few weeks earlier, in September 1997, I had answered a call on my mobile phone, a call that would change my life, shatter my illusions and cause me nights of anxiety. I was in my flat at a secret address in England when I answered the phone and heard a voice I thought I recognized talking loudly, 'Hello, Marty, how are you?'

'I'm fine,' I said, speaking quietly, 'but who's this?'

'It's an old friend calling you from Belfast,' came the reply. 'You know me from way back and I know you.'

That introduction sounded ominous to me so I decided to play it cool. 'Will you give me a name,' I asked, 'and stop keeping me in suspense?'

'You knew me as Mike,' the man replied in a more somber voice. 'I used to work with your two pals Felix and Mo.'

It took me a few seconds to search my memory, trying to remember someone named Mike who had worked with my two SB handlers, Felix and Mo. Suddenly, in my mind's eye, I could see the face and the build of the man but his voice sounded younger than I expected. 'What can I do you for?' I asked cagily for I still wasn't sure he was the man I recalled.

'It's not what you can do for me,' he replied, 'it's what I can do for you.'

'What do you mean?' I asked, fascinated by his approach.

'I'm coming over to England soon,' he replied. 'Can we meet somewhere? Anywhere that's easy for you.'

'What do you want to see me about?' I asked, deliberately sounding suspicious about receiving this call out of the blue.

'I'll tell you this,' he said. 'I've read your book, *Fifty Dead Men*

Walking, and I have some information that you will find very interesting. I don't want to say too much on this line. Let me put it this way. They've taken some liberties with you, and it's not right the way you were treated. I just want to help.'

The friendly bonhomie, the call from a virtual stranger and the fact that he wanted to see me made me deeply suspicious of his motives. I thought, 'What liberties, and who has taken those liberties with me?' It seemed odd, strange even, that someone like Mike, whom I hardly knew, would want to see me. But my interest quickly got the better of me and, I told myself, what possible problem could there be talking to an old SB mate? 'You're on,' I replied. 'When do you want to meet?'

Mike told me he would be traveling to the mainland in the near future and would be staying in Birmingham during a forty-eight hour flying visit to England, arriving by train at New Street Station. We agreed to a date and a place to meet. I felt I could trust Mike because I had met him a few times in Belfast when I was in the Holywood army base recovering from injuries that I had sustained in my dive through the window. I also recalled that he was a good mate of Felix and Mo, which meant I could trust him. If he had just been some Irishman, a stranger whose identity I didn't know, then I would never have dreamed of meeting him. I would automatically have presumed that he was IRA and I knew why they would want to see me. Ever since I had fled Northern Ireland in 1991 I had been suspicious of anyone phoning me, either on my mobile or, more importantly, on my ex-directory BT line at home.

I went to the Grand Hotel in the center of Birmingham one hour ahead of our scheduled meeting to check out the place and see if there were any suspicious characters hanging around. When I walked in, dressed in my black Kicker boots, jeans, shirt and bomber jacket, I felt a bit awkward, for the hotel certainly lived up to its name. I was taking no chances and checked out the various entrances and exits. I was not being hypersensitive or suspicious, just sensible. Felix and Mo had drilled into me during my years with the SB that I always had to take care, check everything possible, ensuring that I didn't walk into some IRA trap. This time I saw nothing to alert me, so I went to the lounge, sat in a corner with a newspaper and ordered a cup of tea.

I recognized Mike the moment he walked into the room. He came straight over to me, a smile on his face and a firm handshake to greet me. I was relieved to see him for now I was certain that this was no IRA trap. 'How are you doing?' he asked, in his baritone Northern Ireland accent. 'You look in fine fettle.'

'Aye, I'm fine,' I said. 'How are you?'

In the back of my mind, however, I was still somewhat suspicious. I had known Mike for only a few months but never as a great friend or confidant. He had always seemed a man full of bonhomie and light talk, yet we had never had a serious conversation despite the fact that he was an SB handler. I still wondered what on earth he wanted to talk to me for some six years after I had left Belfast.

'Do you fancy a beer?' he asked, jovially enough.

'No, not for me,' I replied with a laugh. 'Never drink in the middle of the day and very little at night. It's not good for you.'

'Nothing ever wrong in supping a pint of the black stuff,' he said, and walked over to the bar to buy a pint of Guinness.

I watched him walk away, looked to check whether he was carrying a gun in a shoulder holster or in the back of his trousers but could see no suspicious bulges. As he sat down Mike trotted out all the polite chit-chat, asking me how I was, about my mother and what I was doing for a job. I understood he was trying to be jolly and likable, putting me at my ease, cracking the odd joke, and I kept wondering why. His approach was making me nervous.

After a couple of minutes I had heard enough. I looked Mike straight in the eye. 'What is it, Mike? What do you want? What do you want to see me about?'

'Let me finish my pint and we'll go for a walk,' he said. 'I want to talk.'

The idea of going for a walk, with someone whom I had never had to trust in my life, sent a warning shock wave through my mind. I recalled the times that such an invitation had been made to me in Belfast; that the same invitation had been made to dozens of people; and nearly always such a request meant only trouble - if not a punishment beating, a kneecapping or worse. But then I realized that I wasn't in Belfast but in an English city, crowded with lunchtime passers-by, a place where it was most unlikely that someone would try to knock me off. However, I was taking nothing for granted.

'Why can't we talk here?' I asked. 'There's not many people around.'

'Those days are long gone,' said Mike. 'Stop worrying. We're not in Northern Ireland now. No one's going to take you out. In any case you should know from all your training that neither of us would talk in a public place like this.'

'Honest?' I said and half-smiled, making sure that he realized that I was very much on my guard whatever surprise he had in store for me.

As we walked through the city center we turned into the churchyard surrounding St. Philip's Cathedral and found a bench where we could sit and chat in privacy, where no one could overhear our conversation. I deliberately sat on his right side because I had taken with me my *Olympus* micro-cassette recorder which I kept in my left-hand pocket nearest to him. I was taking nothing on face value, not even someone allegedly bringing me news I would want to hear. In the background, however, was the constant noise of city center traffic. It was a perfect place to sit and chat because no one could overhear our conversation, but I hoped the noise wouldn't drown out his words on the recorder.

'Spill the beans then,' I said. 'What's this all about?'

'This is difficult,' Mike began, 'but I believe the Branch owe it to you.'

'Owe me what?' I asked in my naiveté. 'I've had a pay off.'

'I'm not talking about that,' he said. 'This is far more serious.'

I looked at him, waiting for him to continue, saying nothing.

'I read and I re-read your book *Fifty Dead Men Walking*,' he said. 'I should think most of the RUC and the SB read it. It was good, very good. You caught the mood of Northern Ireland and the risks you ran as an agent working for the Branch. I liked it.'

'Thanks,' I said.

'But I didn't come over here to tell you that,' he went on. 'I came to tell you what wasn't in the book.'

'What do you mean?'

'The ending,' he went on. 'It wasn't like that, wasn't like that at all.'

'Like what?'

He breathed in deeply and looked at the ground as he explained what he was trying to say. 'It wasn't like you wrote in the book. You thought that the IRA kidnapped you, that two of their well-known henchmen somehow took you from underneath the very noses of the Special Branch, spirited you out of Sinn Fein headquarters, then drove you undetected the mile or so to Twinbrook, where you were walked into a block of flats and held prisoner for most of the day.'

'That's right,' I said. 'That's exactly what happened.'

'Well,' he said, pausing and peering into my eyes, a look of anxiety across his face. 'It wasn't like that, Marty, it was nothing like that at all. What I'm about to tell you might shock you but I think you should know what happened. I've talked it over with the others and they think we owe it to you to tell you the truth, so that you won't be taken unawares if anyone tries to have a go at you. It's only fair that you should know what the fuck is going on.'

'You've lost me,' I said. 'But go on.'

'Before I continue, however, I want to tell you that no senior officers know I'm over here talking to you. And I wouldn't have come over if I hadn't read your book. One or two people who care for you, who know you risked your life time and again for the Branch, know I'm here, but no one of authority knows that. And certainly no one in MI5 or the RUC.'

'Why wouldn't you tell them?' I asked in my innocence, not knowing what the hell he was talking about.

'Because if they knew I had planned to visit you, to tell you the truth of what happened, they would have found a way to stop me. I don't know what they would have done but I do know they would have found a way of preventing me seeing you.'

'But why?' I asked, now eager to know what the hell Mike was talking about.

'Because, Marty, it was a set-up,' Mike explained, speaking slowly. 'You were set up, deliberately set up by the intelligence services because they wanted you out of the way. You weren't meant to survive the kidnapping.'

'What!' I said in disbelief. 'What the fuck are you telling me?'

I felt myself go pale and began to shake, not knowing how to answer, not knowing what the hell to say to such a suggestion. I could not believe for one moment that my pals Felix and Mo, my handlers who had taken such care of me over four years, could have arranged to have me kidnapped and killed. My mind raced back to that day in August 1991 and I mentally recreated the whole journey from the moment I drove away from my home in West Belfast to make the fateful trip to the Sinn Fein headquarters in Andersonstown. Now I wanted to know more.

'How do you know this?' I asked, my voice a mixture of anguish and bitterness, as I thought of the trust in which I held Felix and Mo. 'It can't be true, it can't,' I said, feeling a sense of emptiness, of anxiety.

'Listen,' said Mike, 'calm down and let me explain. You knew from the moment you left your home in that green Nissan that the SB were following you, keeping an eye on you. You spoke to Felix when you stopped for a couple of minutes and phoned Castlereagh asking if there had been a change of plan; making sure that the SB wanted you to go ahead with the meeting with Podraig Wilson at Sinn Fein headquarters. And remember how Felix joked with you about your driving that day, dodging here and there in case you were being followed by the IRA? You carried out the plan as instructed, leaving your car some distance from Connolly House, a place kept under regular surveillance by various branches of the RUC. Then you walked out of Sinn Fein headquarters in broad daylight in the custody of two well-known IRA men. You walked to their car nearby and were driven away to Twinbrook. Right?'

'Right,' I said.

'But just think for one minute,' Mike went on. 'Doesn't it strike you as extraordinary that no SB man, no surveillance unit, not even E4A, the RUC surveillance unit, followed you? No one intervened, no one moved a muscle to stop the kidnapping. Marty, you weren't some two-bit tout [informer] but one of the most successful agents the Branch had in Northern Ireland at that time. Your book was right. You saved countless lives, probably far more than the fifty you claimed. You were a vital cog in the intelligence set-up for more than four years, taking the most extraordinary risks but, nevertheless, coming up with great material which helped trap IRA men and save people's lives. You were someone the Branch would have done all in their power to protect. But they didn't. The SB allowed two well-known IRA men to lift you, drive you away and hold you prisoner for a day. You must have known how easy it would have been for the SB, using either a vehicle or a chopper, to track that car. They do it every day. But on this occasion they did nothing.'

'But why? Why did they not raise a finger to follow me?' I interjected, now desperate to hear more, though my heart was pounding at everything Mike was telling me.

'Yes,' he replied, 'that's why I'm here. I thought you should know the truth. The British Intelligence services, the guys who really control the Government's anti-terrorist machine in Northern Ireland, were supposedly protecting someone else, a very senior intelligence agent who had managed to infiltrate the highest echelons of the IRA. They were fearful his identity might have been accidentally revealed if you were ever caught at some future date. They maintained they couldn't take that risk. The Joint Irish Section – you know, the intelligence chiefs – believed that the IRA were on your trail, that you had become too much of a security risk and so the decision was taken to sacrifice you.'

I sat there on the rough, wooden bench facing the church with the cold wind whipping at my jacket, and suddenly I felt lonely and helpless. I put my head in my hands and stared at the patch of bare earth beneath me. I wondered what the hell I was hearing. I wanted to cry, to scream, to stamp around and swear and yell at what had happened, as I suddenly realized that people whom I trusted as my friends had simply used me for their own ends and simply cast me aside as someone of no consequence. The real pain was worse than that; it was knowing that during those four years of working together I had meant nothing to them. I couldn't believe that the camaraderie they showed had all been a sham; I couldn't believe that the relationship we had enjoyed, the jokes we had shared, were nothing more than a ruse, an affectation, a deception to encourage me to keep risking my neck. And for what? For their glorification, their next pay rise, their next rung up the fucking RUC ladder. Maybe they hadn't known of the plot to have me kidnapped; maybe they too had been kept in the dark about the evil machinations going on at a higher level in the Government's intelligence set-up. I took out a handkerchief and blew my nose hard, trying to rid myself of the painful thoughts racing through my mind.

'But you don't know whether Felix and Mo were responsible for the kidnapping?' I asked tentatively, not knowing if I wanted to hear Mike's answer or not.

'I'm sure they weren't responsible,' replied Mike. 'In fact, I'm sure they had no knowledge that you had been set up. We at the SB believe that your kidnapping was arranged by the Joint Irish Section, probably in collusion with the most senior SB officers in Northern Ireland. They would sacrifice their own grandmothers in their fight against terrorism.'

'So Felix and Mo may well not have known about it?' I asked with some enthusiasm, desperately hoping that they knew nothing of the betrayal, giving me something to hold on to, something to believe in.

'That's true,' Mike replied. 'From the way they behaved afterwards I am convinced they knew nothing of the plot to have you kidnapped and murdered.'

'So why did you tell me?' I asked.

'For two reasons. First, because I thought you should know. And secondly, to put you on your guard, to make you aware that the IRA might not be the only people looking for you. To make sure you keep eyes in the back of your head and trust no one. Take it from me, Marty, in this rotten game you can't trust a soul, not even those that are meant to be protecting you.'

'Do you really mean that MI5 would have sold me down the river?'

'Without a doubt,' he replied, not waiting a second to confirm my worst fears. 'They've done it before and they've done it since. And I'm sure they will do it again. This is a rotten, dirty game, Marty, and you were right at the center of it. We suspect that MI5 may even have arranged your kidnapping directly with the IRA.'

'What!' I said, disbelief in my voice. 'I don't believe you. That's impossible. That's fucking treachery.'

'I know it is. I agree with you,' replied Mike, 'but that's the way they work. MI5 have their contacts with the IRA at the highest level and they always have had. We suspect they gave the IRA the wink, told them where to arrange a meet and then told your SB handlers to make sure you attended that meeting at Sinn Fein head-quarters.'

'But I thought the SB were watching over me,' I protested. 'Felix told me that they would make sure I was kept under constant surveillance because they feared I might be kidnapped by the IRA. The last words Felix told me were to take care but not to worry because he was keeping me under constant surveillance.'

'They were,' said Mike. 'But as soon as you parked your car and walked into Connolly House the SB were called off the operation by the TCG who took over its responsibility. Remember, Marty, the Tasking Co-ordination Group comprised members of MI5, the SAS and military intelligence. Remember that the SB have to take their orders directly from JIS and the TCG, and the Special Branch were simply pulled off the case, leaving you to fend for yourself.'

'But that's wicked, despicable,' I said, stumbling over my words in my frustration and anger. 'That's betrayal; in fact it's worse than that, Mike. Basically, they were arranging my kidnapping, knowing I would be murdered. In essence those officers in JIS were guilty of conspiracy to murder. What shits, what cunts. Are you sure, really certain that everything you're telling me is true? I find it hard to believe that MI5 officers would treat people like that.'

'Well, they can and they do,' said Mike. 'There have been others too, Marty; touts, informers and agents who have worked for the Brits during the Troubles and then, when JIS believe they might have passed their sell-by date, they just arrange a convenient kidnapping or so-called "accidental" death. You must remember that MI5 officers and senior IRA men do talk to each other. These things are arranged on both sides. Let me ask you a question: when did you last hear of a senior IRA man or an MI5 officer being murdered? Not for years. And I'll tell you why. Because sometimes they find it necessary to talk to the IRA.'

'Really?' I said. 'Do you mean they conspire together?'

'Sometimes, yes, of course, but it's not really a conspiracy,' said Mike. 'Officially, of course, it is always denied but it certainly goes on.'

'Do you know, Mike,' I said, 'I feel sick, physically sick, at all you've told me. I just didn't believe things like that went on.'

'Marty,' Mike said, 'if you hadn't had the courage to leap out of that window I don't think you would have been tortured. I think the IRA would have just taken you away somewhere and shot you in the back of the head, probably leaving your body in West Belfast, so that some Catholics would have found you. Then the IRA would have issued a statement saying that you had been a traitor, working for the RUC. They would have painted your name as black as possible so even your own mother would have been ashamed to visit the shops or walk out on the streets for fear of what neighbors and friends would say to her.'

'That's horrible,' I said. 'I gave my all for those fuckers. I risked my neck to save other people's lives and they repaid me by arranging for me to be kidnapped by the IRA. That's fucking great, isn't it?'

'Come on,' said Mike, 'let's go and have a cup of tea.'

'Aye,' I said, getting up from the hard wooden bench as though I had the weight of the world on my shoulders. 'I feel deflated, empty,' I said. 'Now everything's gone out of my life. I thought I had done a good job, I felt that my work in Belfast had been worthwhile, that I had contributed something to Northern Ireland. Now it seems the powers that be thought I was nothing but a piece of shit. They had their pound of flesh from me and nothing else mattered to them. They treated me like a bit of scum. God, it makes me angry.'

We found our way to a McDonald's and Mike treated me to a beef burger, chips and a Coke. He ordered the same. We sat across the table from each other and as I munched my way through the Big Mac I looked him in the eye, the anger rising within me as I thought how close I had come to death. I thought back to those moments in the bathroom before making the decision to jump through the window forty feet above ground; moments when I was undecided whether to jump or not; and now I realized that if I hadn't taken that risk I would be a dead man, my mother's reputation would be blackened and tarnished and the rest of my family treated like lepers amongst the Catholics of West Belfast. I shuddered as I thought of the stress that my mother would have suffered, having brought me up as a Republican.

'I really believed in Felix, Mo and Ray,' I said at the end of a long silence, my voice full of misery.

'You still should,' said Mike, obviously trying to cheer me up. 'They believed in you. If they had known that you were entering the lion's den with no chance of escape they would never have let you walk into Connolly House.'

'Is that so?' I asked.

'Hand on heart,' said Mike, 'I know that Felix thought of you almost as a son. He would never have let anything happen to you if he had known such a trap had been set.'

'So you think it was a trap then?' I asked.

'I don't think so,' he replied, 'I know it was.'

'And now?' I asked. 'What's the situation now?'

'What do you mean?' asked Mike.

'Are the bastards still after me? Do MI5 still want me dead or have they given up?'

'I don't think they're still after you. But I can't be sure. They have no reason to be. You left Belfast six years ago and you can't give away any secrets. Everything's changed. Of course they would know your address in England and your new identity. And they haven't tried anything, have they?'

'Not as far as I know,' I said.

'Exactly,' Mike replied. 'I believe you're safe from British Intelligence, but I wouldn't swear on it.'

'But why would MI5 want to bump me off?' I asked incredulously. 'Why didn't they just put me on a flight to the mainland and have done with it if they thought I could have betrayed someone accidentally?'

'I don't know,' said Mike, 'but they have their reasons, no matter how convoluted those reasons might be.'

'And what about the IRA?' I asked. 'I presume they're still after me.'

'Of course,' Mike replied, 'no doubt about it. Look what they did to your brother.'

In July, 1996 my brother Joseph was at home in Moyard, West Belfast, when an IRA punishment team of five men, all wearing balaclavas, pushed their way into his house, tied and gagged him and carried him out to a waiting van. They drove a short distance away, dragged him from the van, tied a rope around his ankles and hung him upside down from a fence. Then they began beating his legs, body and arms with a baseball bat and hitting his chest with a plank of wood with nails embedded in it. The appalling beating went on for fifteen minutes. It left Joseph with two shattered legs, four broken ribs and two broken arms. He was unable to walk for three months. No reason was ever given by the IRA thugs for the beating. But Joseph and I knew why; he happened to be my younger brother and, according to the twisted, cowardly code of

IRA punishment squads, that was sufficient justification to inflict a terrible beating on a totally innocent young man.

After a couple of minutes, I replied dourly, 'Do you think I can ever forget?'

Mike went on. 'Listen, Marty, you're out of Belfast, living at a secret location in England, difficult for the IRA to trace or find you. And it's probably impossible for them to take any action against you while you're living in an English city. They have no back-up here; they have no West Belfast to hide you. No, you've no need to worry now. But keep your head down to be on the safe side.'

'Don't worry,' I replied, 'I always keep something under my pillow just in case. If I thought the IRA were going to burst into my house I would do what I had to do. I would answer to the law later.'

'But always remember,' said Mike, 'never do anything rash and always keep cool.'

'Don't worry, I'm not daft,' I replied. 'Remember, I was well trained by your mob.'

He smiled. 'I never thought you were stupid,' he said. 'Not even when you were a kid. You were a damn good source, your handlers were always singing your praises. Remember what Detective Superintendent Ian Phoenix [head of the Northern Ireland police counter-surveillance unit] said of you?'

'Aye,' I said.

'Phoenix said that Carol, your code-name, was certainly one of the SB's best spies in Northern Ireland in 1990-91. Remember, Marty, they can't take that away from you.'

'What do you think I should do then?' I asked, hoping for some inspiration from Mike.

'That's up to you,' he said. 'I can't make up your mind for you. It depends how hurt and angry you feel. But for now take my advice and do nothing. Go home and sleep on it. See how you feel in the morning; see if the anger subsides. It should do. Look on the bright side, Marty. You're young, healthy, alive and fit; you've got your whole life ahead of you. Forget about Northern Ireland, the

IRA, the RUC, British intelligence and all that shit. Think of the future.'

'What future?' I asked, still feeling despondent.

'Well, put it this way. Have you got a girlfriend?'

'Not really,' I replied, 'nothing serious. I tend to live on my own because of everything that happened in Belfast. I believe the IRA are still after me so I don't like taking any risks. I've had scares but so far no one has actually tracked me down, thank God. None of the people I meet, none of the girls I date, none of my drinking mates, have any idea of my background. I tell them nothing because I don't want to cause any trouble or aggro for any innocents. I don't like girls staying the night. You never know when they might start nosing around. Mike, listen to me, since Northern Ireland I don't trust anyone any more. And after what you've told me today I trust them even less.'

'I understand,' he said. Changing the subject, he asked, 'Do you ever see your wife Angie, or your nippers, Martin and Podraig?'

'No, never,' I told him.

Before we left the restaurant Mike gave me his telephone number and, in return, I gave him my mobile number, but not my ex-directory one. I knew, of course, that he had the number already but I was taking no chances with my home number. He was a member of the SB, he was friends with Felix and Mo, but now, more than ever, I felt I could trust no one. I don't know what I would have done without a mobile phone because it was my link, my one link, with the rest of the world. I could give that number to anyone and no one could trace me. It also gave me a sense of security and, sometimes, I needed that. With the news that Mike had brought me, I needed that security more than ever.

I walked Mike to the railway station and he boarded the next train north. I remembered his parting words: 'Keep your head down and take care. And don't do anything rash. If you want me at any time you know where you can find me. Okay?'

'Okay,' I replied.

'Good luck,' said Mike. And he was gone.

I watched his train gently gather speed out of the station and disappear. I turned on my heel and walked away to find my own train, wondering what the hell to do, wondering why Mike had taken the trouble to come and explain what had happened to me. What he had told me, I could not take at face value and yet everything he had said made sense. I had a lot of thinking to do.

CHAPTER THREE

I had thought long and hard about everything Mike, my SB pal, had told me. I tried to dismiss his theories but the more I turned over the matter in my mind the more certain I became that he had been telling the truth. Everything he had said made sense, making me both worried, unsure of myself and fucking angry. I spent sleepless nights wondering what I should do and days walking through the Northumbria countryside trying to decide what action I should take.

I realized that returning to Belfast, the city where I was born and raised, the city that for more than twenty-five years had been a battleground between Protestants and Catholics, the city where I had turned my back on the IRA and started working for the RUC Special Branch, would be a massive gamble. I knew that I might be risking my life but to me there was no choice. I was determined to discover the truth, to discover who had been responsible for putting my life at risk and whether there had been an MI5 plot to have me kidnapped and killed. The information that Mike had given me during our meeting in Birmingham had come as such a shock that I knew I could not rest until I had discovered the truth. For four years I had risked my life helping to save the lives of British soldiers, RUC officers, prison officers and members of the public, only to learn that British Intelligence had arranged my kidnap in the hope that it would lead to my murder.

Sometimes, as I walked alone in the beautiful Cheviot Hills or Harwood Forest outside Newcastle, I struggled to imagine why those who ran British Intelligence in Belfast could have been so wicked, unprincipled and callous that they would sacrifice one of their own men who had done nothing but work for them and save the lives of innocent people. Yet, seemingly they could, and they did, without blinking an eye. Those thoughts made me both angry and resentful.

My thoughts returned to that day in August 1991 when the IRA sent Carol, a lovely young messenger, to call me to a meeting with Podraig Wilson, at Connolly House, the Sinn Fein headquarters in Belfast. I knew Wilson was the head of IRA discipline, the man who decided who should be kneecapped and who should receive beatings by the IRA's thuggish punishment squads. Before accepting the invitation to meet him, however, I had phoned my Special Branch handler Felix seeking his advice. The very thought of walking into Sinn Fein headquarters scared the hell out of me, and the fact that I had been called to see Podraig Wilson, of all people, made me feel as if I was about to receive a death sentence.

'I'm in loads of trouble,' I said to him, my hands shaking nervously as I clambered into Felix's car an hour later. I had driven through a myriad of back streets for my meeting with Felix that day for I was convinced that if the IRA had called me to a meeting with Podraig Wilson they would be keeping a twenty-four hour watch on my movements. I drove with one eye on the rear-view mirror and zig-zagged in and out of a number of housing estates, making sure that the IRA were not following. And yet I was still shaking like a leaf when I met Felix.

'Calm down,' he reassured me, 'and speak slowly. What's up?'

I explained exactly what had happened and the date that had been fixed for me to meet Podraig Wilson – 10 a.m. the following day.

'I understand,' he said, speaking slowly as he thought what to do. 'Don't worry. I'll have to take advice on this one as to how we're going to play it. But, rest assured, I won't let you down. We'll take care of you.'

For the next few hours I drove around Belfast, keeping well away from my home and from any Republican areas. I was taking no risks. At 3 p.m., I phoned Felix as arranged, expecting him to tell me that the Special Branch would move me to a safe house or even out of Northern Ireland entirely until the danger had passed. My chin was shaking as I heard Felix tell me that senior Special Branch officers had decided that I should attend the meeting with Wilson the following morning. Felix told me to borrow a friend's car and drive to Connolly House, park the car at Andersonstown Leisure Center and tell Wilson that I had taken a black taxi.

As I put down the phone, the palms of my hands were sweating and I was shaking. I walked from the phone box trying to convince myself that with Felix and the Special Branch watching over me I would be quite safe. That night I didn't sleep a wink but tossed and turned, wondering if I was being foolish or whether I should steal away in the night, catch the ferry to Scotland and disappear. As dawn arrived, however, I managed to convince myself that I had become paranoid, that I had never been let down by my handlers and that the two people I trusted most were my two SB friends. Over the four years I had worked for British Intelligence I had developed almost a father-son relationship with Felix, and Mo had always been a good mate. In any case I firmly believed that the IRA would never try to kidnap me at Connolly House, which was kept under constant surveillance by the Special Branch. 'They would be stupid to try that one,' I told myself.

That morning my mother ironed a pair of jeans for me and I looked at her, happy that she was oblivious to the fear that gripped me. I felt a great surge of emotion; I wanted to confess everything to her, about the IRA, the Special Branch and the job that I had been doing during those last four years. I also wanted to tell her that I believed the IRA now knew that I worked for the Branch and that my life was in very real danger. But I told her nothing. I knew it wouldn't be fair to subject my ma to hours, days, maybe weeks of fear and worry over my safety. I didn't even kiss her goodbye that morning, though I desperately wanted to put my arms around her and tell her how much I loved her. But I had never been like that with my mother before and I knew such behavior would alarm her. So I let it go and walked out of her life with a cheery 'Bye, Ma.'

As I drove to Connolly House, however, I suffered a panic

attack, convinced I was walking into an IRA trap. I had to phone Felix to check that all was well and to seek reassurance that I was right to go ahead with what I believed was a madcap adventure. I circled a roundabout three times and stopped at the phone box.

'Is that you, Felix?' I asked when I was put through.

'I can tell you, boy, that you are going to cause loads of shit if you keep on turning circle after circle like that. You're sending our heads in a spin with all your antics.' And he laughed.

His laugh brought a wave of relief to me. The boost to my confidence was wonderful, knowing that the SB were keeping such a close eye on me they even knew how many times I had circled the roundabout. I drove on to my destination, my spirits higher than they had been for days. I parked the car as Felix had advised and walked to the Sinn Fein headquarters. I looked idly around me but saw no one who even remotely seemed like a Branch man in disguise.

The receptionist informed me that Podraig Wilson had not yet arrived for work but said I could wait as I had an appointment to meet him. Twenty minutes later, two IRA men, both of whom I recognized, walked into the office. One, Paul 'Chico' Hamilton, was in his forties; a bearded, overweight man who liked to think he was one of the IRA's hard men. Instinctively, I hated Chico from the moment I met him because I knew him to be an active member of an IRA punishment squad. Some senior IRA men who had known Chico from the 1970s nicknamed him 'Budgie' because he sang to the RUC when arrested in 1977 for his part in the attempted murder of a major in the Gordon Highlanders. He was sentenced to twelve years' jail. I also knew his companion, James 'Jim' McCarthy, a slim-built man in his thirties with a mustache, who also had a reputation for organizing and taking part in punishment beatings. Some years earlier, 'Jim' had himself been disciplined, given a kneecapping by an IRA punishment squad. Jim was known as one of the men who would interrogate victims before deciding their punishment. He also liked to think he had the reputation of being a ladies' man when, in reality, most women despised

McCarthy for they knew he would take advantage of his power to seduce them. In 1977 McCarthy was found guilty of possessing arms and ammunition and sentenced to five years' jail. Later, Hamilton and McCarthy became the trusted henchmen of Sinn Fein President Gerry Adams, employed as his personal bodyguards.

Jim said, 'Marty, are you waiting for Podraig?'

'Aye, I am. Why?'

'Podraig sent us to tell you that he's sorry he can't see you here. You can either go away and make another appointment or we could take you to where he is now.'

For two seconds I thought about the option. I knew that if these two fellows tried to take me away I would beat the shit out of them and walk away with only a few bruises. At heart I knew they were cowards, all mouth and no trousers. I also thought that if Podraig was happy for me to come back another day then the matter couldn't be that serious. 'Okay, I'll go with you,' I said and walked out of the office and down the steps to the road.

'Marty, did you bring a car with you?' Chico asked casually.

'No,' I replied, 'I took a black taxi.'

The three of us walked out of Connolly House and around the corner to a white Ford Fiesta. Jim McCarthy drove, Chico sat in the passenger seat and I clambered in the back. Jim drove faster than I expected, speeding through traffic lights that had just turned red, making me aware that it would be difficult for a pursuing car to keep up. But I felt reassured that RUC-trained drivers would have little difficulty in keeping track of me. I deliberately never looked behind me because that would have given the game away. I kept looking at other vehicles wondering if any Branch men were in them and keeping an eye on me. The further we drove away from Andersonstown the more vulnerable and isolated I became. And the more worried. Throughout the journey Chico never stopped talking, trying to be friendly and chatty, obviously attempting to put me at my ease. Both men knew that I had a reputation for violence if ever I was caught in a desperate situation. We drove out of Andersonstown, through Suffolk and into Twinbrook, a mainly residential area south-west of Belfast. We came to a halt outside a small four-story block of flats in Broom Park, a quiet road which seemed almost deserted. As I walked into the block I noticed IRA graffiti daubed over the walls and doors in different colored chalks and paints and the place smelt of urine. We walked up to the third floor and through a brown front door. I closed the door behind me and my heart sank as the catch clicked shut.

There was a third man whom I had never seen before standing in the kitchen and Jim McCarthy went to talk to him. Then Chico went to join them in the kitchen and I could hear them whispering but I had no idea what they were saying. Then the three men came out into the hallway.

'Listen,' said Jim, 'Provisional IRA. You're under arrest.'

I could see them shaking. Then McCarthy pulled out a hand-gun. 'Lie face down on the floor,' he said, 'and don't try anything.' I felt the stub of the automatic pushed against my head. At that moment I thought they were about to pull the trigger and I braced myself waiting for the shot. Seconds passed and I was still alive. They took off my trainers, made me lie on the sofa and, their hands trembling with nerves, took the laces from the shoes and eventually managed to tie my hands together in front of my body and bind my ankles. Then they fetched a blanket from a bedroom and threw it over me.

'Don't try anything, Marty, don't try anything,' Jim kept repeating nervously as he waved the hand-gun around.

Jim went off to the telephone, Chico turned on the radio and sat at the end of the sofa reading a newspaper; the young lad was sitting in the chair opposite reading a book. 'Remember,' Chico would say every few minutes, 'don't try anything, we've got a gun in the kitchen.'

The radio DJ was playing melodies and love songs and I thought of all the young people leading carefree, happy lives, many in love with someone. And I thought of myself, still a young man in his twenties, lying on a sofa like a trussed turkey, waiting for a bullet in the back of the head. I knew there was no escape for me.

I knew what lay ahead. I knew that I would be interrogated and tortured by what the IRA calls its Civil Administration Team, a polite, innocuous term for a gang of torturers. I knew I was about to be burned with cigarette stubs, given electric shock treatment, beaten and smashed with iron bars and baseball bats, probably given the IRA water torture – my head held underwater until I lost consciousness. And the punishment gang would continue until I confessed to being an informant. Armed with that confession, which I suspected they would tape as proof of my guilt, I would be taken somewhere and shot in the back of the head. Even if I had been entirely innocent the treatment would have been the same. If the IRA thought someone was guilty of an offense against the cause they would be tortured and beaten until they confessed. I always remembered what Felix told me from time to time: 'Marty, remember. If ever the IRA capture you never tell them you worked for us no matter what hell they put you through. Because if you confess you're a dead man. If somehow you can maintain your innocence despite terrible tortures you will at least survive. The IRA will only kill you if you confess.'

And he would usually add, 'I'm glad you understand the score. I don't want you to think this job is just a picnic, a little bit of fun to earn a few quid. This is deadly serious. I want you to know that a number of my close friends have been killed by the IRA since the Troubles began. And some of those were true professionals.'

And those thoughts made me think of Felix and Mo and the other SB handlers I had met. Felix had been like a father to me for years now; advising me, helping and encouraging me, treating me as someone he could trust and whom he had affection for. And yet, as the hours ticked by and I still lay on the sofa, bound hand and foot, I wondered why no rescue attempt had been made. I could not believe that the Special Branch had 'lost' me on the journey to Twinbrook. I knew the sophisticated tracking equipment the SB employed for just such an operation; I knew that Felix and his team had tracked me to Connolly House; I knew that they were outside the building, watching everyone who was coming and going. They would have known Chico and Jim; they would have known they were part of an IRA punishment gang, and yet it seemed the SB had permitted two known IRA men to kidnap me with no rescue attempt to follow.

Every minute that ticked by I listened intently for the sound of helicopters, for RUC police car sirens, for the distinctive engine noise of army Land Rovers. But there was nothing. I listened in the hope that an RUC or Army squad would suddenly come crashing into the flat but as the hours passed I realized that a rescue was becoming increasingly unlikely. And yet, and yet . . . I could not understand how the Special Branch had managed to lose the Ford Fiesta. Although Felix had promised me that everything would be okay I came to realize as the day drew on that I was on my own.

'Shit,' I thought over and over again. 'How the fuck am I going to get out of this?'

Remarkably, I didn't panic. In fact, the more time I remained lying on the sofa, thinking and planning, the more positive I became. Given half a chance, I knew that if Chico or Jim left the flat one more time I would risk all in a stand-up fight with the two remaining men. I checked out the lad and realized that two hard blows to the body and a right cross would send him sprawling if not knock him unconscious. Then it would just be between me and either Chico or Jim. I gambled on the fact that they wouldn't dare use the gun; they would be too scared of their superior officers to risk killing me without permission, or, more importantly, without first gaining a confession. And they had never asked me a single question in the hours we had spent together.

To pass the time I thought of the escapades and the incidents I had been involved in working as an agent inside the IRA. I thought of the scrapes and near-misses and the luck I had enjoyed during the four years I had spent working with the Special Branch; saving lives, helping people and doing my bit to end the IRA's reign of terror in Northern Ireland. I had grown up in the Troubles and my mother Kate had always championed the Nationalist cause. I had seen the way the British Army and the RUC treated the Catholic minority and in my teens I had fought them tooth and nail. I had done all in my power to ensure they didn't catch any Republicans who, I believed, were trying to protect the Catholics from people who were hell-bent on maintaining their authority over us, including the British Army and the RUC, the Protestants and the Orangemen. I had grown up understanding that in Northern Ireland, the Catholics had always been badly treated; given a rough deal over jobs, lousy housing, and poor schools. Every summer I came to expect the dreaded march of the Orange Orders through Catholic areas, showing their strength and their authority; guarded throughout by hundreds of baton-wielding RUC men. I had thrown stones at army and RUC patrols, manned burning barricades, thrown petrol bombs and harassed patrols, but as I grew older I saw the other face of the IRA.

At first I only heard stories of kneecapping and punishment beatings. Then I saw the evidence; young men, some only teenagers, walking on crutches, some bearing the marks of beatings around their head and faces. And I saw the fear in the eyes of young people ordered around by IRA thugs as though they were little more than scum. The beatings and kneecappings came closer to home; young mates, whom I had been at school with, beaten up and left tied to railings in appalling pain; the swaggering IRA men behaving as if the Catholics were little more than stooges or puppets whose duty was to serve those privileged to be members of the IRA. And the more appallingly those IRA thugs treated friends and acquaintances of mine, the more I thought their behavior despicable, beneath contempt. Ever since I had been a teenager I accepted the IRA's argument that their first duty was to defend the Catholic minority of Northern Ireland against the RUC and the Protestants. Far from defending the Catholics it seemed to me the IRA's first duty was to wound, injure, maim and hurt Catholic teenagers. As a result, the older I became the more their actions angered and frustrated me, driving me away from the Republican cause. I had tried discussing the problem with some Republican friends, young men a few years older than me, and they looked at me as though I was mad, speaking some heresy they didn't want to hear. Over and over again they told me that I didn't know what I was talking about, while never answering my questions.

So I agreed to work with the RUC, hoping in my innocence to set the record straight, to stop the IRA thugs from attacking my friends and the other young Catholics from West Belfast. I felt proud when I prevented a shooting or a bombing, though, in reality, all I did was keep my eyes peeled and watch what was going on before phoning my SB handlers and telling them all I knew. But when I eventually joined the IRA and became a part of their intelligence wing I knew that I was heavily involved in serious intelligence work. Once inside the IRA the information I gathered proved invaluable in stopping people being killed, often indiscriminately. And the more lives I saved the more I felt I was indeed carrying out a worthwhile task.

But during those years – from 1987 to 1991 – I also had some fears. I remember that Felix, the handler with whom I had the closest relationship, would on occasions warn me of my fate if ever the IRA suspected I worked for the Branch. But after discussing the shit they would put me through Felix usually ended the conversation by going out of his way to reassure me. 'Listen, Marty,' he would say, 'we will always do all we can to protect you. You can rest assured that we will never put you in jeopardy and if we hear anything about you from any other source we will take you out immediately. I can promise you we will never put you in danger.'

But then I had found myself in August 1991 bound hand and foot and lying on a sofa with three IRA men, at least one of whom was armed, standing guard over me. I thought of all that had happened in the few days before the kidnap when Felix had reassured me time and again that I should go ahead with the planned meeting with Podraig Wilson, head of IRA discipline. Felix knew that I was deeply concerned about the meeting and yet he continued to pressure me to attend. And yet, I remember as I lay there, Felix had never provided me with a proper explanation.

As I lay on that sofa waiting for the interrogation and frightening torture to begin I found myself shaking; sweating with fear at how I would cope with such treatment. I tried to remain calm but as the minutes ticked by and the day became longer I felt that the IRA were deliberately prolonging my agony. I told myself that I would choose the moment to strike back. If the IRA Civil Administration Team did indeed begin to torture me then I was determined not to go quietly. I had never feared anyone and I wasn't going to go down without a fight. I had no idea exactly what I would do, but I knew that I would take at least one of the bastards with me. Those very thoughts gave me courage to face the evil fuckers who carry out this dirty work for the IRA.

When I heard the radio announce the time was 4 p.m., I realized I had been held for more than six hours and knew that, somehow, I had to engineer my own escape. Whatever the reason, it seemed to me that the SB were not about to make a dramatic rescue or, indeed, any rescue. For whatever reason, I was on my own.

But what the hell to do? I was in a flat three floors above the ground and the men guarding me were armed with at least one hand-gun. Then I heard a helicopter overhead and looked up through the net curtains of the living-room window to see a chopper whirring above the block of flats nearby. For a matter of minutes I hoped and prayed that it had come for me and that all my thoughts about being abandoned by the Branch were simply useless fears. But minutes later the chopper flew off and my fears returned once more to haunt me. Then I thought I heard what sounded like an English voice shouting 'shut up' and convinced myself it was the voice of a soldier with an army foot patrol out searching for me. I also thought I heard the unmistakable engine noise of a Land Rover outside the block but then realized as nothing happened that my hopes were dashed once more.

I remembered the day I joined the IRA as though it was yesterday. Davy Adams, one of the IRA's Belfast Brigade intelligence officers whom I had been ferrying around Belfast for over eighteen months, had asked me whether I wanted to join the IRA. Instinctively, I replied 'Yes' with great enthusiasm. I had wondered how my SB handlers would react when I told them of the invitation for I knew they had wanted me to join the IRA ever since I had begun work for the Branch two years earlier. I went by appointment to a house in Andersonstown and the door was answered by a scruffy-looking man in his thirties.

'I know why you're here,' he said. 'Listen to me carefully. I want you to be sure about what you're getting involved in. There are lots of people who have joined the IRA for all the wrong reasons. Some have been caught while on active service and have been sentenced to long jail terms of up to twenty-five years. After being sentenced many have complained that they didn't know what they were getting into, so my job is to make sure you don't make the same mistake. If you want to join Oglaigh nah Eireann [Gaelic for the Irish Republican Army], you have to promise to promote the objects of the organization and obey all orders and regulations issued by the Army and its officers.'

He then told me to go home and think hard about my decision, warning me that joining the IRA could end in either death by the SAS or a long jail term. As I walked back home that night I wondered if I was doing the right thing. I was now within twenty-four hours of finding myself between a rock and a hard place – the SB and the IRA – and I feared I would end up as mincemeat. Yet, the following day I returned to the IRA man's house like a lamb to the slaughter, convinced that I was making the gravest mistake of my life. During the oath-taking ceremony I not only had to swear allegiance to the IRA but review in detail a number of Army orders contained in the IRA's Green Book. I listened with a sickening heart to three particular pledges the man read out: 'One: No volunteer will succumb to approaches or overtures, blackmail or bribery attempts made by the enemy, and will report such approaches as soon as possible. Two: Volunteers who engage in loose talk will be dismissed. Three: Volunteers found guilty of treason face the death penalty.'

Those three pledges came to haunt me during the next two years of my secret life. For no apparent reason the words would come tumbling back into my mind and I would realize that I was forever within an inch of my life. I knew there would be no second chance; I knew the IRA would blow a hole in the back of my head if they thought, for one moment, I was working for the Special Branch. And yet, somehow, I continued doing my damnedest to save people's lives, stop bombings and shootings and try to bring some pressure to bear to stop IRA hit squads from inflicting kneecappings and punishment beatings on high-spirited Catholic teenagers.

Some months later I remember the twinge of excitement I felt the night Davy Adams told me to go to a house in Kerrykeel Gardens in the Suffolk area of Belfast to meet some IRA personnel. Davy was the nephew of Gerry Adams - President of Sinn Fein and the former commander of the Belfast Brigade of the IRA. I knew I was entering the lions' den, still the idea excited me though I carried no weapons and knew I would have to survive on my own wits. A freckle-faced teenager opened the door and motioned me to go into a downstairs room. Once inside, he told me to sit on the single chair which was facing the wall and wait. Five minutes later I heard some people enter the room and my heart beat faster, but at no time did I even think of turning around.

'Okay, Marty,' a voice said. 'Did Davy tell you why you're here?'

'No,' I replied. 'He just told me to come to this address.'

'I'll tell you what it is, Marty,' the voice continued. 'We want to know some things about you.'

That remark put the fear of God in me. In that instant I became convinced that my true identity had been rumbled and I wondered what would happen next. I listened intently for the click of a hand-gun being cocked but heard nothing. After asking a few innocuous questions the voice continued, 'Marty, tell us, why did you join the IRA?'

I had been briefed by my Special Branch handlers as to how to react if ever asked why I wanted to be part of the organization. They never gave me any exact words to remember, but they said that I should reply that I wanted to serve the cause. 'I joined because I believe in what the IRA is doing,' I lied, 'and so that I can help protect the people in the area where I grew up.'

The two men who had been asking the questions wanted to know how I knew Davy Adams and another mate of mine, Harry Fitzsimmons. Then the men trooped out and told me not to move. I feared that I was being watched through a spyhole and never turned round though my heart continued to thump, worrying that I had made a mess of the interview. Ten minutes later they returned. 'Okay, Marty,' said the first voice, 'you can turn round now.'

I recognized the two men who had been questioning me from the Special Branch files I was asked to look through every few days. The man who had asked most of the questions was Spud Murphy. The other face belonged to a man in his thirties, about 5' 7" tall, of medium build with a high forehead. I didn't know his name.

Spud then became much more friendly. 'Now I can tell you why you're here. I'm sorry you had to face the wall while we questioned you, but it's for everyone's safety. We're setting up a completely new IRA unit, a new cell, and we have been told a lot about you. We think you would fit in well for what we have planned. Basically, we need people who can get in and out of areas where UDR soldiers and peelers live, where they feel safe from IRA attacks.'

'Aye,' I replied, 'I've been in that position many times; stopped by the army and the peelers, made to show my license and insurance and things and then told to be on my way.'

'Do you want to come in with us then?' Spud asked, looking directly into my eyes, judging my reaction.

'Yes, I do,' I told him. 'No problem.'

'You're on,' Spud replied. 'Now listen. I'll tell you what I want you to do. I want to put together a new cell and recruit young men who have never been in any kind of trouble, totally unknown to the RUC. I intend to use these recruits to carry out operations where the enemy feel safe: in their own homes.'

At the first meeting of the new cell a week later I searched the faces of all the men present trying to determine if I had ever seen them before while looking through SB files. Except, of course, for Spud, I was sure that I had never before seen a single one of them, which I knew would worry my handlers. So I did my damnedest to remember their faces, their height, weight, color of hair or any feature that would identify them. I knew this new cell would spell real trouble for the SB because the members were unknown to them. I also feared that other new IRA cells, with more unknown recruits, were being assembled. As I went home that night, however, I felt the thrill of actually working with an IRA active service unit, leading a dangerous, secretive life while working for the RUC Special Branch. In that moment of heady enthusiasm I had no fear for my future, despite the fact that I was risking my very life.

However, my initiation into the IRA was not yet complete. I was ordered to attend a meeting in the Turf Lodge area of Belfast where I would become acquainted with a man they called 'The Interrogator'. Felix advised me to go ahead with the meeting to see what it was all about. As he would tell me time and again, 'Remember, Marty, the more we know about the IRA, the better equipped we are to stop their bombings and shootings.'

The Interrogator was a balding, well-built man in his forties with bright intelligent eyes. He told me that if I was ever suspected of being involved in the IRA the RUC could arrest me and hold me for seven days before I was charged or released. He warned that in that time the CID would question me non-stop, taking it in turns to wear me down, trip me up, break me. He warned me, 'Their intention will be to break your spirit so that you will tell them everything they want to know; details of operations, of bombings, the names of other cell members and even names of your friends and relations. But it will be your duty to tell them nothing, absolutely nothing. And I'm going to tell you how to do that. If you are arrested you will say absolutely nothing and you will never answer any question the CID asks you. You will simply tell the custody sergeant that you will refuse to co-operate but that does not mean that you are guilty.'

At another lecture The Interrogator told me what to expect should I ever be arrested. 'They will usually come for you early in the morning, while you're still asleep, some time around five o'clock. They will bang at your door and invade your house, making a lot of noise. They will try to confuse you, order you to dress quickly and come with them immediately. But you must refuse to do that. You must tell them that you have the right, as you do, to make yourself respectable. Take your time; go to the bathroom and wash and shave, clean your teeth, comb your hair, even splash on some after-shave. And remember to dress properly in a clean shirt, a jacket and a smart pair of trousers. They won't like it; they will try to hurry you, but take no notice; fuck them.'

He continued, 'The RUC will take you to Castlereagh and put you in a cell. They will leave you there for a few hours before the interrogation officers arrive. The officers will have known the night before that they are going to interview you and will have showered and shaved, eaten a good breakfast and be on good form trying to make you feel second-rate compared to them. But, because you will have followed my advice, you will feel and look as smart and attentive as they do. They won't like that either. They hope that when they enter the interview room you will look pathetic, unshaven, scruffy and disorientated, putting you at an immediate disadvantage.

'Remember to tell them nothing. Never answer one of their questions, no matter how many times they ask you. Don't look down at the floor and never appear nervous or frightened. Always remember to keep your head up and look them straight in the eye, as though remembering their exact identity. They will hate that. They will fear that you are trying to remember their faces; seal their identities in your memory so that, one day, you will be able to target them and kill them. This worry scares the fuck out of them and puts you at an advantage.'

He also told me how to cope with the stress of the interview which, he warned, might continue for days and nights. 'Exercise, keep fit, walk up and down the cell or the room and keep alert the entire time,' he advised. 'Sleep and eat at every opportunity. Whatever food you're offered, sit down and eat it and try to enjoy it. It will help sustain your energy, help you to resist the bastards' questions. And before any interview remember to go to the toilet because, once they begin to question you, they will refuse to let you go. They know that when anyone wants to go desperately they will say almost anything just so they can go.'

The Interrogator also advised me what to do if the peelers or the Special Branch started to beat me up. 'Hit back,' he said. 'Give them everything; smash the fuck out of them. Don't be frightened to hit back, and the harder they hit you, the harder you hit the bastards back again. They know they shouldn't hit you but they will, especially the nasty, vicious bastards; the hard men who are determined to break you. And if they begin to smack you around while another officer holds you down, curl up into a ball on the floor and try to protect your head and face. They'll probably kick the fuck out of you but then you've got them. As soon as they stop, demand to see your own doctor. Make sure you give his name and address and keep demanding to see him. That will scare the fucking shit out of them because your doctor will note any marks or injuries you have suffered. And that will cause the RUC real problems.'

I was also advised to expect the 'good cop, bad cop' routine that I had heard about before. He told me the 'good cop' would be my friend, advise me to co-operate; the 'bad cop' would shout and swear, threaten and hit me. The Interrogator added, 'You must never show that you are the least bit intimidated or frightened of him. If you do he will know that within a few days he will break you, and that's what he wants.'

A couple of days later I passed all this detail to Felix as he debriefed me. He also told me what the likely consequences would be to me or other IRA members who are picked up by the RUC, detained, questioned and then freed. 'A special IRA security team is assigned to every IRA man freed from custody,' he told me. 'It is their task to follow him, night and day, for the first few days following his release, taking note of where he goes, whom he meets, what he does. A couple of days later he is told to report for questioning. The man goes as ordered to an IRA safe house. Inside is total darkness, no lights whatsoever. The man is taken to a room and told to sit down while men in balaclavas question him, asking him a hundred questions about his time inside, details of the police questioning and the answers he gave. The man is made to feel like a leper, a traitor. They question him harder than the CID ever did. If they think he's talked or betrayed the cause, then he's fucking had it. And if they think he's been turned and become an informant they will beat the shit out of him, torture him and whatever. And before they've finished with him, they will have discovered every tiny piece of information that he gave about members and IRA operations. If he ever admits to being turned, then he's fucked – just a bullet in the back of the head.'

All these thoughts raced through my head, and the more I thought of the IRA operations I had succeeded in ruining, the more I felt a chill running down my spine. I decided to try and cheer myself up but it was difficult. The more the minutes ticked by the more I thought I was nearing the time when questions would be asked by the Civil Administration Team, and I wondered if I had the guts to deny them. I knew only too well that a number of other informants had been arrested by PIRA, questioned and tortured, but I didn't know any who hadn't ended up taking a terrible beating as well as a bullet in the back of the head. I knew that in these circumstances the IRA always demanded a confession to deter others from working for the RUC. But while these two stooges and their underling stood guard over me, I recalled some of the successes when we had thwarted the IRA.

One of the most successful operations began as I was driving Davy Adams across Belfast. He asked me if I would become involved in a major operation being planned by an IRA active service unit, in which they hoped to trigger a massive bomb beside the main road leading from the Larne ferry terminal. The IRA had discovered that every other week a convoy of fifteen British Army trucks would cross from Scotland to Larne bringing supplies to the troops stationed in the Province. More importantly, the IRA had learned that the last two army trucks leaving the ferry on arrival at Larne were usually full of British soldiers. To the IRA this was the perfect target, a spectacular massacre which would shake the British Army to its core. An IRA intelligence unit had managed to plant one of their young volunteers, a lad named Martin, on the ferry, working as a ship's hand.

I met Martin outside a café in the center of Larne, where he gave me the details of the fortnightly crossings of the army supply vehicles. He also told me that the RUC, responsible for checking security at the ferry port, would drive a van to the port and leave it unattended while they checked the ferries arriving at Larne. The following Saturday I drove down to Larne again and counted fifteen British army trucks leaving the ferry. The last two were indeed full of soldiers.

Having reported back to Davy Adams I was sent to discuss the operation with a highly experienced IRA explosives officer named Tony. This man had a formidable reputation and he would be responsible for many of the huge IRA bombs that devastated the center of Belfast during the late 1980s. After explaining the mission to him, and the roadway leading from the ferry, he decided to visit the area with me to see how best to plan the bombing. On the way into Larne, Tony noticed a lay-by on the main road used by the British convoys. 'This is brilliant, fucking fabulous,' Tony said enthusiastically rubbing his hands together. 'If we can't stiff at least a dozen Brits in this operation we're real wankers.'

After passing the lay-by a second time, Tony said he planned to park a caravan packed with explosives in it and then run a command wire from a vantage point from which to trigger the bomb. He also wanted to ensure that the bomber would be able to make a quick and safe getaway. We circled round again so that Tony could check the best place from which to trigger the bomb. As we drove back to Belfast, Tony went on chatting to himself: 'To carry out this job we need 1,000 lbs. of mix [home-made explosives made from fertilizer], enough to blow at least one of those lorries off the road. But this is a chance in a lifetime so I think we'll up the mix to 1,500 lbs. That should really blast the fuck out of the last two vehicles. If both of those trucks are full of soldiers, hardly any will get out alive. Marty, an opportunity like this only comes about once and you have to get it right.'

The following day I reported all to Felix and Mo, two of my handlers, and they took the information with some alarm. I could hardly recall them looking so serious. 'If Tony's involved that means this is a serious job,' said Felix. 'He is one of the IRA's top bomb-makers; he's organized some of their most spectacular bombings.'

I urged Felix and Mo to keep the information secret because very few people knew of the bomb plot and if anyone became suspicious I would be one of the first to be suspected of leaking the intelligence. They agreed to my request and decided, in an effort to protect my identity, to speak directly to army intelligence and tell them of the bomb plot, urging them to stop using the Stranraer–Larne ferry and find another way of transporting men and supplies across the Irish Sea. Not knowing what was happening, I was on tenterhooks wondering if the Branch would accidentally leak the bomb plot. Weeks passed and I heard nothing, so I decided to call on Tony to see how the bomb plot was going.

As I walked into his garden, Tony said, 'Hey, Marty, did you hear about the Larne job?'

My heart leapt. 'No, why?' I asked, trying to keep cool.

'It seems the bastards were only using the Larne ferry for a short while, because they don't go there any more. We had the gear all ready, the mix prepared and packed in a caravan. As usual, before the operation, we took one last look on Saturday afternoon and there were no army trucks to be seen. I don't think they've used the port since.'

'Fuck,' I replied, 'from what the lad told me it seemed the convoy was a regular event.'

'I was devastated when I heard there were no more trucks,' Tony said, looking particularly miserable. 'I thought that job was too good to be true.'

As I lay on the sofa, bound hand and foot, I knew how guilty I was in the eyes of the IRA and I knew exactly what that would mean if I ever confessed to working for the Branch. Even the thought of what would happen made me turn cold. I shivered and yet I was hot as hell under a blanket on a hot August day. I realized I had to face whatever was coming to me and do all in my power to come out alive at the end of the ordeal. Even so, the thought of saving the lives of those two truck-loads of soldiers actually brought a smile to my lips.

By now it was 5:30 p.m. and I wondered how much longer I would have to wait until confronted by the IRA Civil Administration Team. Suddenly, I realized that I had to go to the toilet. I was bursting and I knew they wouldn't want me peeing all over the sofa. I asked the young lad to untie my hands so I could go to the toilet. As I hopped into the bathroom I noticed the bath, full to the brim of crystal-clear water. I knew exactly what that meant and my stomach churned and my mouth turned dry as fear gripped me. I knew that one of the IRA's favorite tortures was putting a man's head underwater and keeping it there until the poor bloke was barely conscious. Then they would bring him out, gasping for breath, question him again and then force his head back into the bath, keeping the ritual of torture going until the man passed out completely or gave them the confession they demanded.

I knew as I looked at that bathwater that if I did not escape from that flat I would be faced with the water torture and, probably, many others just as horrific. I doubted whether I would have the courage or the willpower to withstand such treatment and such interrogation, to keep denying that I had ever worked for the Branch or provided any information to the RUC. I knew that the interrogation unit would arrive at any minute and I also feared that by the time they had finished with me they would either have a confession or I would be dead. The thought frightened the shit out of me. I told myself that if I stayed in that flat, death was a near certainty and I became convinced, in my terror, that I would be unable to take the beatings, the cigarette burns, or the water torture without confessing. I knew that the moment I confessed I would be taken out of the flat, bundled into a car, taken somewhere outside Belfast and unceremoniously shot in the back of the head.

Then a great idea struck me – I made my monstrous plan. I looked at the sitting-room window wondering exactly how far I was from the ground. I had no idea what was below the window – concrete, grass, parked cars, trees or shrubs. Suddenly, it didn't seem to matter. Here was a possible avenue of escape. At that moment I preferred to take the odds of leaping through the window rather than face the IRA's bully boys. I glanced into the kitchen and saw the three of them talking quietly amongst themselves. 'This is your only chance, Marty,' I said to myself. 'Go for it, go for it, go for it.'

My feet were still bound together so I hopped out of the bathroom, across the hallway and into the sitting-room, not daring to look into the kitchen. Ten feet in front me was the window and I hopped faster and faster, frightened that the yobbos might twig what was happening and stop me leaping out of the window. When I was within a couple of feet of the closed window I leapt as high as I could, hurling myself head-first through the pane. I don't even remember hitting the glass . . .

Those memories seemed like only yesterday, so fresh were the details. I had somehow survived, spending a month semi-conscious in the hospital, before being taken out of Belfast and flown to the mainland to a new home and a new life.

I knew that one day I would return to Belfast to discover the truth about what had happened to me; to find out once and for all who had betrayed me and why. There had to be a good reason for MI5 to arrange my kidnapping and orchestrate my death at the hands of the IRA. But that trip to Northern Ireland would have to wait. Other events and circumstances were arising almost weekly in Newcastle-upon-Tyne where I now lived; worrying events seemingly set up to make me feel insecure and vulnerable. I felt that I was being harried and chased by the authorities including the Northumbria Police, the local Special Branch and the Crown

Prosecution Service. I wondered if I was being paranoid but came to realize that there was no arguing that the authorities did appear to be conspiring against me. Before returning to Belfast, I had to first sort out my problems in England and try to determine if everything that had been going wrong in my life there had begun with my abduction in Belfast.

CHAPTER FOUR

I didn't regain consciousness completely for four weeks after my leap from the third-floor flat where I had been held prisoner. And yet for some unknown reason I thought for months afterwards that I had only been unconscious a matter of forty-eight hours. No matter – when I came around, the pain was real enough. I had sustained some serious injuries. My left arm had been nearly severed at the shoulder as the glass from the window cut through the sinew and muscle. I was also suffering from lacerations to the head, a fractured jaw and broken teeth. The severe bruising to the head had caused a deep concussion and doctors at Musgrave Park Hospital, a military hospital, told me that I must have landed head-first on the ground. They told me I was lucky to be alive, joking that I must have a skull made of rubber to have survived such an impact from a height of forty feet. However, whenever I felt pain in my arm or jaw, or dizziness in my head, I was reminded that the pain was nothing compared to what the IRA torturers would have inflicted.

By October 1991 I had fully recovered and left the Province with an armed Special Branch escort, taking the sea route from Larne to Scotland. We took the train to Newcastle and I was handed over to Northumbria Special Branch officers. I had been provided with a new identity, 'Martin Ashe', a bank account, passport and driving license in my new name as well as a new social security number. I was also promised a small flat which would be rented for me until all my papers had been sorted by the RUC and a decision taken as to my needs. I was driven to my new home in Wallsend not far from the famous Swan Hunter shipyards. What I didn't know was that Wallsend was then considered to be one of the poorest districts in the north-east of Britain, where unemployment was high, crime was rife and life hard. The price of property was amongst the cheapest in mainland Britain. Nothing was mentioned about a job or money for a business. I was given no advice except to keep my head down.

The two-bedroom flat was dingy, dirty and disgusting. I looked around the cramped dwelling on the ground floor of the nine-teenth-century house amazed that anyone should be asked to live in such awful conditions. The wallpaper was dirty and torn, the bathroom had slugs on the walls, the bath and wash basin were dirty and stained; the carpets were stained and smelly; the curtains were little more than rags; the furniture was too dirty to sit on; the bed looked more than thirty years old. There was no heat save for a small gas fire in the sitting-room. To me it seemed that the flat hadn't been lived in for years or decorated for a generation.

That night, as I lay in bed waiting for sleep, I thought of Angie and the kids and fought back the tears. A feeling of desolation and loneliness gripped me and I wondered what the hell I had done to end up living alone in such awful surroundings. The following day I went out to buy a few things for the house, hoping to make it more homely and bearable to live in. I bought mugs and some cut-lery, plates, a new teapot and saucepans to cook with. I didn't feel like using any of the dishes or cutlery that were in the flat because they were cracked, chipped and old.

I was missing Angie and the kids desperately and I thought that if I made the house more habitable, more pleasant to live in, then I might be able to persuade her to bring the boys over to Tyneside so that we could live together as a family once again. I feared for Angie, wondering if the IRA bastards might haul her to one of their meetings, occasions when a number of IRA thugs question and cross-question someone, trying to confuse them so that they end up telling the IRA everything they want to know. I had witnessed the outcome of such meetings before; grown men reduced to rambling, babbling figures unable to think or speak straight for fear of what might happen to them. These wretched wrecks usually ended up telling their IRA inquisitors everything they wanted to know whether it was the truth or not. In that way the IRA would not only discover facts and information they wanted but also many other pieces of information they could use on future occasions when questioning any one of the thousands of other Catholics who lived in Republican West Belfast. Allegedly these people lived under IRA protection but in reality, they lived in abject fear of the strict discipline the so-called Army imposed.

I wanted to call Angie every night to tell her how much I missed her, to apologize for leaving her alone with the kids, for involving her in the mess that my life had become since working as an agent for the Special Branch way back in 1987. Very occasionally I did call her, though I knew I was taking a risk. We would weep together during those phone calls for we loved each other and needed each other. Angie had shown remarkable bravery in those months that I had been recovering, understanding that she could not, must not, see me for fear that she might be later picked up and questioned by the IRA. She had no fear for herself but only for Martin and Podraig, frightened that her young sons might be left without a father or a mother.

Angie, in fact, had known nothing, absolutely nothing, of my earlier life as an agent for British Intelligence working inside the IRA's intelligence wing, providing information to the Special Branch. There were two main reasons why I told her nothing of my undercover work; one was the fact that if she knew nothing she couldn't tell anyone anything; the other reason was that she would have thoroughly disapproved and persuaded me to stop working for the British.

In our infrequent telephone calls I would beg Angie to bring the kids to England, to escape the politics, as well as the bombs and bullets of Belfast. I urged her to come to England for the safety of living in peace on the mainland where I would be able to take care of her and the boys in a way I could not while they continued to live in Northern Ireland. Angie, however, was torn between leaving her family and friends with whom she was very close and whom she relied on for support, and living in England, a strange country she had never even visited, in a town she didn't know, surrounded by total strangers.

'Can you understand the Geordie slang?' she asked one night during a phone call.

'Not to begin with,' I told her, 'but the people who live here are really kind, the salt of the earth.'

'But I'm told strangers can't understand what they're saying,' she said, sounding worried.

'It's not that bad; you'll get used to the accent,' I told her, trying to bolster her confidence, encouraging her to take the great leap, leave Belfast and come and live with me in Newcastle.

After three weeks Angie phoned and suddenly asked, 'Would I come across on the ferry?'

My heart leapt and I could hardly contain myself, suddenly chatting sixteen to the dozen as I felt the excitement buzz through my body.

'You'll come then?' I asked, expectation in my voice.

'If you really want me to,' she replied.

'Jesus,' I said, 'I've wanted you to come over here from the moment I arrived.'

'Promise?' she asked, sounding demure.

'I'd cross my heart and hope to die,' I replied. 'Sort everything out,' I told her, 'but remember, tell no one except your Ma. No one must know that you're coming over here because the IRA might somehow come to hear of it and you know what that means. They might tail you all the way to this house, just to get at me.'

'Don't worry,' she assured me. 'No one will know I'm planning on joining you until after I've left.'

'Good,' I said. 'Keep it that way. I'll talk to you tomorrow.'

I put the phone down and punched the air, overcome with happiness at the thought of having Angie and the boys with me once again.

Seconds later I redialed her number in Belfast. 'I suddenly had a panic attack,' I told her, 'thinking you might not come. You promise, don't you?'

'Marty,' she said, sounding so sensible for a twenty-year-old, 'I've told you I'm coming and I will.'

'Promise?' I asked.

'On my mother's life,' she replied.

'Oh Angie, that sounds great,' I said. 'You're a wonderful girl and I love you to pieces.'

One week after arriving in Wallsend I decided it was time to get fit again. I had had no exercise since my leap from the flat in August and I was feeling dreadfully unfit. So I bought a pair of trainers and a track suit and each evening I would run two to three miles along the road by the perimeter wall of the famous Swan Hunter ship-yards. One night in late October I went out as usual and had run my normal three miles around the streets when I suddenly became aware that someone was behind me, running, keeping in step with me. I turned and saw the shadow of a man about one hundred yards behind me but closing fast. I was shattered from my running but somehow found the extra strength to increase my pace. It was no use. This man was gaining fast and he was only yards from me when I reached my front door. I knew, I simply knew the man was an IRA killer.

I fumbled with the front door key, trying to remain calm as my nerves took over. I convinced myself that if I didn't get into my house within seconds I would hear the blast of a hand-gun and I would be done for. Eventually, I managed to open the door and this man put his foot in the door to stop me shutting him out. We tussled back and forth but I did notice that I had not given him time to get out his gun. Suddenly I had an idea and pulled the door towards me knocking him off balance. In the second he needed to regain his balance I slammed shut the door, locked it and then ran like hell through the flat, out of the back door into the yard. I shimmied as fast as possible over the back wall and, without thinking, ran round to the front of the house. The stranger was still standing at my front door, banging on it with his fist. I crept up behind him, grabbed him by the shoulders, spun him round and hit him in the stomach, making him fall forward.

'What the fuck do you want?' I shouted in anger.

'What do you mean?' he asked, gasping for breath.

I pushed him against the wall of the house, held him by the throat and demanded a proper answer to my question. 'What the fuck were you chasing me for?' I asked him again angrily.

'I was after you,' he said.

'What were you after me for?' I asked, unable to fathom what on earth the man was trying to explain.

'You kicked in my car the other night,' he said.

'I did what?' I asked indignantly, wondering if this was a ploy to get me to relax. I still believed he was probably an IRA thug waiting for the chance to grab his hand-gun. I continued to hold him, making sure he couldn't make a grab for his gun.

'You kicked my car in the other night,' he said again.

'I don't know what the fuck you're talking about, but I kicked no car,' I told him.

He appeared to be looking at me more closely. Suddenly the man said, 'I think I may be wrong. I don't think it was you kicking my car; the kids were much younger.'

I let go of the man and he stood by the wall, continuing to apologize.

'I think I've made a mistake,' he said.

'I think you have,' I told him.

'Listen,' he said, 'the other night I came out of my house down the road and saw some kids kicking shit out of my car and I chased them away, told them to stop kicking other people's cars, causing damage which the owner had to pay for. They ran off, jeering and laughing, and I warned them that if I saw them again I would catch them and give them a good clip. When I saw you running down the road past my car I thought you were one of those kids, so I gave chase. I'm sorry.'

His explanation seemed perfectly plausible and I believed him. He had made no effort to escape my clutches and I was sure he was no IRA killer intent on getting me. For a start, he had a strong

Geordie accent. I suddenly realized I had over-reacted. But I couldn't say anything to him; I couldn't explain why I had reacted so violently, nor tell him that I had been within an ace of kicking the shit out of him. I knew it was just a nervous reaction to being chased by someone late at night who seemed intent on breaking into my house. A few minutes later we were shaking hands, exchanging names and he promised to buy me a pint. We said 'goodnight' with a laugh but when I walked back inside the house I leaned against the door, closed my eyes and sighed with relief thinking of what might have been.

'Shit,' I thought, 'I've got to get this IRA nonsense out of my head, otherwise I might end up one day killing some poor innocent bastard.'

As I looked around I also knew I had to do something to improve my dreary, squalid flat so I phoned my old handler Felix and told him of the conditions in which I had been placed.

'You wouldn't put a dog in a place like this,' I told him. 'It really smells and is quite filthy. I've tried to improve things but it really is awful.'

'Listen,' Felix said, 'go and buy a cheap camera and take photos of the place, inside every room, including the kitchen and bathroom, so that people can see how terrible it is. Then send the photos through to the Chief Constable's office, along with a letter, so that he can make a judgment. If it's that bad, Marty, we'll have you out of there, find you some other accommodation.'

'I'll happily send the photos to the Chief Constable. I'm not kidding you, Felix,' I told him, 'you would be disgusted if you came and saw the condition of the place, I promise you.'

'I believe you, Marty. Don't worry. Just get those photos and send them over. But don't forget the letter. Okay?' he said.

'I'll do just that,' I told him. I sent the letter and photographs to the Chief Constable's office and Felix phoned me later to say that he had seen the photographs and wholeheartedly agreed with my description of the place. He seemed more shocked that the Northumbria Special Branch should put one of the RUC's agents in such dreadful accommodation. He said that he would urge the RUC Special Branch in Belfast to speed up the application for the funds which were due to me so that a modest house could be bought for me. Felix knew that I hoped Angie, Martin - then two - and Podraig, who was just six months, would be joining me shortly. He warned me, however, that I would have to wait for a few months for all the red tape and paperwork to be drawn up, finalized and authorized. He assured me: 'Don't worry, I will make sure decent accommodation is found; we can't have you living in some pigsty.'

Ever since I had arrived in Wallsend I would speak to Felix each and every day at exactly 2 p.m. We arranged that I should be standing by a telephone box in Wallsend at that time and he would phone through to check that I was okay and not feeling too lonely. Sometimes we would chat for an hour, talking about everything under the sun. And I noted he was always cheerful, telling me amusing stories, making me laugh as though wanting to keep up my spirits. He wouldn't, of course, call me at home, for fear his calls were intercepted by the IRA. He knew that the IRA had extensive contacts working inside British Telecom which they would use time and again for tracing people in Northern Ireland and sometimes in mainland Britain. Indeed, using the telephone network to track people they wanted to target was one of the IRA's most favored methods of ferreting out people who had gone into hiding.

The IRA hierarchy hated losing anyone who had joined the cause and then worked for the Government or the RUC. Agents and informants such as me were always high on the IRA's target list because to catch and kill a former IRA member worked wonders as a warning to any other person planning to defect, or even contemplate working for the RUC. For the first four weeks of my life on the mainland I also had the company, for at least an hour a day, of two RUC Special Branch officers who were detailed to watch over me and care for me. During their stay in England they lived in Northumbria police accommodation and would drive over to see me. I believe that the reason they came visiting was to ensure that

I didn't high-tail it back to Belfast, for they rightly concluded that I was feeling lonely and miserable and obviously missing Angie and my boys. The Special Branch had known other informants who had been taken out of Belfast and housed in safe accommodation on the mainland, provided with new identities, passport, etc., and then, feeling homesick, had made their way back to Belfast without informing anyone.

These people worried the shit out of the RUC because, on occasions, they had highly sensitive material locked in their memories which the IRA would have loved dearly to learn about. Sometimes the RUC managed to intercept them, explain the risks they were taking and arrange for them to return to England. On other occasions the IRA reached them first and they had been taken away, questioned by the IRA's feared Civil Administration Team and then shot.

Throughout those first few weeks I wanted to speak to Angie on a daily basis but I realized the potential danger for both me and, more importantly, for Angie and the boys. My SB friends told me to be very wary of calling her at her home number and to try instead to call a phone box at a prearranged time. But I was so happy that she was coming over to England and bringing the boys with her that it was with great difficulty that I refrained from calling her. I was also worried that she might have a change of heart; that her mother might persuade her to stay in Belfast. But she didn't – she was as good as her word.

I was a bundle of nerves when I traveled by train to Stranraer, praying that nothing would go wrong, so keen and eager to see Angie and the boys. But I didn't let the occasion go to my head. I knew there was every possibility that the IRA might, somehow, have heard of Angie's plans to join me and I was taking no chances. I didn't walk all the way to the disembarking point but stayed in the background, finding a vantage point from where I could see Angie coming off the boat without anyone seeing me. I checked everyone as they walked from the ferry just in case I recognized someone from my days with the IRA. But I saw no one and when I felt the coast was clear I ventured out to welcome my family to Britain. Angie looked tired and worried and the children hardly recognized me at first because they had not seen me for four months. I gave Angie a hug and a kiss and told her how wonderful it was to see her again. She seemed nervous and somewhat strange, as though holding back.

'Are you all right?' I asked.

'Sure I am,' she replied. 'Why do you ask?'

'Are you sure no one tailed you?' I asked, worried in case Angie had been told by the IRA to act normal when she met me, warning her that giving any hint she was being tailed would result in instant death for her and the boys. That was a typical IRA ploy which they had used time and again, especially when planting bombs.

I looked around, checking to see if anyone suspicious was hanging around nearby, but saw no one.

'You're like a cat on a hot tin roof,' Angie said, smiling. 'Will you calm down, relax? I told you no one knew we were leaving and no one's tailed us.'

'Are you sure?' I asked, still not certain that Angie was telling me everything.

'Yes, I'm certain,' she said. 'Now stop worrying, pick up these cases and give me a hand with the kids.'

Suddenly I realized I was being paranoid and foolish, that I had been living on my own for too long, letting the IRA dominate my thinking rather than pushing those fears to the back of my mind and getting on with my life. As we walked to the railway station to catch the train to Newcastle I realized how lucky I was to have Angie and the boys with me again. I felt a warm glow of happiness as the train sped through the wild and beautiful Scottish countryside but I realized that Angie, sitting across from me, seemed concerned and apprehensive. Seeing her look so young and vulnerable, I made a mental note to stop feeling so pathetic and show some strength of character. Then she caught my eye and smiled, looking more confident, as though a great weight had been lifted from her mind. I leaned forward, gripped her hand and squeezed it gently.

We said nothing but looked into each other's eyes as the train rattled along, each of us holding one of the boys as they slept beside us.

I had warned Angie of the terrible conditions in which we would have to live but explained that the RUC were trying to sort out something else; though the red tape and paperwork necessary would mean we would have to put up with the present accommodation for a few months. In fact, I had no idea when our housing would change, but I hoped, for Angie's sake, that it wouldn't be too long. I had persuaded her to come and live on the mainland and she didn't deserve to live in a slum, especially as the health and safety of Martin and Podraig were uppermost in her mind.

'My God,' she said, as she walked into the flat and looked around at the dingy surroundings. 'From what you said, Marty, I thought things would be bad, but I never realized the flat would be this bad.'

'I know,' I told her. 'I warned you. But remember I had no choice. This has been rented for me by the Northumbria Police and nothing will change until the RUC find me some accommodation. I'm sorry, Angie, I really am, but there's nothing I could do. I wanted everything to be nice for you and the boys but I couldn't do any better for now.'

'We'll make the best of a bad job,' she said. 'Now give me a hand with the cases and let's get the place sorted out.'

Within a week of Angie's arrival Felix phoned with some good news. The RUC had forwarded £4,000 for me to buy a second-hand car, a Ford Fiesta. This allowed me to drive Angie and the boys around, enabling us to feel free and mobile, rather than being holed up in a dreadful flat day and night. For Christmas that year I was determined to get away from Wallsend because we were certain to feel very lonely while everyone else around us was enjoying festivities with members of their families. So I rented a cottage in Scotland for a week and we had a wonderfully romantic holiday. Although the boys were still very young, Martin, in particular, loved opening his presents. Angie relaxed, laughed and smiled but on Christmas Day there were tears for she missed her family terribly. She thought of her parents, brothers, sisters, cousins, aunts and uncles enjoying themselves together at their Belfast home and realized that she would not be seeing any of them this year or any year in the future.

I believe on that Christmas Day Angie realized for the first time that coming to England had been a permanent move; that she would never again be able to return to Belfast, even for a fleeting visit, and that she would, in effect, be cut off from her family forever. She fully realized that once the IRA knew she was living with me they would always be waiting for her to return, to question her and find out all they could about my whereabouts. By moving to England, Angie had exiled herself from Belfast as permanently as I had and I could see she found the break with her family very, very hard to take.

Throughout the cold, hard winter that was Newcastle in January and February, 1992 I could see that Angie was becoming more restless and homesick, though she tried to hide her feelings. However, in late February we had some good news. I was informed by my Northumbria Special Branch contact, a man called Alan, that I had been given permission to look for a house in their force area which the police would purchase for me. I would also be given £6,000 to equip the house from top to bottom with everything from curtains to carpets, beds to sofas, a washing machine and dryer. But £6,000 would be the maximum. My expectations soared, as I realized that a lovely new home might help to make Angie feel better and perhaps persuade her that life in England was not so bad after all. I knew that a new home wouldn't stop her from missing her parents, but I just hoped it would make her see that life with me and the boys was a big enough compensation. I couldn't be sure.

Seconds later my expectations were dashed when Alan told me that the RUC had informed him that I could only buy a house for a maximum of £25,000.

'What?' I said, in amazement, '£25,000? What the fuck are they on about? You can hardly buy a rabbit hutch for that amount in Newcastle. I've got a girlfriend and two children living with me; I can't buy a one-bedroom flat somewhere.'

'It's nothing to do with me,' said Alan. 'I'm just passing on messages. You'll have to take it up with the authorities.'

'Fucking right I will,' I told him angrily. I felt dejected and miserable, as I became aware that once again I was being screwed.

The following day I phoned Felix in Belfast and told him what I had been offered by RUC headquarters in Belfast, who had passed the message to me via the Northumbria Police. He could hardly believe his ears. 'Jesus, Marty,' he said, 'they're fucking you about something rotten. I don't know what they're doing giving you a maximum of £25,000. Let me look into it. They can't do that to you. It's not as though you're living on your own, not now that Angie and the kids have joined you. I'll be in touch.'

Felix urged me to get the local paper and search through the 'Houses for Sale' notices to see what the current prices were for modern, three-bedroom houses in and around Newcastle. Later I would tell him that to buy a good, modern house in a respectable area of Northumberland the cost would be about £50,000 but that older, cheaper houses in less salubrious areas could be bought for about £40,000.

Some weeks later I was informed that the RUC department responsible for resettling agents and informants in England had decided to permit me to buy a modern, three-bedroom house for about £50,000. I began looking around again and found a brand new home at South Beach, in a new private development in Blyth. The cost was £52,500. The RUC agreed to purchase it for me and we moved in during May 1992.

Angie and I had great fun buying everything for the home with the £6,000 we had been given to furnish the place. She seemed happier than ever and loved the new home. She felt this was the right place to bring up the boys; a good, clean, tidy and hygienic house where she didn't feel them to be at risk. But that same month, Europe's biggest shopping complex south-west of

Newcastle, the Metro Center, was fire-bombed by an IRA active service unit, just forty-eight hours after Angie and the boys had spent the day shopping in the place. Seven fire-bombs exploded in seven separate shops, causing minimal damage but striking fear into the 120,000 shoppers who were there at the time. Three other incendiaries were discovered and successfully defused in three other department stores at the Center. But the fire-bomb attack would have been far more serious if an off-duty RAF serviceman had not spotted an incendiary device – something ordinary shoppers would not have noticed – at a sports shop.

That night, news of the Metro Center bombing was splashed on every TV news station complete with pictures showing the damage and the risk to shoppers and passers-by. Anti-terrorist police chiefs believed a team of four IRA bombers – two men and two women – had traveled across from Larne to Scotland and then by train to Newcastle in exactly the same way Angie had come over with the boys only a few months before. The police chiefs believed the active service unit had been staying in a safe-house somewhere in the north-east of England, probably around the Newcastle area, where they had been handed the fire-bombs and trained how to prime them.

Angie sat on the sofa that night and I could see her shaking, trying to control her fear and her emotions. There were tears in her eyes and I felt so terribly guilty that I had been responsible, utterly responsible for persuading her to share her life with me. I had never asked her permission to work for the RUC as a secret intelligence agent; I had never even hinted to her that I had joined the IRA. She had known nothing of my double life and had never asked me. Now, here we were hundreds of miles from the bombs of Belfast and it seemed the IRA bombers had followed us to where we were trying to live in peace and safety. Those fire-bombs unnerved Angie. In her years of growing up in Belfast she had never shown signs of fear or nervousness, though members of her family had been touched by the violence. Though she had grown up in Belfast, where fire-bombs and massive explosions had often been a weekly occurrence, the torching of the Metro Center in Gateshead sent shock waves through her.

'What are we going to do?' she said looking at me, sounding both miserable and sad.

'There's nothing to do,' I replied. 'Those bombs weren't aimed at us.'

'But it means the IRA have people living here in Newcastle. They might even be in our neighborhood, in our street and we wouldn't know. If they see you and recognize you then we're done for.'

'Don't worry,' I said, trying to reassure her, desperate to rebuild her confidence.

'But I can't help it, Marty,' she continued. 'I can't help worrying. I have a fear that they'll never give up; they'll continue to chase and to hound us forever and I can't take that. I don't think I would be able to live fearing that at any time they might plant an under-car booby trap, killing or maiming Martin and Podraig, or put a fire-bomb through our letter-box. You know what they can do, Marty, you've seen it time and again in Belfast and it's always the innocent who get maimed and killed.'

'But it's much worse in Belfast,' I protested.

'It may be,' Angie said, 'but somehow I can face the troubles and the violence in Belfast. It's my home, Marty, and I don't feel so vulnerable there. Here I wake at night and stay awake for hours worrying myself about what might happen to us. It's just me, Marty, I can't help it.'

'I understand,' I told her. In fact I understood too well. I knew that night that Angie would make the decision to return to Belfast and take Martin and Podraig with her. She knew she was taking the risk of being interrogated by the IRA but I didn't try to dissuade her from returning. To have stopped her would have been unfair, especially if I had been taken out. It would have been even worse if the IRA had got one of the boys by accident. She would never have been able to forgive me for stopping her from returning home, telling her that everything would be fine in England when, in reality, I had no assurance whatsoever that she and the boys would be safe with me. In some ways I agreed with her thoughts because I knew I was a prime target. I had been told so by Felix and other SB men. I also knew that the IRA would never stop looking for me and that in itself was too much baggage for Angie to carry around. It was hard for me but it had been my decision to work for the RUC and now I would have to learn to live with it.

The worries about Angie's imminent departure returned to haunt me after a few weeks when I noticed that she still had that faraway look in her eyes. It was nothing Angie said to me, but I saw the fear and felt her slowly but irreparably drawing away from me. I would sometimes drive out alone to Kielder Water during those spring days and go for long walks trying to think of the right words to say that would persuade her to stay in England. But I always came up against the same difficulty and could find no way round it. I felt that I wasn't safe in Newcastle and so I didn't have the conviction to tell, or even try to tell, Angie that she should stay with me. I wanted her to stay more than anything else, and I knew that I would miss the boys horribly if they went back. I wanted us to remain together as a family, and so did she, but she couldn't take the risk; she simply couldn't risk the lives of the boys.

A few nights later Angie returned to the matter that we had both deliberately refused to speak of since the fire-bombing of the Metro Center, a subject I hoped she would never refer to again. But that had been wishful thinking.

'I want to go home, Marty,' she said, speaking quietly as we sat in the sitting-room which we had furnished together. Angie was looking at the carpet as though not wanting to look me in the eyes. I was glad she did that because I was so close to tears.

'I thought so,' I told her. 'I've felt it for weeks.' I didn't want to tell her that I knew for months past that she would one day give me the news I didn't want to hear. In my innocence I hoped that by not raising the subject she might, just might, forget about the matter and come to accept that life was quite safe and quite happy in Newcastle, away from the violence of Belfast. But the bombing of the Metro Center had been the final straw.

Then she turned and looked at me and as I looked back at her I fought back the tears that were choking in my throat. I felt so vulnerable and so helpless because I knew there was nothing I could say that might persuade her to change her mind.

'Can I say anything, Angie?' I asked, feeling wretched and incapable.

'No, Marty,' she said. 'I've made my mind up.'

'But we haven't discussed the issue,' I said, now feeling somewhat desperate. 'We must talk about it for Martin's and Podraig's sake.'

'There's nothing to discuss, Marty, nothing left to say,' she said, speaking quietly. 'I've thought about it for months but I can't stay here. I feel so vulnerable somehow.'

'But you've been here seven months and nothing's happened,' I said, trying to sound confident.

'But they haven't caught the bombers who live in or around Newcastle,' she said.

'But in Belfast there would be dozens of bombers and loads of gunmen, Angie, you've just never seen one.'

'I know, I know,' she responded, 'but I can't help the way I feel. I can't stop worrying. Every night I finally fall asleep worrying about you and the boys. Marty, you know they're after you and I just fear that one day they will get you.'

'There's no way they'll find me. You don't have to worry about me,' I said, not meaning to sound selfish but desperate to find any chink in her armor that might persuade her to stay.

'Even after we've made love and you've gone to sleep,' said Angie, 'I lie awake afterwards worrying about what might happen to you. I couldn't face seeing you taken out by the IRA and I wouldn't want the boys to witness such a thing. It would affect them for the rest of their lives. And that's not fair either, Marty.'

There was silence for a minute and I found myself fidgeting, wanting to find a solution that would persuade Angie to stay.

'But it doesn't mean I don't love you,' she said. 'You've been a wonderful father since we came over here and I do love you, Marty. You're always so kind and generous.'

Suddenly I felt her voice break with emotion and I looked across and saw the tears dropping slowly from her eyes on to the carpet below. I didn't know whether I should pretend not to notice or put my arms around her to comfort her. I decided to hold her, as tightly and closely as I could, to show her how much I loved her and how much she meant to me. But the closer I held her, and the more I kissed her hair, the more the tears flowed. Her body began to shake, gently but uncontrollably, and the tears that had been silent were now more anguished and clearly audible. I knew in that moment, if I hadn't known before, that Angie truly loved me. In those minutes I knew that I would be capable of facing the fact that Angie was leaving me because she had shown she truly loved me. I hoped too that, once back in Belfast, she might realize that she and the boys missed me enough to return to England. I didn't want to contemplate anything else for that gave me the strength to stop my tears and dry my eyes. That night together was one of the most emotional I had ever experienced in my life. It was also one of the most traumatic.

The following day I asked Angie just one question: 'Are you definitely going back?'

'Aye,' she said, 'I think it's for the best. You know how much my family fear for the kids if I stay here. Marty, I've got no choice. I have to go.'

'I'll arrange everything,' I said, 'leave it to me.' I knew there was no point in prolonging the agony either for Angie or myself.

I drove to Kielder Water later and walked slowly around the almost deserted place trying to gain inspiration, hoping that I could think of some magic formula which would convince Angie that it was safer for her and the boys to stay with me in Newcastle. But every argument I could think of ended in dust as I came to the conclusion that I was the problem because I had made fateful decisions earlier in my life to try to thwart the IRA's attempts to kill and maim innocent people.

The evening I drove Angie and the boys back to Scotland was the worst of my life. One hour out of Stranraer and with plenty of time to spare we stopped at a lay-by. The boys were fast asleep in the back seat. Angie became very emotional and asked me, for one last time, to make love to her. Silently we kissed and hugged each other and finally made love. Outside the night sky was filled with stars, the Milky Way clearly visible.

'I hate leaving you, Marty,' Angie whispered.

'I know, I know,' I said, stroking her hair and brushing away her tears.

For most of the time that three-hour journey was dispiriting, unnerving and miserable. Every mile I drove I kept hoping that Angie would change her mind, tell me to stop and turn around, tell me that she could not go ahead with her plan to return with the boys to Belfast. I wanted to beg and plead with her to change her mind but I knew that I had no right to try and persuade her to stay with me in England. And so, though I was feeling despondent and near to tears, I never tried to dissuade her from the path she had chosen.

At Stranraer I had said that I would stay at the terminal as she walked with Martin and Podraig the two hundred yards to the ferry. Angie was weeping and wailing, the tears streaming down her face as she kissed me goodbye and turned to walk away, out of my life forever. Podraig was sleeping peacefully, his head on her shoulder, unaware of the trauma that was ripping apart our family. Martin, however, did not want to go, did not want to leave me, and Angie had to drag him along the quay by the hand as he kept looking back, screaming for me to go with them. I don't know how I managed to control myself for I desperately wanted to run after them and bring them back to the terminal, to plead one last time for them to stay with me. Up to that moment I had never realized how much I cared for the three of them and how much I wanted to protect and look after them. As I watched them walk out of sight and on to the ferry I felt in that moment I had nothing to live for.

That wretched feeling of desolation and loneliness never left me during the long, long journey back to Newcastle; driving through the dark, isolated countryside of southern Scotland lit only by the stars that seemed in that darkness to be so very bright. I could think of nothing to cheer myself; could think of nothing to help relieve the feeling of despair or to stop the tears that erupted every few miles. And I cursed myself for the stupidity of youth that had led me into this terrible state. Little did I realize then that my troubles were only just beginning.

CHAPTER FIVE

Within a couple of weeks of Angie's return to Belfast the dreaded knock at her front door came early one morning. The IRA demanded that she attend a meeting at Sinn Fein headquarters to answer questions. It was, of course, the same place – Connolly House – from where I was kidnapped by two of Gerry Adams' henchmen, Paul 'Chico' Hamilton and James 'Jim' McCarthy. Though understandably nervous and frightened, Angie agreed and went along as 'requested'. She knew that she had no option but to attend, otherwise the next request would probably be far more forceful. She feared more for Martin and Podraig than for herself, for she had no idea what course the interview might take. Angie knew that she would be asked where I was living, my address and telephone number and full details of my car.

The man who called at Angie's front door after her return from England was Joseph Mulhern, a twenty-three -year-old IRA sympathizer who was well known in Catholic areas of West Belfast as a ruthless thug and bully, a member of an IRA punishment gang who delighted in terrorizing, bullying and beating young Catholic teenagers, sometimes kneecapping them, at other times simply dragging them from their homes and beating them senseless with iron bars and baseball bats. Angie would have known that such an invitation from such a well-known thug could not be ignored.

For four long hours Angie was questioned by 'Jim' McCarthy and another IRA interrogator before being allowed to return home. She had told them everything she knew of my whereabouts. At the end of their questioning the IRA interrogators told her to inform Sinn Fein headquarters if she should hear from me or, more importantly, if I should return to Belfast for a visit.

Before I drove her and the boys to Stranraer for their return journey to Belfast I told Angie that if she was ever questioned by the IRA that she must tell them the truth, hide nothing and answer whatever questions they asked to the best of her ability. I told her that within twenty-four hours of her arrival in Belfast I would have moved house, changed my car and changed my identity. In fact, I had no idea exactly where I would be twenty-four hours later but I had been telling her the truth for the Special Branch had informed me that I would have to immediately sell both the house and the car, as well as change my mobile phone number.

As it turned out, I stayed in my own home. To my great surprise Alan, my SB officer who maintained contact with the Newcastle Special Branch, told me during a conversation in a pub car park only days before Angie left that, having discussed the matter with headquarters, they advised that I should not move house.

'Not move anywhere? Stay put?' I asked, totally perplexed.

'Aye, that's right,' Alan said. 'The SB say that they've had a word with the powers that be and they believe you're in no danger; just stay where you are.'

'But the odds are that Angie will be questioned by the IRA and I've told her to tell the truth,' I replied.

'Don't let it worry you,' Alan said. 'Our SB boys know what's what. You're okay.'

'How can they possibly say that?' I asked, amazed at their lack of concern for my safety.

'You'll be okay, Marty,' Alan said. 'Don't worry about a thing.'

The nonchalant attitude to my possible danger shown by the Newcastle Special Branch surprised and, to a certain degree, alarmed me. The Special Branch knew that I had been moved to the mainland and given a new identity because, according to the IRA, they were determined to kill me. I had been judged guilty of treason to the Republican cause and, accordingly, my penalty was death. But this didn't seem to have any effect on the SB hierarchy or their advisers in MI5.

I couldn't understand their laissez-faire attitude. Throughout my four years working for British Intelligence in Belfast I had always been told to take no risks whatsoever, to leave nothing to chance and to always assume that the IRA were a thoroughly ruthless and intelligent organization which should be treated with respect. It seemed Newcastle Special Branch and MI5 thought otherwise, happy to leave me to my own devices even though there was now every chance that the IRA knew of my current home address.

Before she left Newcastle, I had warned Angie that the IRA men who interviewed her would pull no punches during her interrogation but that she would probably be well treated if she told the truth. However, I also knew in my heart that the IRA would be capable of taking any action towards her if they thought by doing so they could beat a path to my front door – and kill me. Many people were under the impression that the IRA never ill-treated or tortured Republican women but showed them respect. Nothing could be further from the truth. On most occasions, if IRA interrogators believe a woman is withholding information from them, they will treat her in the same way as a man who refuses to answer their questions. And it is a rule that if a Republican man or woman is found to work for the RUC Special Branch or British Intelligence they will be interrogated, tortured and murdered after being branded a traitor to the cause.

However, neither Angie nor I knew that Joseph Mulhern was also working for the RUC as an informant, running the same risks as I had run during my years as an undercover agent. He tried to cover his work for the police by showing a brutal side to his nature, happy to take part in savage IRA beatings of young teenagers and anyone who dared to cross the path of the petty IRA volunteers. Ten months after summoning Angie to her cross-examination, Joe Mulhern was also called to attend a meeting where he would be questioned by the dreaded IRA Civil Administration Team. Joe Mulhern, whose staunch Republican family was well known throughout West Belfast, was taken for a ride – south of the border – and held prisoner for ten days. During that time he was tortured until he finally cracked, admitting working for the RUC since 1990. Ten days is a long time for a man to be held, even by the IRA's standards, but immediately after his confession Joe was taken to a lonely spot near the River Derg, close to the Ballymongan border crossing near Castlederg, and shot. His carcass was found dressed in a khaki boiler suit, his hands tied in front of his body. He was wearing no shoes. He had been summarily executed in the IRA's traditional way – shot twice in the back of the head.

From the day I took Angie and the boys to Scotland to bid them farewell, I kept a low profile, ignoring the advice of the Newcastle Special Branch and changing my home from month to month, determined to keep at least one step ahead of any possible IRA assassination squad. I also changed my car on a couple of occasions just in case the IRA had stepped up their efforts to trace and pursue me. I knew full well that if an IRA active service unit was dispatched to England to 'get' me there would be no question of them kidnapping me. I knew they would simply be ordered to kill me whenever and wherever they found me.

There was another reason I stayed out of the limelight. For some months following the fire-bombing of the Metro Center there had been no further bomb attacks in the northeast. It seemed the IRA bombing team had left the area, presumably returning to Belfast. But, in December 1992, an IRA warning was issued saying that a bomb was to be placed on the Newcastle Metro system. In fact, no bombs were ever discovered but the warning caused chaos for many hours, closing down the system while bomb teams and police checked for possible devices. Four months later, on April 23,1993, IRA terrorists blew up an Esso oil terminal at North Shields near Howdon on the north side of the River Tyne. Two months later another IRA explosion rocked Dunston, Gateshead, when a bomb blasted the Redheugh gas holder, ripping a huge hole in the side of one of the three gas tanks. Hundreds of residents – many pensioners – were evacuated from their homes. On the same day – Wednesday, June 9, 1993 – explosions rocked another Esso terminal in North Shields but fortunately no one was injured. It was part of the IRA's strategy to bomb industrial targets on the mainland, hitting places which had never previously been attacked by IRA active service units. The campaign was intended to strike fear into the people who had never been touched by the Troubles in Northern Ireland. It also made me realize how close the IRA squad must have been to my Newcastle home.

One year after Angie and the boys had returned to Belfast my troubles with the authorities began to mount. Looking back on those heady days I can now see everything falling into place but at that time I must have been remarkably naive, believing I had friends in the Special Branch both in Belfast and Northumbria who would gladly keep their eyes open and protect me. I had no reason to think otherwise. For four years I had been cosseted and protected by my handlers, made to believe that I was a vital, all-important cog in the fight against terrorism and, in particular, against the IRA gunmen and bombers. Sometimes the praise I received made me believe I was a hero, particularly during the two years I was working inside the IRA intelligence wing. The fact that my work resulted in saving the lives of many innocent people made the risks I was taking each and every day seem absolutely worthwhile.

To pass the lonely days after Angie and the boys had left, I would often recall my life as an agent in Northern Ireland. I recalled driving through Belfast, ferrying one or more top IRA activists around the city, and feeling a warm glow as I listened to their conversations, taking a mental note of their 'hush-hush' plans to bomb and blast shops, offices, factories and RUC and Army bases, not caring a damn how many innocent people died in the process. Within an hour of hearing such information I would find a way of passing on the intelligence to the SB. My handlers were always totally supportive, offering advice and encouragement. But I never needed any praise for I knew that the lives of wives and sweethearts, husbands and sons were being saved.

As events unfurled throughout 1993, however, I was left with the strong impression that the Northumbrian authorities seemed hell-bent on getting me before a Magistrates Court. They knew that I was living in secret in Northumbria because I had been targeted by the IRA and my life had been threatened. They knew it was their duty to protect my identity to the best of their ability. And yet their actions towards me screamed that they were intent on exposing me and revealing my true identity.

I didn't know why; I hadn't a clue why the Northumbria Police Force would wish to expose me, and announce to the world my secret address where for two years I had been trying to keep a low profile living under my new name. Everything was under my new name; my bank accounts, my mortgage, my driving license, my social security number, my passport. No one in Newcastle, including my closest friends, had any idea that I was not really Martin Ashe – my new name – but in reality Marty McGartland. I had been smuggled out of Northern Ireland by the Special Branch and every precaution taken was designed to ensure my real identity and new address would be kept secret. Only the Northumbria Special Branch and, of course, the most senior police officers were told of my arrival on their patch.

They were informed that I was a prime target for an IRA assassination squad, that my life was in permanent danger from an IRA attack and, as a consequence, urged that everything should be done to ensure no one, but no one, knew of my real identity and background. The SB in Belfast knew from their sources within the IRA that the word had gone out: 'Get Marty McGartland'. They knew that I had been responsible for betraying many of the IRA's plots to bomb and shoot soldiers, prison officers and RUC and Army personnel; they knew that I had been responsible for stopping the IRA carrying out major attacks on British soldiers, preventing police officers being blown up by UCBTs, and that I had also given the Branch a stream of names and addresses of the IRA's top hit-men and bombers. That information had also been passed through the Joint Irish Section, the top-level British-staffed covert organization which even I knew very little about except that they were responsible for advising the Tasking Coordination Group, always called TCG. I had been told by my handlers that every effort would be made to take care of me and stop an IRA active service unit from getting to me. For, they told me, if an IRA unit did murder me my very death would put the fear of God into every agent and informer working for the Branch or British Intelligence in Northern Ireland. At a stroke it would have cut off the supply of information which the RUC, the Branch, military intelligence and MI5 relied on for more than eighty per cent of their intelligence in the Province. And without good intelligence sources, the security services in Northern Ireland are a spent force.

My contacts with the uniformed branch of the Northumbria Police Force began in earnest in late 1992 after a fracas with a number of Northumbria police officers. I had been sitting in my car, minding my own business, when a police officer I had never met before approached the car, telling me to move the vehicle. At the time I was parked in the library parking lot in Newcastle, a public place where I was perfectly entitled to leave my car. I refused to move away and the officer began shouting at me. I wound up the window and sat in the car listening to the radio. Suddenly he began banging on the window with his truncheon. I got out of the car to discuss the matter with him and he made a grab for me, intending to arrest me. He pushed me against the car and I turned round and pushed him. A scuffle developed.

'What are you doing?' I shouted at him.

'I'm arresting you for resisting arrest,' he said.

'But that's madness,' I told him, 'I've done nothing wrong.'

'You have,' he protested. 'You have refused to obey the order of a police officer.'

'Don't talk crap,' I told him. 'I've committed no offense.'

'Don't you fucking talk to me like that, you little prick,' he said. 'You're nicked, you little bastard.'

I began to get back into my car and the officer made another grab at me, this time threatening me with his truncheon. I saw red and though he struck out at me with the truncheon, hitting me around the head and shoulders, I managed to get the better of him. He called for assistance on his personal radio and I grabbed hold of him, pinning him face down on the bonnet of my car. Within two minutes four police cars and a police van arrived and I suddenly found six officers trying to pull me away from their colleague, everyone shouting and yelling. Eventually they handcuffed me and put me in the van. But while I was being driven to the police station the officer riding with me said, 'You're nothing but a fuckin' Irish mick . . . We know who you are . . . you're nothing but a mouthpiece . . . you're no fucking hero.'

I was amazed at what he had said. At that moment I realized that ordinary cops on the beat knew all about my background and the fact that I had worked for British Intelligence in Northern Ireland. I had not the faintest idea where those cops had been given that information and for what reason. It seemed unbelievable that Northumbria police officers should know all about me when every detail about my previous life was meant to be a closely guarded secret.

That fracas with the patrol officers was the start of a four-year campaign of victimization against me conducted by the Northumbrian Police. From that moment I was repeatedly pulled over by traffic patrol officers for alleged speeding offenses. I was also stopped and questioned by ordinary uniformed officers who seemed determined to incite and provoke violent arguments which would culminate with me being accused, and sometimes arrested, for alleged public order offenses. During those four years I was stopped on more than fifty separate occasions by traffic police, not only for speeding but just so that the officer could examine my car, check my lights, tires, brakes, etc. They were deliberately targeting me, hassling me, trying to provoke me into arguments so that they could accuse me of committing public order offenses.

I was in an impossible position. I was accused of more than half a dozen public order offenses all brought by the same small group of Northumbria police officers who seemed to take a delight in stopping and questioning me for no reason whatsoever. I would be taken to court and then have to listen to a torrent of lies by the officers as they gave evidence on oath in the witness box about my latest alleged misdemeanor. And, of course, the magistrates, accepting the word of the police officers, would find me guilty, levying fines of between £100 and £250 on each and every occasion.

Later, however, I became friendly with one Whitley Bay police officer. He told me, 'Martin, I think you should know that some police officers really enjoyed baiting you. They would try and get you to overreact so that they could arrest you and take you to court. They all thought it great fun, finding different ways to haul you before the magistrates. In the evening, we would all sit around having our tea or dinner and laugh about you, discussing different ways we could think of to provoke you so that you would respond by telling us to 'piss off' and leave you alone. That was our excuse to accuse you of a public order offense.'

'Are you kidding me?' I asked him.

'Not at all,' he replied. 'They knew details of your background in Northern Ireland and I think they were jealous of you. They wanted to show that they were top dog and try to make you look like some little prick.'

It seemed extraordinary that those police officers should not only try to take the piss out of me, but also go to court and actually relate a tissue of lies – on oath! In court the officers would allege that I had been swearing, pushing and kicking them, distressing passers-by with my behavior when, in reality, I had done no such thing.

I asked this friendly cop, 'Why did they want to wind me up?'

He told me, 'Because you had made them look like shit. They felt embarrassed the first time they tried to arrest you in the car park and it took six of them to hold you down. You made them look pathetic and they couldn't forgive you. Eventually, over time, arresting you became a huge joke, a way in which they could regain their self-esteem. I did it too for a while but now I want to say sorry. We were taking a liberty.'

But many other Northumbria cops continued their harassment. They continued to target me, almost on a weekly basis. It continued for years and cost me hundreds of pounds in fines and court costs, though for much of the time I was totally innocent.

When I was stopped by police during the hours of darkness I was sometimes exceeding the speed limit, but for a reason. I did fear that the car tailing me could well have been IRA hitmen intent on pursuing me. At night, the police cars following me would only flash on their blue lights and sound their sirens after they had been tailing me for a few miles, putting the fear of God into me before I knew it was really them. In Northern Ireland I had been advised by my SB handlers to take evasive action if I found a car had been tailing me for some miles, with the driver making no effort to overtake. When you know you are a targeted man you don't wait around, driving slowly; you get the hell out of the way as quickly as possible, not waiting until those tailing you open fire.

Within weeks, however, I found myself being tailed by unmarked police cars. They would usually follow me at night, driving close behind me, harassing me and making me feel nervous and threatened. When I sped up and tried to lose the chasing vehicle the unmarked cop car would tailgate me for a few miles, almost encouraging and forcing me to drive faster. Only when I had exceeded the speed limit for a few miles would the cops pull out, sound their siren and order me to pull over. Even then I wasn't sure they were cops. I would wait while they got out of their vehicle and walked towards me, keeping the engine running and the revs high, in case, just in case, they were IRA gunmen and I needed to make a rapid getaway. For people whose lives have never been threatened, particularly by a terrorist organization, all this may seem far-fetched and over-dramatic. It isn't. In such circumstances one is struck with deep fear at the thought that someone chasing you in a vehicle could well be a gunman hell-bent on killing you.

And I had a major problem to contend with. When the cops did stop me, usually for speeding, there was no excuse that I could offer. I could not explain the reason why I had been speeding; I could not pour out my history and just tell them that I was in permanent danger because I had spent four years working undercover in Northern Ireland. So I would simply produce my driving license and say nothing. In a bid to lay a false trail for the IRA, however, I had taken the precaution of obtaining two licenses at two addresses, one in Northumberland, the other in Durham. So, because of the extraordinary number of times the police were stopping me I decided to make use of both licenses. I would offer first one and when stopped the next time, hand over the other. In this way I escaped a driving ban for almost two years. Of course, I knew that technically I was breaking the law but I believed the extenuating circumstances heavily outweighed the offense. My luck could not last and because of my constant fear of being targeted, my numerous speeding offenses piled up until I eventually did exceed the twelve-point tally; eventuating in 1995 to a statutory six-month driving ban. During that appearance at North Tyneside Magistrates Court I simply pleaded guilty, offering no excuse or reason to the magistrates as to the real reason why I had been caught speeding so frequently. At that time, I did not want to attract attention to myself or reveal the circumstances behind my frequent breaking of the speed limits.

As soon as I regained my license, however, the Northumbria traffic cops were back tailing me. The motor-patrol units continued to follow and harass me, making driving a real problem. And though I presumed it was traffic cops following me I could never know for sure. So I adopted a new technique, though a far more risky one, which would not have been approved by Special Branch officers. Instead of speeding away, I would draw into the side of the road and stop whenever I felt a vehicle had been tailing me for too long, though making no attempt to overtake me. In that way the cop cars either had to stop behind me or overtake, permitting me to continue my journey. But it was a real hassle.

In January 1995, my troubles escalated when the police discovered that I held two driving licenses. It seemed they had been waiting patiently to throw the book at me and now they had found the opportunity. I had learned during my time inside the IRA that it was possible for IRA computer experts to hack into the DVLA computers in Swansea to gain names, addresses and car registration numbers. I knew that if the IRA were determined, such information on the DVLA computers could expose me to attack. Two officers came to my home and asked me to accompany them to Blyth police station in Northumberland. They escorted me to the station and put me in an interview room.

'What are you arresting me for?' I asked.

'You'll find out at the station,' replied one of them.

'Why can't you tell me now?' I asked.

But the officer simply repeated his statement that I would learn everything at the 'nick'. At the station I was put before the custody sergeant and then taken to an interview room to await questioning. After a few minutes two officers came into the room, asked my name and address - which I gave them - and then proceeded to question me. 'We have reason to believe that you have two driving licenses,' one officer told me. 'Have you anything to say?'

I looked from one to the other, wondering if they knew of my background or whether they were genuine. I realized that perverting the course of justice was a very serious offense and I had no wish to face a jail sentence. I knew that if I tried to argue my way out of this accusation the police would simply apply for a search warrant of my home and discover that I did indeed hold two licenses. I decided the time had come to tell the truth.

'That's true,' I replied, 'but there is a reason why I have two licenses.'

'Oh yes,' said one of the officers, sarcastically, 'pull the other one.'

'It's true,' I told them, 'and I can prove it.'

They didn't want to hear my story but simply accused me once more of 'trying to pervert the course of justice', asking me if I had anything to say in my defense. We were in a police interview room and, of course, a tape recorder was running. I asked them to stop the recording as I had something of extreme importance to tell them, something that would satisfactorily answer all their questions. After some further discussion, they finally agreed to turn off the recorder and listen to what I had to say. I spent the next ten minutes explaining in some detail my background, my real identity and the fact the Northumbria Special Branch knew of my history and the undercover work I had carried out in Northern Ireland. I told the patrol officers the SB would be able to verify my story.

Seemingly, my undercover work in Northern Ireland made not the slightest difference and I was served notice to appear at Newcastle Magistrates Court in July, 1996 charged with attempting to pervert the course of justice. I was surprised and angry. I attended the Magistrates Court and, as I expected, was then sent for trial at Newcastle Crown Court. The hearing was scheduled to go ahead in May, 1997. This meant that from the date the case was forwarded to the Crown Prosecution Service in July, 1995, I had to wait one year for the case to come before the Magistrates Court and a further ten months for the case to be heard in Newcastle Crown Court. I began to wonder why this was so – a total of twenty-two months!

It was, allegedly, the Crown Prosecution Service that had taken the final decision to prosecute me, for my solicitor received a letter in June, 1996 from D.K. Hyland, a special case worker for the Crown Prosecution Service, saying that I would be prosecuted for attempting to pervert the course of justice. In talks with my solicitor later, Mr. Hyland admitted that the case was 'both complicated and sensitive' and told my solicitor that if the case became embarrassing for the Government he would be prepared to 'back off a little'.

Looking back on that episode it seems unbelievable that the CPS should demand I stand trial, for I knew that the CPS, part of the British Government's legal system, would have been aware of every detail of my life and work as an undercover agent. They would have known that I had no intention of perverting the course of justice but had been taking such action to ensure I kept ahead of any assassination squads. I couldn't understand why they should want to expose me in such a public way, by dragging me into a Crown Court, a place where members of the public could gather to listen to the evidence, thus exposing me to possible IRA retaliation.

But later I would understand only too well. My Belfast SB mate would put everything into perspective when he told me of MI5's plot to have me kidnapped and killed by the IRA.

I discussed my forthcoming trial with Inspector Denzil Gibson, my Special Branch contact in Newcastle, who knew all the details of my work in Belfast. He advised me: 'Plead guilty, man, and no one will know anything about your past life.'

'But if I plead guilty,' I told him, 'there is every chance that I will be sent to jail.'

'Don't worry about that, man,' he said. 'If you have to do time that's the penalty you must pay to keep your background under wraps.'

I told him, 'My solicitor has warned me that if I don't fight this case and win it the Crown Court judge is bound to send me to jail and not just for a few weeks. I'm not prepared to go to jail when I had very good reasons for what I did. I'm innocent and I don't see why I should plead guilty.'

'Have it your way,' he told me, 'but I'm telling you that the only way to escape exposure is to plead guilty and do the time. It might only be a year or so inside; you can take that.'

I was flabbergasted. It seemed extraordinary at the time but Inspector Gibson continued to press me, always urging me to plead guilty and never suggesting that I should fight to clear my name.

'But if I plead guilty,' I told him, 'no evidence will come out. And I want the judge to hear the way the traffic cops here have treated me over the years. I want a jury to know the full facts, including my undercover work in Belfast, so that then I will get a fair hearing. If I just plead guilty I will be seen as nothing but a toe-rag. I won't do it.'

I knew, of course, why the police wanted me to plead guilty. They were scared that the jury would find me innocent. They also didn't want the ignominy of being seen harassing and bullying someone who had served his country in a dangerous, life-threatening job for four years.

The magistrates committed me to Newcastle Crown Court for

trial on indictment on May 14, 1997. Under my new identity, Martin David Ashe, I was charged with 'Doing acts tending and intended to pervert the course of public justice between June 8, 1993 and April 29, 1994, in that he surrendered two or more separate driving licenses for endorsement with a view to avoiding disqualification'.

But in December, 1996, my book, *Fifty Dead Men Walking*, the story of my life as an undercover agent, was published. It seemed that because I had decided to come out into the open and tell my story the authorities had made the decision to make my life as difficult as possible. The Northumbria Police stepped up their efforts to hassle and provoke me, taking me to court seemingly every other week or so for offenses I did not commit. I talked to journalist friends and former Belfast SB friends and they all told me that the actions taken against me were typical of the authorities doing all in their power to create problems for me; to make my life as difficult as they could. It also seemed that senior RUC officers, including the Chief Constable, were determined to downgrade the part I had played in Northern Ireland, fearing that I would take the limelight that they believed rightly belonged to them. Initially, there was nothing that I could do to counteract their sly, spiteful attacks but, in a matter of months, the difficulties being put in my way escalated to such a degree that I could hardly step outside my front door without fresh problems confronting me.

In late December, 1996, nearly one month after my book was published, I was informed by a friend whom I was staying with at the time that two men were knocking on the front door of his house looking for me. They asked him where I could be contacted and he told them that he had no idea. They asked what car I was driving at the time and my friend surprised them. 'Lately he has been riding a bicycle around. He hasn't got a car at the moment. Can I take a message?' he asked, but they refused point blank to give their names or where they were from.

My friend, who knew nothing of my past in Northern Ireland, thought the two men wanted to give me a good hiding, especially when they told him they would be returning later. When he informed me what had happened I went immediately to the local police station and asked if any officers were looking for me. The police officer on duty checked and informed me that no officers had been to my house. He tried to reassure me that he didn't think I had anything to worry about. I wasn't so sure. I then called at the local council offices and the DHSS but was informed that no one had been looking to contact me.

Later, I would learn that the Northumbria Police were also concerned. They made their own checks within the force, with the DHSS and North Tyneside Council, but all checks proved negative. I never discovered who my two mysterious visitors were and neither did the police. I was fearful that they could well have been IRA hitmen who had learned of my whereabouts, so I decided to phone my SB mates in Belfast to see if they had heard if any IRA team were actively searching for me.

'We've heard nothing to alarm you,' an SB man named Chris told me. 'But keep your head down and your eyes peeled. Trust no one, Marty, because they will never give up. If you want us to help in any way just call, night or day.'

Despite the SB assurances I decided to move out of my friend's house that very night, going to stay with another acquaintance.

But my problems with the Northumbria Police continued unabated. One example of the way I had been hassled occurred in January, 1995 after I had driven home and parked the car as usual at the back of my house. As I did so, half-a-dozen or more police officers leapt out of the bushes where they had been hiding and ran to my car, making me feel like some armed terrorist. They snatched the keys from the ignition and ordered me out of the car. Then one of them opened the bonnet and after checking the engine number told me, 'We are arresting you for being in possession of a stolen vehicle.'

'Don't be daft,' I told him. 'This is my car and I can prove it.'

'This car has been stolen,' he replied, 'and you are under arrest.'

I replied, 'Don't talk rubbish. I bought this car months ago and it was in terrible condition. I've spent the last few months rebuilding it myself with the help of some mates. I don't know what you're talking about; you need your fucking head examined.'

'You will still have to accompany us to the police station to make a statement, you little bastard,' he said.

'Wait a minute,' I replied, 'I can prove this car's mine.'

'Don't come that one,' said the officer in charge, 'that's bullshit. We know you've nicked it.'

'Hold on a minute,' I demanded, 'inside the house I've got photos taken at different times showing how I rebuilt the vehicle from scratch after it had been involved in an accident. Perhaps that will persuade you that I'm telling the truth.'

'Okay,' said the officer in command, 'show us.'

Once in the flat I found the photographs and showed them to the police. The photographs seemed to calm them and they agreed that perhaps they had been misinformed. In the meantime, however, the other officers were poking around my flat as though looking for other things to embarrass me with.

Suddenly I heard a yell from my bedroom and I ran in. 'Don't move,' one shouted at me. 'Stay exactly where you are, don't move a fuckin' inch.'

To the other officers he shouted, 'Arrest him; cuff him; this place is full of fuckin' guns and ammunition.'

'What the fuck are you talking about?' I asked, half laughing at this officer who seemed to have lost his senses.

'Don't talk, don't say a fuckin' word. Just shut up,' he shouted.

I tried to intervene to explain everything but he wouldn't even allow me to speak.

'Cuff him, handcuff the fucking Irish bastard,' he yelled at one of the officers standing next to me.

I went to move forward to pick up one of the guns and explain everything to the screaming officer but before I had moved one foot forward he leapt towards me, pushing me away from the arms and ammo, shouting, 'Get back, get back, don't move; stand still; you're under arrest.'

To one of his officers, he yelled, 'Grab him, arrest him; don't let him near the guns.'

On his police radio he called his Operations Room and urged them to send specialists from the Northumbria Police Fire Arms Team as a matter of urgency. He explained that an IRA arms dump had been discovered in the bedroom of a private flat.

'Will you listen to me?' I said when he had finished his conversation. 'This is no IRA arms dump, these guns aren't real, they're only replicas,' I insisted.

'Shut the fuck up and keep quiet,' he shouted.

I could see that he was in a blind panic, stumbling over his words, perspiring profusely as though he had indeed come across an IRA arms dump and that I was an armed terrorist.

I tried again. 'Let me show you, let me prove to you that they're only replicas,' I suggested.

'Don't fuckin' come that with us,' he said. 'We'll wait until the experts get here. They know what's what.'

I started to laugh, unable to control myself as I witnessed the officers rushing around my flat in a panic, searching for more weapons and ammo. I shrugged my shoulders. If they wouldn't listen to my explanation then, I felt, fuck 'em, let them show their senior officers how stupid they were. In fact, I had the weapons and the ammo as protection, just in case the IRA were to burst into my flat; but I couldn't tell the police the real reason.

Though nobody listened, or appeared to take the slightest notice of anything I said, I did in fact manage to say a few words once they calmed down a little and their panic subsided. I explained that I collected such replicas. But they were still all on edge and I could tell they were too nervous to pay attention to what I was saying. When one of the officers finally found the courage to kneel down and examine the sacks containing the guns and ammo, the man in charge yelled, 'What the fuck are you doing? . . . Get back . . . get back . . . don't move . . . they might be booby-trapped . . . we know what these IRA bastards are like.'

After the specialist officers had arrived at the house and

checked the weapons they were put in clear plastic bags and taken downstairs. A number of neighbors had turned out to see what was happening, wondering why four police cars had arrived at my flat with their sirens screaming, bringing attention to this quiet backwater which had never seen such police activity. They witnessed me leaving, handcuffed to a police officer, while other officers walked out holding the guns and ammo in the plastic bags. That night my neighbors were left in no doubt that in fact I was an IRA gunman and my flat an IRA arms dump.

Eventually, when I was allowed to explain things in the police station, the arms expert and others inspected the life-like weapons more closely. Despite the fact that they appeared to believe they were harmless replicas the decision was nevertheless taken to have them sent to the forensic arms headquarters in Huntington. Despite proving the weapons were only replicas, the police detained me in a cell for a full four hours. I could hardly contain myself from laughing out loud at the reaction of the officers that day. Eventually I was released without charge and driven home. I had to be escorted by the police because, despite producing papers proving the Ford Orion was my property, they wanted to double-check the vehicle to ensure it had not been stolen. In fact, the police kept the car for four days before saying I could collect it. I noted they never apologized for the inconvenience they caused me nor did they apologise for doubting my word. It seemed to me the police were taking every opportunity they could to harass me. A few weeks later, my replicas and the ammo were returned to me. But it wasn't the end of the matter.

Some months later I was in the kitchen of my flat on the first floor of a terraced house in Northumberland when I was disturbed by a heavy 'thud, thud, thud' on the back door below. After a few minutes the thumping began again and I looked out of the window to see two men, dressed in everyday civilian clothes, standing by the door. 'What do you want?' I shouted, fearing that these could indeed be IRA gunmen. They somehow seemed shady, standing with their heads down as if not wanting to be recognized.

'Are you Martin Ashe?' one shouted.

'Who wants to know?' I called back, for I didn't recognize either man.

'We're police officers; we want to talk to you,' he said.

'Have you any identification?' I called down.

'Yes,' he said, and produced his police warrant card, showing it to me as I was leaning out of the window. I looked down and they seemed genuine enough but I wasn't absolutely certain. I decided that they were probably not IRA gunmen and went down to check their IDs more closely.

'We're from Cumbria Police,' one explained, showing me his police ID, 'and we understand from Northumbria police that you own an AK47 assault rifle and ammunition.'

'That's not true,' I replied, 'but I do own a replica AK.'

He continued. 'Well, recently there has been a bank robbery at Windermere and the robbers were carrying an AK47. We're checking everyone in the north of England who is known to own such a weapon.'

I looked at them and shook my head for I sensed this was a deliberate set-up by the Northumbria Police to either hassle me or frighten the shit out of me. 'Come and inspect the AK if you want,' I said, and explained the reaction of the officers from Northumbria when they had discovered an IRA arms dump in my bedroom. The officers inspected the weapons but were still skeptical. They demanded I tell them where I was on the day of the Windermere robbery and I told them I was with a girlfriend, a Customs and Excise officer. The detectives asked for her phone number and while I stayed in the room one placed a call, checking the details I had supplied to them. Only when they were satisfied that I had told the truth did they apologize for troubling me and left. I sighed with relief that yet another police attempt to frame me had failed. But I was also angry at the treatment I was receiving at the hands of the local police.

But those incidents were nothing compared to what I was to discover. I had been led to understand by both the Belfast Special

Branch and the Northumbria SB that when I was relocated to Blyth my previous names, official documents, even my life history would be eradicated and I would henceforth be known only as Martin David Ashe. I was informed that for all intents and purposes the person known as Martin McGartland would cease to exist.

But somehow, someone had decided to resurrect my former name and surreptitiously make it known. It was inserted on police computer files, the DVLA computer database and given to officers of the Crown Prosecution Service. I would learn later that within months of my secret arrival in England, many police officers, court officials, and persons with access to police files or the DVLA computer knew that Martin McGartland, one of the IRA's prime targets for execution, was alive and well and living in Blyth, Northumberland. I could not believe that the insertion of my former identity on those files was a mere accident. Someone or some Government agency, or even some police force, had to be responsible for such an action. It seemed to me that I was being set up for the IRA to discover my new identity and my new address. But why?

I determined to discover what precisely was on my police computer files that warranted such continued interest in my affairs by the Northumbria Police. I wanted to find out if by examining my computer files I could ascertain why I was being targeted by the local police force. And, if possible, I wanted to discover who had taken that decision to have me targeted.

My suspicions had first been aroused during one of my many appearances before local magistrates on the dozens of spurious motoring offenses I was accused of by the Northumbria Police motor patrol unit. During one such court appearance in 1995, before North Tyneside Magistrates, both my solicitor Paul Dodds and myself happened to look over the shoulder of the Crown Prosecution Service lawyer. We both read on his files that my two names, Ashe and McGartland, were prominently displayed for all to read. This would have meant that anyone dealing with the paperwork concerning the dozens of alleged motoring offenses brought against me would have been aware of my real identity which the Special Branch in Belfast and the authorities in England had been at great pains to keep secret.

There and then Paul Dodds approached the CPS lawyer, Mr. Stuart Michie, and asked him to explain why my two names were on the file he had brought to court. Mr. Michie was taken aback by our concern and said that he had no idea how this matter occurred. I told him that I had never, but never, told anyone that I was known by any other name than Martin David Ashe. Even Paul Dodds, my own solicitor, had never known until a short time ago, that I was anyone but Martin David Ashe!

As a result, Paul Dodds wrote on my behalf to John Stephens, then Northumbria Chief Constable, asking for a meeting to discuss what to me was a very serious matter. Within days, Chief Superintendent Gordon Hay, head of Northumbria Police Complaints and Discipline, contacted my solicitor and a meeting was arranged. At that meeting, Superintendent Hay assured Mr. Dodds that the 'offending alias' (McGartland) would be removed immediately from police files. But there would be worse to follow. I had discovered from a friend of a friend that my two identities were also on the Northumbria Police computer file and had been for years. This news came as a total surprise to me but, at that stage, I had no proof. I could not believe that the name McGartland would be included in the file on Ashe. I told my solicitor what I had learned and, as a result, he wrote again to the Chief Constable demanding full details of any intelligence referring to me on the Northumbria force's intelligence computer file.

Superintendent Hay wrote back informing him that the offending material concerning my two identities – McGartland and Ashe – had indeed been filed on the Northumbria Police computer but had been removed from all computer files in August, 1995. It seemed extraordinary that Superintendent Hay should report that my file had been removed from the computer exactly one week after my solicitor's original letter demanding the files be forwarded to him.

In August, 1995 my solicitor, Paul Dodds, had written to the

Data Protection Officer of the Northumbria Police demanding that all the files concerning me, under the name Martin David Ashe, be sent to his office. I had been advised that the Northumbria Police were legally bound to hand over those files as part of an individual's 'Subject Access' rights. But the Northumbria Police seemed most reluctant to carry out what they were legally bound to do, all but ignoring my solicitor's letters and writing disingenuous replies which gave no reason why the Data Protection Officer was refusing to forward full copies of my computer file. Three months later, the Data Protection Officer for Northumbria Police sent to my solicitor what she claimed was a full copy of all that had been included on my file in the police computer. There were just six pages.

Now I was even more suspicious. I knew that the six pages could not possibly be a comprehensive account of my file; simply because of the unbelievable number of times I had been stopped by traffic police, arrested, taken to police stations for other offenses, and, as a result, ended up in court on countless occasions. I urged my solicitor to continue to press the Data Protection Officer for a complete and full copy of all the material on police files. Finally, in July 1997, two years after my solicitor first demanded my records, and two months after my court appearance at Newcastle Crown Court, the Northumbria Police sent through a complete resume of my computer file. It was twenty-five pages long!

The police file was full of inaccuracies, falsehoods and downright lies. The brief description of me on the file recorded that I spoke with a strong Southern Irish accent, was of a violent disposition and that I was to be approached with caution because of my propensity for carrying firearms. Now I knew why the Northumbria Police had been so reticent in sending me the file that I was legally entitled to see. First, I always spoke with a Belfast accent; secondly, I was not of a violent disposition unless aroused; and third, I had never carried or used firearms in my life. What concerned me was the fact that whenever a police officer asked for my personal data file over the radio, the only details they would receive included those three damaging and inaccurate descriptions, under the headline: 'Warning. Violent. Firearms'. That revelation made me spit with anger for it was obviously one of the reasons why I had received such close attention from Northumbria Police. What I didn't know, and what I wanted to know, was who had been responsible for putting those warnings on my personal data file. And why?

Unbelievably, that was not the end of the matter. Despite the assurances and the promises from senior police officers, my two identities were not removed from computer files. Two years later, in June 1997, I found out that my two names – Ashe and McGartland – and my address were still both on the Northumbria Police computer information system. That meant that for an additional two years the computer would reveal my records to any police officer who accessed my records. As a result of that cock-up five thousand police officers, who had immediate and direct access to those files, could have known that McGartland and Ashe were one and the same person. And they would have known from those computer files that McGartland had been an RUC Special Branch informant working inside the IRA, who had been relocated to the northeast after his cover had been blown. As a result, an internal police inquiry was ordered to determine exactly how and why my two names had been entered into the computer. Surprisingly, after what the police described as a thorough three-month investigation, a Northumbria Police chief told me that it had been impossible to discover who had entered my name on the computer despite the fact that access can only be gained by police officers entering their own personal code.

But I was not going to accept that explanation, so I wrote to the Police Complaints Authority complaining about what had happened and asking them to investigate. Eight months later the PCA wrote to me saying, 'It has not been possible to trace the officer responsible for placing the name on your record. This is due to a fault with the computer system at the time the information was entered.'

'Balls,' I thought to myself, 'the lying shits.'

But the PCA also revealed that my two names – Ashe and McGartland – were still on the DVLA computer files. The files also included my home address. And, once again, I was led to understand that it had been impossible to trace the person who had put both names and addresses on the DVLA computer due to a fault. The PCA added: 'There is no evidence to show that the name was entered maliciously or that there was any intention to place you in danger. There is also no evidence to suggest that any officer, apart from those entrusted with the information, was informed of your background.'

The Chairman of the Police Complaints Authority, Peter Moorhouse, wrote to Ronnie Campbell, my MP: 'I have now read the investigation file . . . Northumbria Police of course acknowledge that Mr Ashe's other identity was on the force computer. They maintain with some justification that Mr. Ashe's continued breaches of the Road Traffic Act had brought him to the notice of a number of traffic officers, one of whom accessed Mr. Ashe's name on the DVLA computer and there learned of Mr. Ashe's other identity. The officer entered the alias on the police computer with the result that when Mr. Ashe requested a data protection report the entry came to light. There is nothing unusual in the fact that this item of intelligence was entered on to the computer and nothing sinister should be read into the entry.'

The letter went on to accuse me of being indiscreet and of being regularly stopped driving a car for which the owner was listed on the Police National Computer as one 'Marty McGartland' (sic). I was furious by the response because it was totally untrue. At no time had that car been registered under the name McGartland.

Of course, the police should never have entered the name McGartland on that computer file, or any file that could have been accessed by officers, giving details of both my identities, background and particulars. Indeed, the names of all British agents – which also provide details of their work for British Intelligence – is never under any circumstance put on a police computer file for the same reason. To permit thousands of police officers access to such material is a serious breach of security. It is well known in the security services in Northern Ireland that the IRA send political activists to be trained as computer experts in Britain, learning how to hack into computer systems, so that they can trace names, addresses, phone numbers, social security numbers, car registration numbers, etc., of anyone they want to target. Instructions are regularly issued by the Home Office to every police force in Britain ordering them to make sure that no such information is input into any police file. At first, I believed in my innocence that the instruction was simply ignored. But I began to suspect the hand of MI5 was behind this despicable act of duplicity. It seemed extraordinary that the Northumbria Police had found it impossible to trace the person or persons responsible and yet, as a result, anyone with access to those files would have been able to find exactly where I lived.

But now I had to attend to a more pressing personal challenge, facing an open court with a jury sitting in judgment. My ordeal in Newcastle Crown Court before Judge Denis Orde began at 10 a.m. on 16 May 1997, when I was charged with attempting to pervert the course of justice. I pleaded not guilty. The first legal arguments centered around the question as to whether the media should be permitted to cover the court case on a daily basis. The prosecution, headed by Mr. Mark Styles, argued that the hearing should be in public. He contested that I was in no danger from any source and had pleaded not guilty in an effort to gain publicity for *Fifty Dead Men Walking* which had been published five months before. As a consequence, my defense, headed by Mr. Glenn Gatland, was forced to tell the judge the reason why the press should be banned from reporting the case until after it was over. Mr. Gatland explained that because the Northumbria Police had refused my application for police protection throughout the court case, he feared there was a danger that IRA men intent on killing me could take the opportunity to shoot me as I entered or left the court.

As I sat in court throughout that first day I wondered who it was that had persuaded the prosecution to put forward such a legal argument, all but forcing my defense lawyer to reveal my background at the very beginning of the trial. I felt suddenly lonely and unprotected, as though all the forces of the British legal system, including the police, were intent on revealing my identity and my home address. I knew that the Crown Prosecution Service would have been fully aware that the line of argument they had taken in court could only end with my two identities being revealed. As I looked round the courtroom from my position in the dock I felt a sense of desolation and hopelessness; that I was unable to take action myself that could retrieve the situation. My mind went back to that awful day in August, 1991 when I lay on the sofa in that stiflingly hot flat in Twinbrook, Belfast, waiting for the IRA execution squad to arrive. I wondered what the judge could do on this occasion to alleviate my anxieties, particularly as he too was a member of the British legal system. I realized that he was also in a difficult position. Thus I was greatly relieved when Judge Orde decreed that no publicity or photographs whatsoever be permitted until after the trial was ended, thereby allaying fear of someone tipping off potential assassins. The public gallery remained open, however, and reporters were allowed to attend court and take notes. It wasn't a perfect solution from my viewpoint but it was a better one than I had anticipated as I listened to the spurious legal arguments put forward by the prosecution.

Although I felt somewhat of a fool, I entered and left court each day wearing a hooded coat, scarf and dark glasses. The suggestion had been made by one of my old buddies in the Belfast Special Branch. He advised me to take no chances. I told the court that one of the licenses in the name of Ashe had, in fact, been organized by the Special Branch. I also told them that every time I appeared before local magistrates for speeding offenses, I could not tell them the real reason for my offense because I would have blown my cover and exposed my two identities, something which RUC Special Branch officers had advised me not to do under any circumstances. I told the judge that I had obtained the two other licenses using false addresses to avoid details of my true whereabouts being held on record. I also emphasized that I never had any intention of perverting the course of justice.

I was indeed fortunate that I had friends who came to my rescue during my four-day trial. Sam Cushnahan of Families Against Intimidation and Terror, a Northern Ireland pressure group for peace, gave evidence saying that I was one of two people heading the IRA's most-wanted list. He told the court, 'People who are caught informing on the IRA are tortured and then murdered. As far as the IRA is concerned, it would be a great propaganda coup to murder Martin McGartland. His death would be seen as a lesson to others who infiltrate their security.'

My lawyer, Glenn Gatland, explained to the jury that each time I was stopped by police I could not explain my true identity because I feared detection from 'moles'. He explained that throughout the early 1990s Britain's anti-terrorist police knew an IRA cell was living and operating in the north-east targeting high-profile establishments, and would have certainly informed their IRA commanders in Belfast if they had discovered that I was living in Newcastle.

I had to bite my tongue on several occasions, however, when Mr. Mark Styles for the prosecution tried to dismiss what I and others had done on behalf of the people of Northern Ireland in risking our lives to save others. But what I found even more despicable was Styles' efforts to dismiss the savage beating of my brother Joseph by an IRA punishment squad as of little consequence. In July 1996, only ten months before the court case, Joseph was left with two shattered legs, four broken ribs and two broken arms. The jury was shown photographs taken shortly after his savage IRA treatment, carried out solely because I was his brother. Every member first looked at the pictures and then glanced up at Mark Styles, a look of revulsion on their faces. I felt like shaking the hand of every man and woman in that group after I saw their heartfelt reaction.

Mr. Styles also tried to play down the threat to my life by the IRA, stating in open court that he had spoken to a Special Branch officer outside the court who informed him that the threat against me was 'minimal'. So I immediately asked Mr. Styles and the judge to bring the SB officer into court so that he could be cross-examined. Mr. Styles immediately changed the subject and refused to produce the so-called SB man to the court.

But on occasions there was also humor. When Sam Cushnahan was being questioned by my barrister, he was asked what his views were in relation to the threat on my life by the IRA. Cushnahan replied that, with his knowledge of the IRA, I would need to look over my shoulder for the rest of my life.

Cushnahan was asked to put himself in my shoes concerning the speeding offenses. 'What would you have done if you had been in Mr. McGartland's position?'

His reply was, 'I would not only have been exceeding the speed limit but I would have been driving through ditches, over rivers and, if my car had wings, I would have been flying.'

The entire court burst into laughter.

Seconds later the jury looked anxious and some of the women close to tears when Mr. Cushnahan told them, 'There are probably young men from this area that served with the security forces in Northern Ireland walking the streets today who are unaware of the fact that this man standing in the dock saved their lives at great risk to his own life.'

In his summation to the jury Mr. Styles went further, attempting to refute my courtroom testimony about why I had obtained two driving licenses by alleging that I was at no time in any danger while living in Newcastle. He instead claimed that I had used a deliberate course of conduct to deceive courts over my driving record. Getting different licenses had been pre-planned and he claimed I had acted with a total disregard for the law. After a two-hour summing up Judge Orde sent the jury to consider their verdict. They came back within ten minutes and unanimously returned a verdict of 'not guilty'. I tried to contain myself but couldn't do so. The sense of relief after nearly two years of stress and anxiety while waiting for the case to come to trial had overwhelmed me. I sat down in the dock and wept.

In a statement made following the case my solicitor Nigel Dodds said: 'The prosecution has deliberately exposed my client to further danger. He will now have to move house, relocate to a different area and change his identity once again. My client should never have been brought to court in the light of his services in Northern Ireland. The prosecution has exposed him to danger which his resettlement on the mainland was meant to avoid. It appears he has been thrown to the wolves by the Special Branch.'

My acquittal at Newcastle Crown Court was welcomed by MPs, the newspapers and Tynesiders who believed the case should never have been brought against me. Former Northern Ireland Minister Peter Bottomley was one of a group of MPs trying to establish a new identity for me. Both Labour and Tory MPs from the New Dialogue peace group approached Northern Ireland Secretary Mo Mowlam and Home Secretary Jack Straw urging them to arrange a new ID for me. In a nationwide TV program, Peter Bottomley said, 'Without trying to turn Martin McGartland into a saint, I think what he was doing was saintly, trying to reduce the effectiveness of a killing machine which has helped put three thousand people into cemeteries.'

Thousands of Tynesiders signed a petition in the days following the court case calling on the Government to give me a new identity as a matter of urgency. I was touched that so many people from Tyneside should stand up and be counted when I was a stranger in their midst, an Irishman who had come to the north-east seeking sanctuary. Tynesiders had revealed how kind and generous they are to total strangers. But despite the great support and the wonderful court victory, I was a deeply worried man.

CHAPTER SIX

As I walked into my home at the end of the court case, feeling exhilarated and vindicated, I knew that I had to discover why the Northumbria Police had gone to such lengths to embarrass me; charging me not only with trying to pervert the course of justice, but also ensuring that my two identities and my home address were revealed in open court. It seemed to me that they couldn't have done more to identify me and my home if they had made an announcement in the press!

But I was convinced that the answers to these conundrums lay not at the Northumbria Police headquarters in Newcastle-upon-Tyne but, more than likely, in Belfast. To my knowledge the Northumbria Police, even the Northumbria Special Branch, had nothing against me. They hardly knew me. I had had a few minor problems with one or two SB officers on my arrival in Blyth in 1992, but since then my dealings with them seemed purely motivated by their intention to antagonize and prosecute me on nothing but trumped-up charges. They had been vindictive towards me, but it still surprised me that they had gone out of their way to expose me in such a blatant manner.

Of course, I understood that the Northumbria Police had been informed by the Special Branch in Northern Ireland of my arrival on their patch. They would have been told that I was being relocated to the mainland for security reasons and I knew that the Northumbria Special Branch were asked to 'keep an eye on me'. The SB in Belfast had told me that there was a special department in the Home Office in London whose specific duty was to relocate and take care of agents and informers who had worked for the Government in Northern Ireland in a variety of different jobs, and who were at risk of being taken out by the IRA. This office inside Whitehall found suitable homes for targeted people and their families to settle on the mainland, provided them with a new identity, a new passport, and, on occasions, a job too. Some of those forced to flee the Province were provided with money to set up in business on their own, while others were provided with training for skilled work. Nearly all were bought houses or flats by the Home Office, though only after they had been invited to view them along with their spouses. Special attention was given to those with children so that homes were purchased near suitable schools.

It is, of course, always difficult for former informants that have been relocated to mainland Britain to find a job because with new identities, new National Insurance numbers and driving licenses, their actual work experience has been obliterated. And, of course, prospective employers could never be told what these men, and sometimes women, had really been doing for the previous few years because that would defeat the whole object of the exercise. As a result, many former undercover agents have tried to find self-employment, also difficult because they usually have little or no experience in commerce or business.

And yet, when it appeared that I had broken the law by having two separate driving licenses under two different names, the reasons for them were totally ignored both by the police and the Crown Prosecution Service. I explained to the Northumbria Police the reasons why I had the two licenses; one under the name Martin Ashe, with an address in Durham; the other under the name Martin David Ashe with an address in Northumberland. I was laying a false trail in an effort to thwart any PIRA investigations into my whereabouts because after Angie's return to Ireland, I feared they might redouble their efforts to trace me. Before taking out the new license in Durham I had been to the Northumbria Special Branch, pleading with them to move me from my home to another residence, but they refused. I urged the Northumbria authorities to check my story with the Special Branch in Belfast and yet, despite my appeals, they still decided to go ahead and prosecute.

As my appeals for the truth were ignored and the story of my years inside the IRA treated with derision, it became increasingly obvious to me that someone, somewhere, was pulling strings with the authorities, ensuring that I would be taken to court and my two identities exposed to the public at large. I came to the conclusion that someone in authority had 'had a few words' with the Northumbria Police authorities and the Crown Prosecution Service, suggesting that my legitimate defense should be ignored and that every action should be taken to get me to court. In doing so, of course, the Northumbria Police would have been fully aware that there was every danger that my real identity – Martin McGartland, a man the IRA had sentenced to death – would be revealed to the court and the world at large, exposing me to the danger of being targeted by an IRA active service unit. I knew from former friends in West Belfast that the IRA were actively searching for me in England. If found, I was to be summarily executed for I had revealed my 'guilt' in the book I had written. Now there was no need for the IRA to kidnap and torture me. All they required was my execution.

I sensed the work of MI5 behind the machinations designed to expose me. As a result of everything Mike, my SB friend, had told me, I was now deeply suspicious of all the secret intelligence and security services, not knowing if, and when, they might strike. But what worried me and what spurred me on to continue my investigations was the fact that if any government agency, such as MI5, decided to kill me, they could then quite conveniently blame my 'execution' on an IRA active service unit seeking revenge for my 'treachery'. If it was true that MI5 had organized my kidnap back in Belfast in August, 1991, then I had to take great precautions in case the bastards were still intent on having me disposed of.

The thought made me angry. Hardly a day had passed without me thinking about what Mike had told me. I had come to the conclusion that he had told the truth, that my abduction and kidnapping had been deliberately planned by MI5 and their associates in Northern Ireland. And yet, what frustrated me was the fact that I had no real idea why they should have wanted to carry out such an evil scheme. I racked my brains trying to find a logical reason why they would have wanted me out of the way to such an extent that they preferred to make me go through the horrors of an IRA kangaroo court, torture and eventual execution rather than simply put me on a boat to the mainland and arrange a new identity.

I had to assume that they were irritated by my survival, for they obviously wanted me to dissappear for reasons I knew nothing about. I would think back to my long conversation with Mike trying to make sense of everything. I had no idea who this unknown and mysterious senior British Intelligence agent could be that Mike had told me was the real reason for the plot to have me murdered. But the fact that I had survived, ruining MI5's little game of espionage, had probably annoyed the Tasking Coordination Group that covered the Belfast area. On a number of occasions Special Branch handlers had told me that the MI5 hierarchy considered their agents and informers nothing but 'touts'- local Catholics who could be used and treated like an inferior underclass until their services were no longer required. To them, it did not matter a damn that someone had risked his life for four years saving other people's lives. I could not escape the fundamental fact that in my case it had obviously been far more important in MI5's judgment to sacrifice me, in case my very existence should jeopardize their great espionage plan for the Province. To me, that seemed the only possible reason, yet I could not believe that senior MI5 officers would behave with such callous disregard for human life.

I had to assume that the same senior intelligence officers who enjoyed having the power of life and death were probably behind the machinations which had resulted in my two identities being revealed in open court. I suspected that those officers also reserved the power to influence both the Northumbria Police and the Crown Prosecution Service, ensuring that the charges brought against me went ahead. They wouldn't mind if I was convicted or set free, for their objective would have been achieved – the revelation of my identity in open court.

I made myself a cup of tea and walked into the sitting-room, thrilled at being a free man but thinking all the time of the possible alternatives now facing me. However much I tried to give MI5 the benefit of the doubt, I found it all but impossible to count them out of the equation. Of course, those officers behind my kidnapping could have been members of the RUC Special Branch, though I doubted it. I knew those men, I had enjoyed a good relationship with them for four years. It could all have been an accident of fate but the more I examined precisely what had happened to me that August day in 1991, the more I came to the conclusion that the whole wretched business had been a set-up. Now in my heart, I was certain that I had two enemies to contend with; two sets of people hell-bent on killing me: MI5 and the IRA. But accepting that meant that I had to redouble my efforts to safeguard my identity. More importantly, I had to be on my guard against not only some IRA killer but also against any other authority who might decide to take me out and make my death appear to be an IRA vendetta.

Now, more than ever, I was on my own. My first thought was to move from the northeast, tell no one of my plans, but simply try to disappear somewhere on the mainland, change my name by deed poll and adopt a new identity in another major British town or city. But then I would have no passport, social security number or chance of getting a job and making a living. Often during the years I had lived in the northeast, my mates had ragged me, giving me the nickname 'Semtex'. I would take no notice and never take offense because I realized it was their way of showing friendship. But the nickname carried a warning to me. With my strong accent, getting a job anywhere on the mainland would be a major problem - especially when the IRA were still bombing major targets, making ordinary people and employers wary of hiring any young Irish labor.

Before reaching definite conclusions, I was determined to try and uncover the facts for myself, to see whether the information Mike had given me was in fact true. Before I fell asleep that night I decided to go to Ireland, to see friends who had close links with the IRA and in the security services, the RUC and the Special Branch. In returning to Northern Ireland I accepted that I was taking an enormous risk; and yet, in a funny sort of way, I knew I would feel safer back in Belfast visiting than sitting in my flat in Blyth waiting for a knock on the door, checking my car for UCBTs every time I drove off and never knowing whether the person across the street might be watching and targeting me. Getting to the bottom of this puzzle was paramount, even more important to me than my own safety. I preferred to return to Belfast, grasp the nettle and risk all rather than stay at home like a sitting duck.

After reaching that decision I went out to celebrate my court victory. I went to my favorite café in Newcastle, ate a great plate of the finest fish and chips, then drove out of town to enjoy a few pints of Newcastle Brown in a pub where no one knew my identity. There had been newspaper photographers outside the court throughout the four-day trial but I had ensured my anonymity by walking in and out of court with my face covered. I was almost certain that no one could have recognized me. As I drank my beer and thought of what was happening to my life, I became aware that I had to melt into the background once again and keep a low profile. As soon as possible I needed to start a new life, move to a new city, and take yet another new identity.

It saddened me to leave my mates in Blyth and Newcastle, the people who had known me as Martin Ashe and who nicknamed me 'Ashie' and 'Semtex'. The people had been kind to me, in fact wonderfully friendly and generous, accepting me as one of their own, giving me a break and even offering me the friendship and hospitality of their own homes. In Blyth and Newcastle I had felt comfortable and safe among friends, but now I would have to throw away those years and start all over again. It made me feel angry that someone in authority had decided to do all in their power to ruin my life, and for what?

'Fuck it,' I said almost audibly and downed another pint. That made me feel better, though the anger wouldn't go away. But as well as anger there was jubilation for, finally, after seventeen months of worry and anxiety, I had persuaded a jury of six women and six men that I was not some reckless young tear-away who had tried to cheat justice. Indeed, the jury had made the Northumbria Police and the Crown Prosecution Service look like a bunch of amateurs who were determined to punish a young man on trumped-up charges. Put simply, the jury had refused to believe the tissue of concocted evidence put before them and, instead, had put their faith in me and my evidence, believing that the story I told in court had been the truth.

I believe that my vindication in front of the jury was made largely possible by three tributes made during the trial. In court, Sam Cushnahan of FAIT had verified the work I had done in Northern Ireland and the fact that I was at the very top of the IRA's death list. And there had been two other pieces of evidence, both from beyond the grave, which had highlighted my work for British Intelligence.

Six months before my trial, a book entitled *Phoenix – Policing The Shadows: The Secret War Against Terrorism in Northern Ireland* had been published, jointly written by Jack Holland and Susan Phoenix, the wife of the late Detective Superintendent Ian Phoenix, a former head of the Northern Ireland police counter-surveillance unit who died in June, 1994. Phoenix died alongside twenty-five other senior anti-terrorist intelligence officers, when a Chinook helicopter crashed into the side of the Mull of Kintyre. There were no survivors. But in his diaries Superintendent Phoenix wrote at length about me under my code-name 'Carol', saying, 'Carol was certainly one of the Special Branch's best spies in the 1990s'. Phoenix's diaries revealed various intelligence reports that I had made to the Special Branch enabling lives to be saved.

There was a further tribute from a former Assistant Chief Constable, Brian Fitzsimons, who was in charge of the Special Branch during the early 1990s. He too had died in the same Chinook helicopter crash. After my kidnap by the IRA, Fitzsimons had said, 'McGartland was a very productive agent'.

I knew that going alone to Belfast would be a risky affair, yet there was no other way to make contact with the people I needed to question and cross-examine if I was to discover, once and for all, who, if anyone, was behind my kidnap. To telephone anyone in Northern Ireland would have been suicidal because I knew that in the cauldron of Northern Ireland politics and the fight against terrorism, many phones are monitored or bugged by the various security agencies. Any person I could talk to in an open, indiscreet conversation manner would know that their phones were tapped by the security services. I knew from my time working with the SB that security services in the province maintain a highly sophisticated phone-tapping operation.

I had been to Northern Ireland once since being relocated to mainland Britain. In October,1996 I was asked to appear at the Lisburn County Court to give evidence regarding my claim for compensation from the Government concerning the criminal injuries I received when escaping from the IRA following my kidnap. The Compensation Agency had refused to give me any assistance because they claimed that I had been a member of the IRA, a terrorist organization, and therefore was not entitled to a single penny. Of course, I informed the court that I had joined the IRA on the specific instruction of the RUC Special Branch and had worked as an agent inside the IRA providing valuable intelligence to the security services.

The Compensation Agency also informed my solicitors that I could not be provided with any money because I had failed to comply with instructions to submit my medical records, detailing my injuries. There was, however, a very good reason why this occurred. Within days of my departure from the Royal Victoria Hospital in Belfast and transfer to protective custody in Palace Barracks, the Special Branch had taken possession of my records and had them destroyed. As a result, there were no records whatsoever of my injuries.

Within days of receiving the date to attend court in Lisburn, I called the Special Branch in Belfast asking whether I could be given police protection during the twenty-four hours I expected to be in

Northern Ireland. I was told that this would not happen while I was in the Province. This both surprised and perplexed me. It seemed extraordinary that I should be given no protection, for the Special Branch, more than anyone else in Northern Ireland, knew that the IRA were intent on finding and, more importantly, killing me.

I had more than half-a-dozen phone conversations with RUC officers at their headquarters in Belfast as well as contacting senior Special Branch officers over a period of four weeks but those conversations only referred to my forthcoming court appearance. From each and every one of the officers I spoke to I received the same answer – a categorical 'no'. Some of the conversations were remarkably candid in tone.

'There is no way the Branch would give you protection,' one senior SB officer told me.

'Why not?' I asked.

'We're nothing to do with you any more, Marty,' he said.

'Since when?' I replied.

'Since you got a pay off and left the Province,' he said.

'But if I'm to come back to attend a compensation court, I'll need police protection,' I argued.

'Your compensation is fuck all to do with the RUC.'

'What do you mean?' I said. 'It's only because of the work I did for you that I ended up jumping from the flat,' I explained, feeling more irate at the obdurate attitude he used.

'Listen, Marty,' he went on, 'can't you get it into your skull that you're nothing to do with us any more? We owe you nothing. If you want to fight for compensation then that's your business. But don't expect the RUC to spend their time watching your back. It's down to you.'

'So that's all the thanks I get for risking my fucking neck for four years,' I said, shouting at him, enraged that the RUC should treat me so appallingly.

'Marty,' he said again, 'any favors that were afforded to you, you blew by your antics. We owe you nothing.'

'What do you mean?' I asked.

'You know well enough,' he replied.

I knew full well that he was referring to the murder of Private Tony Harrison, the twenty-one year old soldier of the 3rd Parachute Regiment who was gunned down by two Provo killers in June, 1991. Harrison had been staying at the home of his fiancée, Tracey Gouck, on Nevis Avenue off the Holywood Road, Belfast. Later, Tracey had described how at 6.30 p.m., on 19 June, she had answered a knock at the door to see two men standing there. One man had put a gun to her head and forced her into the living room. The second gunman then fired five shots at her fiancée, hitting him in the head and body before fleeing to their getaway car. Later, one of the gunman named Paul gave details of the operation to the IRA cell of which I was a member. He told us, 'It was a piece of piss. The bastard didn't even move. We got him still sitting on the sofa in the living room. I let him have it, firing into the body and the head, just to make sure.'

I stood there listening to this sickening tale of cold-blooded murder, my mind racing, my body shaking, a terrible empty feeling in the pit of my stomach for, in that PIRA operation, I had been the driver of the getaway car. In fact I had no alternative but to drive the car ferrying the two gunmen to the victim's address. Four weeks earlier my cell member, a young man named Jimmy, told me that they had heard a paratrooper was living in a house off Holywood Road but had no precise address. They thought he would make an easy target and decided to find out where he lived. I reported all this to my SB handler Felix but I had no name for the soldier and no address. He said the SB would do all in their power to find the young man, warn him and move him. Felix was so concerned that later the same day he and I returned to the area, driving up and down the streets in a vain search for him. I heard no more and believed my IRA active service unit had dropped the operation.

But on the morning of Wednesday, June 19, 1991, I was contacted by one of the IRA messengers and told to report to my IRA cell commander 'Spud Murphy'. When I arrived he told me, 'This is not a meeting, Marty, we've got a job for you. You're to drive Stephen and Paul on an operation.'

My heart sank. Though I had no idea what the operation entailed I feared the worst, knowing Paul Lynch to be one of the IRA's principal assassins, a ruthless bastard who had a reputation for carrying out the most daring attacks and a man with a ferocious hatred of anyone who opposed the Republican cause. Even his mates believed he was a man without feeling.

Spud said, 'The car's outside. It's hot, it's just been hijacked, so dump it immediately afterwards.'

As we drove away Stephen asked, 'Do you know East Belfast, Marty?'

'Aye,' I replied.

'That's where we're heading,' he said. 'A house in Nevis Avenue off Holywood Road.'

I knew instinctively that I was driving to the home of the soldier whom they had planned to shoot in cold blood. I wondered what I should do, wondered what the hell I could do to save this poor man's life. As we drove along I prayed that the soldier was away from home because I knew that with Paul Lynch there was no question of his life being spared. If he was at home I knew he would be shot dead. I debated whether I should try any trick, like stalling the car or crashing into another vehicle, as if by accident. But Stephen, sitting beside me, was armed with a hand-gun and I knew that if he suspected I was not playing straight, he would shoot me and walk away without a second thought. I was already convinced that Spud Murphy was seriously suspicious of me and had brought me in as driver on this 'op' to test me.

'Stop here,' said Stephen, as we turned into Nevis Avenue. 'I'll be back soon.'

A few minutes later Paul arrived in another hijacked car and parked nearby. As Stephen got out of the car I was driving and walked away, I prayed to God that the Branch had spirited away the soldier like many of the other IRA targets I had discovered. I knew that the Special Branch, and all the security services, did everything possible to save all targeted men, not just police officers and army personnel. But during the past month the Branch had told me nothing to indicate whether their search for this particular soldier had been successful or not.

I wound down the car window so that I would hear if any shots were fired. 'Please God, please God,' I kept repeating to myself, praying I would hear nothing. I waited what seemed an age but it was probably only a couple of minutes. Then I heard the shots – one, two, three, four, five. I counted them, wincing at every one, while waves of nausea and rage gripped my body. I knew in my heart that the poor bastard had been murdered. My hands were shaking and I broke into a cold sweat as I rammed the car into first gear and drove towards the two IRA killers as they walked from the house. I slowed down and they jumped into the back seat of the car.

'Fuckin' drive,' said Paul, 'fuckin' drive.' I said not a word but drove, screeching the tires as I sped away trying to put distance between us and the scene of the shooting. Two hundred yards down the road, Paul said, 'Stop the car.' After I braked and stopped, Paul shouted, 'Dump it, dump it here, then fuck off.'

I knew that my involvement in the murder of Tony Harrison caused a ferocious argument within the Special Branch and the RUC at the highest levels. There were those who believed that I should be arrested and charged with conspiracy and with being an accessory to murder. But my RUC handlers fought tooth and nail for the matter to be dropped, arguing that I had no option but to do as I was told by my IRA cell commander. They knew that there was no way I could have gotten out of that operation unless I were to have blown my cover, yet my instructions were to do all in my power never to reveal that I was working for the Branch. That confession would have signed my own death warrant, and also meant that another agent had been rumbled by the IRA, putting the fear of God into every other informant working for the RUC or the SB. Nonetheless, I knew from my Branch friends that my involvement in the murder of Tony Harrison had put a giant question mark against my name, many RUC officers believing that the Branch should, at the very least, have gotten rid of me.

But all that had been in the past. They must have known that I needed police protection if I was to visit Belfast in broad daylight. Yet I also knew that my friends in the Special Branch would be unable to assist me in receiving police protection because of the constraints placed on them by their senior officers. Fortunately I had a number of influential friends who came forward to argue my case. One such person was Pastor Jack McKee, a community worker in Belfast who had never met me but heard of my predicament. Appalled by my treatment at the RUC, he immediately wrote to Secretary of State Patrick Mayhew and Sir Hugh Annesley, the former Chief Constable of the RUC, urging them to wield their influence with the RUC so protection could be provided for me during the twelve hours I was expected to be in the Province. The lobbying worked to a degree that surprised me, leaving me wondering why I was suddenly being treated like a VIP.

On Monday, October 7, 1996, I flew heavily disguised on a scheduled flight from Manchester to Belfast. I wore a new suit, spectacles, a beard and a wig, as I had been advised by the RUC. When the aircraft came to a halt, two armed Special Branch officers boarded the plane and told me to stay in my seat until everyone had disembarked. I wondered why they were taking such remarkable precautions. We eventually descended the steps to an unmarked RUC police car. Pastor Jack McKee sat beside me in the rear seat while the RUC driver and the other armed Special Branch man sat in the front of the vehicle. Immediately behind our car was another unmarked RUC car with two armed officers. We drove from the tarmac directly through Customs without stopping, all the way to Lisburn. Police in cars, on motorcycles and standing by the roadside lined the route, on occasion nodding and giving a surreptitious wave to our driver as we passed by. I kept wondering why the authorities were going to such lengths. Did they know something that I didn't? And if so, what?

While we drove the eight-mile route to Lisburn County Court

I chatted with the Branch officers . For most of the time we talked of the remarkable eighteen-month-long IRA cease-fire which had surprised many government officials and security service chiefs. Those who accompanied me explained they were keeping their fingers crossed, hoping the cease-fire would continue and maybe, maybe, become a permanent reality.

Once inside the court building I was taken immediately to a private room where two armed officers stood outside, acting as bodyguards. We arrived at the court building sometime after 11 a.m., but our case was not called until shortly before 4 p.m. I was not permitted to leave the safety of the room and sandwiches were brought in for our lunch. Sitting with me was Pastor Jack McKee and my solicitor, Frank Roberts, from a Belfast law firm. I was giving evidence to the court, explaining to the judge 'You must always remember that the IRA are a very professional organization . . .' when suddenly my evidence was interrupted by a massive explosion which rocked the building. The judge turned white and looked to the police officers but they turned on their heels and raced outside, ready to help in any rescue operation. Fifteen minutes later another huge explosion stunned everyone in the court, with people looking at each other, checking whether the court should be adjourned. These bombs announced in the most spectacular fashion the end of the IRA cease-fire, blasting the biggest army base in Northern Ireland. The two bombs, the first estimated to be a large 500-kilo bomb, the second an estimated 250 kilos of explosives, had been driven through the main entrance of Thiepval Barracks in Lisburn, and were a huge embarrassment for the British Army. They exploded within fifteen minutes of each other, causing extensive damage and reminding the British Government, the RUC and all the security services that the IRA could successfully target even the most well-protected and vital military camps.

It was a callous act for two reasons; primarily because the second, smaller bomb was designed to explode at a site inside the barracks which they obviously knew would be used as an evacuation point. Such despicable planning fitted a long-established IRA pattern of maximizing the carnage and confusion at an attack site. Secondly, no warning had been given by the IRA. As a result, twenty people were injured, five seriously, including an eight-year-old girl. The first blast was close to the administration building manned mainly by civilian staff; the second appeared to have been designed to catch casualties being taken to the medical center, which was badly damaged. A nearby hospital unit which looks after severely disabled adults was also caught in the blast. Prime Minister John Major described the bombing as 'wicked beyond belief'. The bombing was also seen as a direct attack on the Province's Protestant community, for Lisburn is a staunchly Protestant town.

In court, the first blast brought my case to a quick resolution, the judge telling me that as the law concerning it was set in stone, he had no authority to grant me compensation for the injuries I had received escaping from the IRA. However, he suggested that my solicitor should approach the authorities asking for a discretionary award to be made. By offering such advice it seemed to me that the judge believed that I should receive compensation for the injuries I had received and from which I was still suffering.

'Let's go,' said one of my Special Branch bodyguards only seconds after the case had finished. 'Just do exactly as I tell you.'

'Okay,' I replied.

'Right, follow me,' he said. 'Keep right behind me.'

He called to a number of other SB officers who were outside the court, telling them we were ready to go. 'We're going out the back, that should be safe,' he said as though talking to himself.

At the door we stopped and officers, all carrying hand-guns, moved outside checking if the way was clear. 'Don't move,' I was told, 'and keep back.'

I could see a number of RUC officers with hand-guns, army personnel with assault rifles and sub-machine-guns, guarding the rear entrance to the County Court used by judges, court officials and police officers attending the court. Twenty yards away I could see two unmarked police cars and officers checking underneath them for fear of UCBTs, one of the IRA's favorite methods of assassination.

'Okay,' someone shouted.

'Run,' said my officer. 'Follow me.' And we took off, sprinting the twenty yards to the cars. Other officers took up positions, checking the entrance and the perimeter walls. No one was permitted to enter the car park.

As we clambered into the vehicles the RUC man told his driver, 'Airport, and don't stop for anyone. We've got to get him on the next flight out.'

The eight-mile drive to Aldergrove was one of the hairiest I have ever experienced. The entire area around the court and across Lisburn seemed chaotic and confused. Army personnel and police officers were struggling to control the traffic as well as hundreds of people who had spilled out into the streets following the two explosions. I saw scores of children who had just been let out of school running around not knowing where they should be going, or what they should be doing, to escape the mayhem. There were mothers herding children away from the town center, police officers carrying young children and babies.

I saw one young soldier, dressed in combat gear, body armor and a camouflage helmet, carrying two small children who must have both been under five. Slung over his shoulder was an assault rifle. He was following a young mother who was carrying a third child. She seemed distraught as she ran away from where she believed the bombs had exploded. As we sped past them I turned to check if they were all safe, worried in case they should have been running in the wrong direction, perhaps towards another IRA bomb. There was a look of fear in the young mother's eyes and I wondered if all this terror had taken place because I had returned to the Province.

'Were they after me?' I asked my RUC bodyguard, feeling guilty and full of regrets that I might have been responsible for the bombs which I prayed had injured or killed no one but which I feared may well have done so.

'I don't know,' he replied, 'but we do know they're after you.

Did anyone know you were coming over here today?'

'Not as far as I know,' I said, 'I told no one. In any case I don't think I'm that important. I'm sure it's just a coincidence.'

'Let's hope so,' he replied.

I will never forget that drive from Lisburn. The roads around the town were choked with cars, all going in different directions but causing snarl-ups and long lines of vehicles at a standstill.

'Take no notice,' my RUC officer told the driver. 'Switch on the sirens and the lights and make sure we keep moving. We don't want to be caught in a road block or at a standstill because then we would be sitting ducks. If the road ahead is blocked then use the footpaths.'

And we did. We drove on the roads and the footpaths, bouncing up and down curbs and pavements and, when the road cleared, at speeds in excess of seventy miles an hour. Throughout the trip, the back-up unmarked police car was driving only ten feet behind us, manned by four armed police officers. They were taking no chances. There were about eight police and army road blocks along the way, all heavily guarded with the police and army personnel in full body armor and all armed, mostly with assault rifles and Heckler and Koch sub-machine-guns. We were automatically waved through while all other vehicles were being stopped; details of the occupants noted and many drivers searched and checked. I had been struck at how impressive and speedy the army and police reaction had been to the explosions. It seemed that within minutes, police and army personnel had flooded the center of Lisburn and road blocks had been set up. I knew all the while that the authorities were angry, perplexed and extremely concerned that the IRA had managed to infiltrate the British Army's most important location in Northern Ireland and blow the place to bits. I also believed that the blasts were a dramatic declaration by the IRA that the cease-fire was at an end and that they were intent on bringing their campaign of violence back to Northern Ireland. The bombing was also organized to create the maximum political affect, exploding on the eve of the Conservative Party conference.

Back in Newcastle the following day I read that a soldier from that area had been seriously injured in the bomb blasts and subsequently died. It seemed poignant and frightening that I should have been in Lisburn that day and that the poor man who died carrying out his duty should have come from my area.

After returning to Newcastle, I made up my mind to visit Northern Ireland again in my quest for the truth. My next trip there would prove far more dangerous, for this time I was to travel alone and unprotected.

CHAPTER SEVEN

Back home all seemed so peaceful and life so ordinary, but it would not stay that way for long, for my battles with various authorities were proving difficult and complex. My court case victory in May, 1997 did not go down well with the Crown authorities, the Home Office, MI5 and the Northumbria Police and I felt an increased threat. Following my court victory I did not know where to turn, or whom to turn to, for I felt exposed and vulnerable.

While MPs, my solicitors and other kindly Tynesiders took up my case and demanded I be given a new identity and accommodation elsewhere in Britain, I decided that the safest course for me was to disappear. I talked to my former SB friends in Belfast and they advised me to get as far away as possible from Newcastle.

'If you stay there, Marty, you'll be a sitting duck,' one said. 'Take our advice and get the fuck out of it. Remember the IRA got hold of you once and you managed to escape, next time you might not be so lucky.'

'Do you think I'm that much at risk?' I asked.

'Think?' he said, raising his voice. 'I know you're at risk. Now get the hell out of Newcastle until this thing's blown over.'

'Okay, I will,' I replied. 'Thanks for the advice.'

'And whatever you do, don't sleep at your own home for the next few weeks,' my former handler went on. 'Don't take the risk even for one night. You remember the way the IRA gunmen and bombers keep one step ahead of us all the time. They never sleep in their own beds more than two nights a week. Now take the hint and get the fuck out of there. If you're in any trouble you can always call. And one more thing.'

'What's that?' I asked.

'Keep your head down at all times and keep a low profile; you never know who might be after you.'

'Are you being serious?' I asked, feeling somewhat worried.

'I'm just being cautious,' he replied. 'If you keep your wits about you, you'll have nothing to worry about. Now fuck off.'

'Cheers,' I replied. But as I left the phone box and walked off into the summer rain I realized with increasing nervousness I was totally on my own. During the years I had been working for the Branch, I had always had a feeling of great security; that I was a member of a team who would always come to the rescue if ever I was in deep shit. Now, all that had changed. Despite the fact I was living in Northumbria, a place without any of the dangers of Northern Ireland, I felt somehow vulnerable. I was uncomfortable, unsure of myself, and it worried me. As I walked to my car and started the engine I had a tremendous urge to drive to Stranraer, take the ferry to Ireland and drive home to Angie and the boys. I felt lonely and miserable and I yearned for my family. I wanted nothing more in the world than to go home to Belfast and walk indoors to a cup of hot tea and the smiling faces of Angie and the kids. I knew, however, that it was an impossible wish and had to bite my lip to stop the tears and emotions from taking over.

In reality, I had not the faintest idea where I could hide or where I could go. My only friends lived in and around Newcastle and I had no intention of putting pressure on them. They had all known me as 'Ashie' or 'Semtex' but now it was no joke. This was for real. I couldn't ask them to put me up or stay at their place for a few days or weeks because that would be unfair. They may have been my mates for a couple of years but they weren't family and I had no right to ask such favors. Before my trial they had no idea I was a wanted man. Now they knew everything, and I had no wish to ask them to pit themselves against the IRA.

My solicitors had issued a statement immediately after my court case saying, 'It is Mr. McGartland's view that the prosecution should never have been brought in the light of his services to the public in Northern Ireland. The prosecution has exposed him to further danger which his resettlement on the mainland was meant to avoid. Mr. McGartland believes that the prosecution was brought with total disregard for his own safety and that the Crown showed no insight into the real and particular dangers encountered by those living in the shadow of the IRA. Mr. McGartland now faces the prospect of having to make a new life all over again.'

In many respects the revelation that I was not really Martin Ashe, but a former undercover agent who had infiltrated the IRA, put the fear of God into some people but also, thank goodness, won me a number of friends. Janice, the lovely lady who lived in the flat beneath me in Blyth, wrote a letter to her MP, Ronnie Campbell, stating: 'Since I found out that my neighbor is really Martin McGartland, I have been extremely concerned for my personal safety. I am aware that his identity and his address are now known by a large number of people in Blyth. He has been staying away from his flat since the court case but I am worried that he might move back in. I think that something should be done as a matter of urgency as I am extremely worried and the stress is affecting my health.'

A few days after my trial a group of women from North Tyneside who knew me as Martin Ashe organized a petition demanding that the Home Secretary provide me with a new identity and a new home. It read, 'Martin McGartland risked his life to save others. He now deserves the full support of the British Government.' Blyth MP Ronnie Campbell wrote to Northern Ireland Secretary Mo Mowlam asking her to intervene and put pressure on her colleagues to relocate me and give me a new identity. Mr. Campbell told me that his constituents had inundated his weekly surgery with letters and personal appearances on his doorstep all arguing my case. He mentioned he would be raising the issue with the Home Secretary. Within a few weeks more than three thousand people had signed the petition urging quick action to ensure my safety. I found it very embarrassing but also very kind that people who did not even know me should go to such trouble because they feared my life had been put in jeopardy. I later learned from Mr. Campbell that he personally spoke to both Jack Straw, the Home Secretary, and Mo Mowlam about my case.

Following a television program screened in England in June 1997, detailing my life on the run, a number of Members of Parliament came forward, all urging the Home Secretary to provide me with a new home and identity in a different part of the country. Labor MP Harry Barnes, who represents northeast Derbyshire, commented, 'It is absolutely crucial McGartland is given a new identity and I want to see this unfortunate situation resolved. His life is in considerable danger.'

A month later my solicitors received an offer from Burton & Burton, a Nottingham-based law firm acting on behalf of mysterious and unknown 'Crown Authorities'. I was offered a new passport, drivers license, National Insurance number and NHS card; but not a single penny towards the purchase of a new property or removal costs. In fact, they stated categorically that, 'it was not possible for the authorities to make any financial provision towards moving home'. In exchange for a new identity, the authorities expected me to somehow pay for everything, including selling my small Blyth flat and buying a new one in a different part of Britain, paying for all legal fees, buying and selling costs, surveyor's fees as well as removal costs. They refused to understand the difficulty of my situation, for Blyth was one of Britain's poorest areas, and purchasing similar accommodations in another part of the country would be double the cost. It seemed to me the Crown authorities were deliberately offering me a deal which I could only refuse, for to say 'yes' would have meant sinking me into heavy debt from which I would have had no way out. I knew from past experience and from talking to SB officers in Belfast that most former informants and agents were given generous awards by the authorities because it was felt that society owed them a reward. My treatment seemed Machiavellian; I could not believe the Home Office would stoop to such tactics.

During the weeks following the trial and all the publicity I did not return to my home, save on the odd occasion to collect clothes or papers I needed to pursue my case. I used my car and, on occasions, trains and buses, criss-crossing the north of England, staying at many different places. I visited a couple of old mates but only stayed with them a night or two before moving on somewhere else. Sometimes I slept the night in my car, which was parked in inconspicuous places; but every morning brought cramps and the effects of sleeping rough. In the damp, the shoulder wound I had sustained after my leap from the window would cause me grief and pain; but after a few hours, a cup of tea and a hot breakfast I would feel better. Most of the time I showered and shaved in motorway restrooms to ensure I didn't end up looking like some ruffian or young alcoholic. I kept going by convincing myself that living like this was far better than meeting an IRA gunman at home or exploding a UCBT when I jumped into my car, but it was still a miserable existence and I hated the idea that I was running away from the IRA.

During the weeks of traveling across the north of England, only once did I suspect that I was being followed, which made my heart leap with fear and a sense of anticipation. I had come to discover that being on the run could be unutterably boring and a complete waste of time and yet, sometimes, I felt I was back in Northern Ireland, excited, even trembling at the very thought of running risks. Sometimes the frustration and the fear gnawed away at my subconscious and I would wake from my dreams with a start, expecting to find a gun pointing at my head. I had been far less worried during my years inside the IRA, though the danger was far more real and ever present. And yet, being on one's own, not knowing from where the problems would come, made me more nervous than ever. Sometimes as I sat in a motorway café I would start trembling nervously for no apparent reason. I would try to control my nerves but that often proved difficult so I would quickly finish my meal, drink a glass of cold water and take a walk outside for a few minutes or so to regain my composure. For some reason or other those little tricks worked for me and I would manage to regain my nerve and take off again, often driving down a highway with not the faintest idea where my next port of call would be.

One day, I tried getting far away from the world of traffic, lorries, cars and the hundreds of people who congregate at motorway cafés. I drove off the M6 and made my way to Wales, a country I had never visited before. I found myself in North Wales heading towards the glorious slate-colored mountains of Snowdonia; the low, dark, cloud-filled sky hiding the top of the mountain range, and for a while I enjoyed the sheer peace and wild beauty of the desolate surroundings. I felt an urge to drink from the streams that were like torrents, falling sharply from the mountains above, sometimes cascading fifty or sixty feet before hitting more rocks and spraying the surrounding grass and moss. I parked the car by the roadside and walked up the steep rock-face of the mountain to a stream that seemed to encompass the memories of Northern Ireland where I used to walk as a young boy with my mother and sisters, a time when I had never heard of the Troubles. I cupped my hands and drank the cool, crystal-clear water, quenching my thirst and thinking how much I needed my family. I turned and looked out across the wonderful green expanse of country, dotted here and there with sheep minding their own business, and wondered if I could live in such a place. In my excited impetuosity I thought of climbing to the top of the mountain but as I looked up the sheer face of the cliff I realized this was impossible so I turned and walked back down to my car. I had been driving leisurely for another ten minutes or so around a host of mountain bends, looking down at the occasional sheer drop to the bottom of a ravine, when, all of a sudden, a large 32-ton truck came sweeping around the bend towards me, the driver having problems keeping the vehicle on the correct side of the road. That awoke me from my day-dream like an ice-cold shower and I instantly realized that I was more at risk here in the friendless mountains of Wales than in the maddening cauldron of motorway mania.

So, like a lonely traveler desperate for company, I turned around and headed back to civilization, a feeling of warmth and bonhomie surging through me, as though I had rejoined the human race. As I queued for my cup of tea in a motorway service station, I smiled in my happiness at the couple standing next to me. They looked at me as though I was mad!

The real scare, however, occurred in the washroom of another motorway service station in Yorkshire. I was standing in front of a mirror when two men with Irish accents walked in. I noted they seemed to be paying particular attention to me. They left and I followed some time later. As I was buying a newspaper the two men reappeared and one seemed to be watching me while the other moved outside into the car park. My heart began to beat faster and my mouth became dry. I walked out and returned to my car and the two men followed, walking only a matter of ten yards behind me. I had to presume that they were IRA but I also knew I had to keep my cool and act as though nothing whatsoever was strange about them being there. When I reached the car, I immediately bent down to check for a possible UCBT; while I did this one of the men walked up and stood beside me.

'Have you lost something?' he asked. I froze, the sound of the voice reminded me of the dangers of living in Belfast.

'No, just checking everything's okay. I think I've got a fucking oil leak,' I said.

'Do I know you?' asked the more heavily built man.

'I don't think so,' I replied, now all but convinced that these two men were people I didn't want to know. I wasn't sure who they represented but in the manner of their dress, and their ages, they looked more like RUC plainclothesmen than members of the IRA.

'Isn't that a Belfast accent?' I asked, hoping to diffuse the situation which became more tense by the second.

'Aye,' said the other one. 'Are you also from the Province?'

The very fact that the man had used that phrase 'from the Province', immediately raised my hopes because that turn of phrase is used in Northern Ireland by Protestants, not Republicans.

'Aye,' I replied, 'though I've lived here for some years now.'

'We just thought we recognized you, that's all,' said the taller man.

'Don't think so,' I said. 'I'll be seeing you.' I then opened the car door and slipped into the driver's seat.

I watched as they clambered into a Transit van. Written on the side and the back was the name of a major road construction company. I drove away wondering if I was becoming paranoid or just taking sensible precautions. I knew I had just been sensible.

Following my acquittal in May, 1997, the authorities argued back and forth about the real and immediate threat to me by the IRA. All correspondence to my solicitors, Alderson Dodds, came from Northumbria Police headquarters or Burton & Burton, who steadfastly refused to reveal whom they were representing. It seemed odd in 1997, when the new Labor Government promised more open representation, that a firm of solicitors would take on this attitude, and indeed on a number of occasions, my solicitors asked them to reveal their connections. So I called my pals in the Branch in Belfast and they told me that the agency involved was in fact a Government one. I suspected MI5 was the link.

Within days of the conclusion of my trial, my solicitor wrote to the Chief Constable of Northumbria Police pointing out that my new identity – Martin David Ashe – had become publicly known and, as a result, my safety had become considerably prejudiced. He asked that I be granted a new identity immediately. Several applications for a new identity were made over the ensuing weeks, emphasizing that a quick decision needed to be made, but no reply was received from the Northumbria Police, whose responsibility it was to grant me this request.

In the meantime, my life was not without incident. A few weeks after my trial I returned to my home late one night to collect a change of clothes. I parked my car at the bottom of the lane behind the house and went to the door. As I was about to put the key in the lock I realized the door was almost off its hinges and the thought crossed my mind that the flat might have been booby-trapped. I was deeply suspicious. I believed that if a burglar had broken in, the door would have simply been left open, not pulled almost closed again. I now had to presume that the IRA were aware of my new identity and my address and I also knew the sort of tricks they would play to get me. One was to booby-trap either my home or my car.

I immediately retraced my steps and, on my mobile phone, dialed '999'. I gave the police officer my name and address and asked him to send two officers immediately there as I thought my flat had recently been broken into. I also told the officer to phone Blyth police station and report this incident. I explained that they would understand the seriousness of the report.

Within minutes a police car arrived and I explained to the officers that I was Martin Ashe who had recently been acquitted at Newcastle Crown Court on a charge of perverting the course of justice.

'Aye,' one replied, 'we know who you are. You used to work undercover in Belfast.'

'Aye,' I replied, not wanting to give anything else away.

'Have you been inside?' one asked.

'No,' I replied, 'it might be booby-trapped.'

'Fuck,' one officer said to the other, 'call the station and get a couple of dogs down.'

As we waited the senior officer told me, 'As we were driving here I told my mate that I knew who you were. I also told him that if we saw anyone with an AK47 or anyone hanging around looking suspicious, turn 'round the car and get the fuck out of the place.'

Minutes later a police van arrived with a handler and his Alsatian. The Alsatian was sent in to search the place. We stood well back in case the door had been booby-trapped. Five minutes later the police decided it was safe to go in. Nearly all my expensive goods had been stolen but, thank God, there was no sign that it had been an IRA related incident. It was an ordinary, run of the mill burglary. But that tiny incident, and the reaction of the police, at least assured me that the Northumbria Police finally did realize that there was a real threat to my life.

To me and my solicitors it seemed extraordinary that Burton &

Burton should be stopped from revealing the identity of the agency that they represented while Northumbria Police dragged their feet on providing me with a new identity, ensuring that my two identities and my address, which had been revealed in open court, should become common knowledge. Finally, on 11 June, I was informed that I would be issued with the necessary documentation to support my request but only if I agreed to accept certain terms.

In September 1997, four months after my court case, Burton & Burton finally outlined the new terms on which they would agree to relocate me with a new identity. I would have to agree to behave discreetly, maintain a low profile and not visit Northern Ireland. After pressure from Members of Parliament and my solicitors, the government authorities finally made me a new offer, a derisory £3,000 to cover all my removal costs. A move to a similar small flat in a different area on mainland Britain would probably have cost me at least £20,000 after I had sold my Blyth apartment. I just didn't have that kind of money. It seemed from their risible offer that the various authorities and agencies were happy for me to have a new identity, provided I continue living at my old address, a laughable situation at best. The government agencies would have been fully aware that such protection would be absolutely useless. But why? Why were the agencies continuing to take advantage of situations such as my low financial state to continue what appeared to be a vendetta against me, making me insulting offers which they knew I could not accept? They must have known that the longer I stayed living at my Blyth address the easier target I would become for anyone determined to find me, including the IRA.

My SB friends in Belfast believed that a main reason the Crown authorities were happy for me to stay in Blyth was not just to facilitate the IRA in their search for me but to save money on my protection. The agencies would have known that my Blyth home was now a property publicly targeted by the IRA. As a result, trying to sell the flat would be very difficult because no one would want to live there, fearing a fire-bomb attack or an unwelcome visitor in the night. The authorities knew that if they were forced to sell my home on the open market it would fetch very poor money, thereby doubling the total cost of my new identity and relocation. It was a cynical view but I believed it because I recognized that the authorities no longer needed my aid or assistance. I had done my duty and was now considered a nuisance, no longer a hero.

My solicitor wrote to Burton & Burton explaining the financial implications of a move away from Blyth which many authorities aware of the Northern Ireland terrorist threat knew to be essential if my life was to be safe. My solicitor wrote: 'Mr. Ashe must clearly relocate. He presently has a mortgage on his flat and has spent some £15,000 upon it which will not be recoverable on a sale. He was obliged to sell his car as its number had become known in the court case and he lost approaching £3,900 on that. He has incurred considerable expenses in living away from home while the authorities have been endeavoring to resolve this matter. Mr. McGartland's house was burgled in his absence where a considerable loss was incurred as he received only second-hand value on his insurance claim. Clearly he will need new accommodation which should either be provided or alternatively financed . . . To deal effectively with the cost of relocating will cost Mr. McGartland something in the region of £30,000. Your offer of (£3,000) removal expenses is in our client's view impractical, unrealistic and derisory.' He was right in every instance.

Every aspect of my life now seemed dogged by red tape – the Home Office, mysterious government agencies, the police and my old employers, the Royal Ulster Constabulary. But throughout these weeks and months, which grew into years, the various authorities continued to hide the truth at every turn in an effort to deny that my identity and my address had been revealed in open court by the Northumbria Police.

Solicitors working with Burton & Burton, as well as the Northumbria Police and the Crown Prosecution Service, denied time and again that the police, while giving evidence, had revealed my home address in Blyth, in open court. They would go further, claiming that I had been responsible for revealing my name,

'McGartland', during the Newcastle court case. Of course they were right. I had done so because the prosecution had forced me to do so. The Crown Prosecution Service, together with the forces advising them, knew that by taking me to court on trumped-up charges they would force me to reveal my career as an undercover agent, and my real name – my one and only defense. There was no other way I could convince the jury of my innocence, not to cheat justice, but to escape from the IRA. But for two years the CPS had debated my prosecution. In that time I was led to understand that they had taken advice from the Home Office and, of course, the security services, including MI5. They knew that by taking me to court I would be forced reveal my name to prove my innocence. It seemed, without a doubt, that they wanted me to reveal my true identity in open court.

And yet, shamefully, after the court case, they used the fact that I had revealed my true identity in a manner against me. Did they really think that I would have happily done this in open court knowing that I was among the top five people the Provos had vowed to kill?

Their chicanery made me sick. Both the Northumbria Police and Burton & Burton's clients, whom I would forever believe were representing MI5, steadfastly denied any responsibility for revealing my identity, arguing in their immorality, that I had been the guilty party. The Northumbria Police had for years exposed the name McGartland on their computer files so that every one of their officers would know that Ashe and McGartland were one and the same person; my two names had been blazoned on the front cover of the Crown prosecution files which were taken into open court; and a Northumbria police officer had readily given out my full home address in open court. And yet, despite this overwhelming evidence, the police and MI5 had the audacity to blame me for revealing my identity.

Once again I wondered why the Crown authorities were so determined to make me the guilty party when I had won the court case so handsomely, making the Northumbria Police and the

Crown Prosecution Service look, at the kindest, incompetent and, at the worst, vengeful. Others, particularly my friends from the SB back in Belfast, wondered if there had been another reason to drag me into court on a flawed charge that was thrown out in just ten minutes.

In one letter to Burton & Burton my solicitor related in no uncertain terms how serious the question of my security had become: 'The matter of problems with Northumbria Police needs to be addressed as quite clearly further breaches of security would render the whole exercise of producing a new identity worthless. It was of course Northumbria Police which made our client's identity public knowledge, but unfortunately there had been previous security lapses. One former employee of that force was dismissed for making disclosures about Mr. McGartland. There were other breaches made known to our client's previous solicitor . . .'We would remind you that it was not our client's media attention that led to the disclosure of his identity nor his book *Fifty Dead Men Walking* but the actions of Northumbria Police. You will be aware that we have previously been in conflict as to the details of our client's address being given out in court. Our client has now had confirmation from Mark Blacklock of the *Daily Express*, who apparently took a shorthand note of all the proceedings, that PC Weldon, in his evidence-in-chief, gave out our client's full present address. There was a substantial public gallery at that time. His name and location is in any event known and of course he appears on the DHSS computer system relating to his benefits. You will know that the IRA have access to this.

'Our client is now known and recognized in this immediate area. He has received conflicting advice from Northumbria Police as to his security position and what he should do about it. We must make it very plain that we do not believe that he is safe at his present address and should be relocated forthwith. The longer this goes on the more danger he is in.'

Because it seemed that neither I nor my solicitors were making any headway with the Northumbria Police or those mysterious government agencies fronted by Burton & Burton, my solicitors decided to take up my case at the highest level – with Home Secretary Jack Straw. They asked him to personally intervene in my case. He was informed of my situation, emphasis placed upon the fact that authoritative commentators on the Northern Ireland scene believed I was in 'real and immediate danger'.

Three weeks later I received an extraordinary letter from the Home Secretary claiming once again that I had been responsible for revealing my own identity, repeating the lie that the prosecution had not disclosed my address in court. Inspection of the official court transcript of my trial before Newcastle Crown Court, revealed that while giving evidence on oath, PC Weldon, under pressure from the Crown prosecution lawyer, did in fact state my full home address in open court. There was no doubt whatsoever. And despite the fact that the court transcript was available to the Home Secretary, his advisors, the CPS and the Northumbria Police, all continued to deny that my address had been revealed by the police during my trial. It seemed to me beyond any reasonable doubt that MI5, the Crown Prosecution Service, the Northumbria Police and the RUC, as well as the Home Secretary himself, were ranged against me in my battle for protection, a new identity and relocation to a safe place. And all I had done was to try, in some small way, to play my part in bringing some security to the Protestants and Catholics of Northern Ireland.

The authorities who worked against me also claimed that in writing my book *Fifty Dead Men Walking* I had been further responsible for revealing my identity. That accusation was without foundation. In fact I had taken extreme precautions to ensure that no photographs for the book or publicity purposes were ever taken of me without my appearing in heavy disguise and that no one knew that my new identity was in the name of Ashe. I may well have raised my profile by writing a book but I never once revealed to anyone that I was 'Martin Ashe' in any article or TV or radio program. Not a soul on Tyneside where I had lived for over six years knew that my real name was McGartland and they would never have done so if it hadn't been for the Northumbria Police. All these facts were explained forcefully by my solicitor in letters to our adversaries.

One such letter from my solicitors, Alderson Dodds, to solicitors Burton & Burton read: 'Our client wishes to know which organ of the state he is in effect contracting with. Our client reserves the right to make public his legitimate complaints to the tardy approach that has been adopted towards his resettlement. It is doubtful whether anything would have been forthcoming but for public pressure. Our client has never appeared undisguised in any media appearance. He has no intention of altering that. For several years he kept the identity of Ashe secret and the area of his relocation. Such contact that he did have with the media and his publishers was as McGartland. He has no plans to change that.'

And my solicitor raised with Burton & Burton the question which had become of the greatest importance to me – my future security. 'Our client remains concerned about the proposed arrangements for his security. The suggestion that it should be the responsibility of the senior officer at his local police station inspires no confidence at all. That was how his identity in this area was exposed . . . Our client requires to have contact with a named senior officer whom he can speak to if there are problems of a security nature. Our client has a perfectly valid reason for requiring that his new identity and his new name should not be linked with Ashe or McGartland on the computer systems of the police because of matters outlined above. Northumbria Police should be able to confirm what occurred.'

To ram home to Burton & Burton once and for all what really occurred concerning my identity, my solicitor wrote: 'Ashe's address was disclosed in the criminal proceedings. He was committed from that particular address. It is the same address which appears on the driving license which was a document produced in open court. There is no doubt that the prosecution process made Ashe's address known and available . . . There is no doubt in Mr. Ashe's mind that he needs to relocate. It is quite clear that if anything does happen to Mr. Ashe the authorities will bear a very heavy responsibility.'

I was continually pressed to accept all the proposals put forward by Burton & Burton's mysterious clients, proposals which would have meant I was given a new name, a new driving license and new National Insurance number but which condemned me to stay in my flat in Blyth, a place well known to everyone living in the district. To me, my solicitors and my Special Branch friends in Belfast, the offer made by the mysterious government agency seemed madness.

But no matter how hard the Crown agencies were pushed they steadfastly refused to give an inch. Three months after the trial, while I was still living rough moving from house to house, I was told that the Chief Constable of Northumbria was still satisfied with the current arrangements for my security, saying 'the threat against Mr. Ashe is not such that it requires him to move immediately'. In the meantime, the Crown Agencies, which I was now satisfied were headed by MI5, refused to admit to any liability for my situation and as a result claimed they had no legal obligation to assist in providing me with a new identity.

And yet one month later, in September 1997, Home Secretary Jack Straw, the minister responsible for MI5, said in an interview: 'I have an absolute duty to ensure agents' lives are not put at risk.'

In October 1997 I received a further letter from the Home Secretary which once again showed extraordinary intransigence towards accepting the truth of the disclosure of my identity. It read, 'I note all you say regarding the way in which your identity as Martin Ashe and your role as an agent came to be more widely known but I understand that it was you and not the prosecution who revealed your past during your court case. Indeed I understand that the prosecution, contrary to what you say in your letter, took considerable care to ensure that your precise address was not disclosed in court.'

I was amazed at the effrontery and the extent to which the Crown authorities accepted their responsibility. We had proved by producing shorthand notes that Police Constable Weldon, PC 481 of Northumbria Police motor patrol, had revealed all in open court and still the Home Secretary refused to accept responsibility.

My solicitor later wrote to the Home Secretary: 'Our client has met with quite clear obstruction, difficulty and a complete lack of will to ensure his safety . . . We have to say that if anything does happen to Mr. McGartland the Home Secretary will bear a very heavy responsibility.'

Taken aback by the Home Secretary's refusal to accept responsibility for the disclosure my solicitor wrote another letter to Burton & Burton in which he told the Crown authorities, 'It would appear that an attempt is being made to divert responsibility for the disclosure of our client's identity in his trial to our client and his representatives. His name and address were disclosed in the Crown evidence. The Crown knew that his only conceivable defense involved the disclosure of his identity. The Crown was in a far better position than the defense to evaluate the impact of the prosecution as they had full insight as to Mr. McGartland's precise role and position in Northern Ireland, whereas the defense team simply had the bare instructions of their client whose importance and security problems were being belittled by the Crown. You well know that the case would not have been heard in camera unless that application had been supported by the Crown. You will appreciate that once our client's identity was revealed he would become immediately traceable in any event by way of the social security computer which you will again know is not secure.

'Our client is resigned to the fact that there is no genuine wish to securely relocate him and without that there would be no security in a new identity. He is accordingly taking what steps he can to see to his own security in this area. He would see any threat to his safety as being very clearly at the door of the authorities.'

Determined to prove that there was a real threat to my life, my solicitor wrote to Ronnie Flanagan, the Chief Constable of the RUC, asking him to make an assessment of any threat posed to me from the IRA and associated bodies. During the following month the Police Division of Stormont House launched a surreptitious

campaign writing to concerned members of the public who wanted action taken to provide me with proper security and a new identity. The letters made no comment suggesting to the recipients that
the matter was of little importance.

But one month later no such assessment had been received by
my solicitor and another letter was sent to the Secretary of State for
Northern Ireland. This letter asked Mo Mowlam if she would exert
some influence over the Crown authorities, and even consider personal intervention, because 'we do not know with whom we are
negotiating'.

Slowly but surely it appeared that the RUC had come to the
conclusion that I was still under threat from the IRA and now they
seemed prepared to admit it. In October 1997, Chief
Superintendent G.W. Sillery of the RUC's Command Secretariat
replied on behalf of Chief Constable Ronnie Flanagan stating that
there was a continuing threat against me from the IRA while offering me a new identity and finance to help me relocate.
Superintendent Sillery went on to advise me to take up the offer of
the new identity in a new location as soon as possible, to keep a low
public profile and keep out of Northern Ireland. It seemed from the
tone of the letter that the RUC were intent on persuading me to
hurry in reaching a decision, and I wondered why.

Days earlier there had been an even greater surprise for me. It
appeared I was nearing the truth about my abduction at the hands
of the IRA. On Monday, September 29, 1997, I was surprised by
an appearance on the BBC television program *Here & Now* from
a former RUC intelligence officer who was answering questions
about the treatment I had received at the hands of the authorities.
In fact, the RUC officer had been one of my handlers. He told the
viewers, 'I think Marty has been treated unfairly. He saved a lot of
lives and did a lot of good. He seems to have been dumped. Agents
like him are extremely valuable. And they should be looked after a
lot better than Marty has been.'

Interviewer Wendy Robbins asked: 'Why do you think the case
of perverting the course of justice was brought against Marty

McGartland in the first place?'

My handler, who was sitting in dark silhouette in the TV studio, replied, 'I think there was a hidden agenda.'

Those words struck home hard. I had never spoken a word to that handler since I had left Northern Ireland in 1991. And he had no reason whatsoever to make such a suggestion. Now, here he was telling the entire nation on TV that there had been a hidden agenda in what had happened to me. I didn't know whether he was referring to what had happened to me since my relocation to England in 1991 or to what had led to my kidnap, or both. But his statement on television convinced me that there had been some plot against me. I also believed at that moment that the campaign against me was not an accident of fate but something intentional and probably vindictive. But why? Now, more than ever, I was determined to discover the truth.

However, the Northumbria Police headquarters had been given details of the prerecorded program and had prepared a 400-word 'News Item' in advance which had been sent to the Belfast newspapers with a strict embargo. It read: 'The Crown authorities reject any suggestion that Mr. McGartland has been treated unreasonably. Individuals who have given valuable service to the country and who may be at threat as a result deserve – and receive – considerable support at public expense to ensure their safety. The techniques used to resettle and protect such individuals are obviously sensitive and cannot be discussed publicly. They have a proven track record but problems are bound to arise if the individual in question:

1. Disregards security advice he has been given.
2. Draws attention to himself by writing about his work against terrorism and giving media interviews.
3. Engages in activities which draw him to the attention of the police.

'Despite the difficulties which have arisen, the Crown authorities remain committed to providing the necessary and appropriate support to Mr. McGartland. Northumbria Police, while not directly involved in the negotiations over Mr. McGartland's future, also support the approach which has and is being taken.

'While there continues to be a threat against Mr. McGartland, it has not been such that he needs to immediately abandon his current residence or obtain immediate police protection. He is encouraged to take up the offer, repeatedly made, of a new identity as soon as practicable in order to provide for his long-term security in the event that the threat should change.'

The statement continued, 'We must emphasize that, no matter what services an individual may have performed in the public interest, he is not above the law and cannot be immune from prosecution if there is evidence to put before the courts. In such cases a decision to prosecute is taken by the Crown Prosecution Service in the light of all the facts. In the Crown Court case involving Mr. McGartland in May 1997, the CPS was able to prosecute without reference to his past history and identity. Mr. McGartland chose to reveal those details to the court in his defense and at no time requested that the case be heard in front of a camera to protect them.'

If this was not bad enough, the Northumbria Police, the force given the responsibility of protecting me from the IRA, also sent their statement to the Belfast newspapers thus, at a stroke, providing the IRA with absolute information as to what part of England I was living.

Most of the statement criticized me for writing a book about my exploits as a Special Branch source and yet no one in Britain had known that Martin McGartland and Martin Ashe were one and the same person. I had taken the utmost precautions to ensure that no one knew that. And no one had known until a Northumbria Police officer had read aloud in open court my full home address. Even my next door neighbor of four years had told the media that she had no knowledge that my name was Martin McGartland until my trial at Newcastle Crown Court.

What angered me the most was the Northumbria Police force's attempt to blame me for revealing my past as an RUC informant during my trial. That, of course, was my only possible defense and they knew it. They had gambled on me not revealing my personal history, making sure that they would secure an easy conviction, having brought a case, flawed in root and branch, against me. In ten minutes the jury had seen through the prosecution's deceptions and found me not guilty. The only question I could not answer and which the police shed no light on in their statement to the press was, 'Why?' Why did the Crown authorities, with all the knowledge they had about my background, decide to go ahead with such a flimsy case, thus ensuring my two identities and probably my home address would become public knowledge? I was more convinced than ever that it couldn't have been an accident. That TV program, and my handler's candid assessment of my treatment by the authorities, had given me the proof for which I had been agitating. Now all I needed to know was, why?

I had become frustrated by the stalemate which now seemed to prevail over my problems with the authorities and I was determined to try and discover what really lay behind the Crown's antipathy towards me and their scant concern for my security. I felt the time for me to take decisive action had arrived. I still believed that despite all the chicanery surrounding my case someone, or some organization, authority or agency was determined to expose me to a possible IRA attack in exactly the same way as I had been deliberately led into an IRA trap in the August of 1991. Telling no one, I packed a change of clothes in a small bag, left my home early one autumn morning and made my way to Stranraer. I was returning to Belfast. Alone.

CHAPTER EIGHT

A cold autumn wind whipping the waters off Stranraer greeted me as I drove into the town at the start of the most important journey of my life. I had decided to leave my car in Scotland for fear that the registration number would be known to the RUC authorities in Belfast. I drove around the town for I had some time to spare before the ferry departed. I parked in a side street outside the town center some seven minutes' walk from the Sea-Cat terminal.

As I sat in the waiting-room I took stock of the other travelers that morning, wondering if there was anyone I knew or, more importantly, if there was anyone who might recognize me. I knew that the most favored crossing for IRA personnel traveling to Scotland and parts of the UK was the Larne–Stranraer ferry but there were many IRA sympathizers who took the Belfast–Stranraer crossing because of the speed, giving less time for the security services to check and identify possible suspects. I had considered flying to Belfast but judged that to be an even greater risk for I knew that RUC personnel check passenger lists both on and off those flights. If there is the slightest suspicion that some wanted person is on board, a photograph of him or her is taken off the CCTV and flashed to Belfast International airport where it is checked by a unit of the RUC Special Branch against the extensive photographic files they hold.

I sat in the café drinking a cup of tea and watched everyone like a hawk while not to appear too observant. Inside, my heart was thumping with anticipation and nervousness but I managed to smile, telling myself how pathetic I had become during my years living in the comparative safety of the British mainland after my time of far greater risk living in Belfast. I knew that Scottish SB officers also constantly manned the ferries, checking everyone coming and going and I guessed and hoped they had no ID of me. Then my old luck returned. As we trooped from the café to the boat a young woman was struggling with three small children and their luggage.

'Can I help you?' I said as I moved quickly to her side, picking up one of the young toddlers.

'Thanks very much,' she said, checking me from head to toe to ensure I was a genuine helper.

'Think nothing of it,' I said. 'I've got a couple of little ones and you can always do with an extra pair of hands.'

'You're right,' she said, 'especially when they're a handful like these lot are.'

'Going home to Belfast?' I asked, trying to be as chatty as possible, so that any police personnel on the quayside might believe we were a family unit and ignore us.

'Aye,' she replied, 'I've been seeing my Ma.'

Simply walking on board holding one of the children and a piece of luggage gave me confidence, for by seizing the initiative, and picking up a child as a decoy, I realized that I hadn't forgotten my old SB training. Once on board I wondered if I should continue to use the young mother as cover but that was not to be. She had obviously been somewhat suspicious of my kindly act of good manners. She thanked me for my help in a dismissive manner and went to sit on her own with the children. I walked away realizing that I hadn't done such a wonderful 'Sir Galahad' impression as I thought.

As I sat on my own trying to look as inconspicuous as possible there was one further fear haunting me. I remembered that for months at a time the IRA would station a young sympathizer on the ferries, officially employed as cabin staff or cleaner but in reality ordered to report back to senior IRA commanders if anything suspicious was happening. These lads were responsible for information concerning many of the British Army troop movements, the comings and goings of the thousands of British soldiers who were, and still are, constantly on the move across the Irish Sea. But one of the reasons I chose the Sea-Cat crossing is that most of the IRA members take the big, slower ferries as do the soldiers traveling back and forth on their tours of duty. I bought a newspaper as a shield and read it slowly from cover to cover trying to make sure that I didn't look too ridiculous.

Before setting off for Belfast I had reread Ian Phoenix's diaries. They explained in some detail how he and other members of the Northern Ireland police counter-surveillance team were aware before I started out on my journey to Connolly house that morning in August 1991 that I was to be 'kidnapped' by the IRA. Phoenix's diaries made plain that he had been made aware what was to happen to me – that I was to be 'debriefed' by the Civil Administration Team. I reread that sentence time and again because I had never been told that I was to be debriefed by the ruthless IRA interrogators, euphemistically entitled the Civil Administration Team. In fact, my SB handlers had encouraged me to attend that meeting after having taken advice from their senior officers. I had such faith in Felix that I agreed to attend the meeting because he urged me to do so and, more importantly, because he said they would be watching me every step of the way with a full back-up surveillance unit in attendance.

If I had not believed that I was to be chaperoned in this way I would never for one moment have agreed to attend that meeting with Podraig Wilson, the head of IRA discipline throughout Belfast, the man who decided who should receive a punishment beating and who should be kneecapped. I had, of course, known that if the IRA had discovered I was a Special Branch source I would be taken before the organization's Civil Administration Team to face questioning, deep interrogation, torture and a bullet in the back of the head.

My handlers had never given me a single reason why I should go to Connolly House that day to see Podraig Wilson and yet they had encouraged me to attend as though I had no option. Having read Detective Superintendent Ian Phoenix's diaries I knew that the SB and members of the all-powerful Tasking Co-ordination Group which comprised senior officers from MI5, the SAS, the Special Branch, the 'Det' (military specialist surveillance unit), the RUC and the British Army knew I was to face the IRA's most ruthless interrogators. And yet no one had warned me, no one had given me a chance to back out and no one had offered or even suggested to me that I had a choice. No one had told me that I was taking the most enormous risk in going to Connolly House; no one had said that I could skip the meeting at the Sinn Fein headquarters; no one had told me that I was to face the IRA torturers and no one had suggested that I might prefer to be taken out of Belfast to a safe haven outside Northern Ireland.

As the Sea-Cat bounced across the water I felt despondent and bitter that I had been treated so despicably after all I had tried to do to help people in Belfast. It made me feel physically sick that anyone, let alone the people I had risked my neck for, could have handed me over to the IRA knowing I faced interrogation, torture and certain death. But that had been the reality facing me. Now I wanted to expose the evil shits that could have done that to me and reveal them for what they were.

In his diaries Phoenix had revealed that he believed that a (SB) surveillance team saw me leaving Connolly House only a short time after entering the building, and that he had been informed that later I had been observed by the surveillance team on the spot walking across the road to the Busy Bee shopping complex. Ian Phoenix then wrote: 'The surveillance team was mistaken. The informer had been snatched from the Busy Bee car park, bound and gagged, and whisked to a flat in nearby Twinbrook. There he was guarded by two Provisionals who were waiting for the arrival of the CAT interrogators.'

To me, it seemed extraordinary that Ian Phoenix, one of the top twenty-five anti-terrorist intelligence officers in Northern Ireland, should have written so inaccurately of my kidnapping. When he wrote his diaries he must have had access to the latest, most thoroughly detailed account of what really happened to me. Within weeks of my leap from the window I had given a detailed account to the Special Branch of exactly what occurred. Phoenix had apparently entirely ignored the SB accounts. But why? It just didn't make sense that such a senior officer as Detective Superintendent Phoenix should have written such an inaccurate account. And it wasn't that he didn't acknowledge me, treating me as some run-of-the-mill informant, for in his book he states that I was one of the Special Branch's best spies.

When RUC officers came to interview me about my abduction I had been told by Special Branch handlers not to say a word to the CID (Criminal Investigation Department) officers of the RUC, to tell them nothing whatsoever about what happened to me that day or the names or descriptions of the IRA men who had taken and held me. Even at the time I thought that advice was strange. I wanted those bastards caught, charged, convicted and jailed and I wondered why the hell I was being advised not to help bring them to justice. Senior Special Branch officers told me that I should simply say that I could remember nothing of the incidents immediately before, during or after my kidnap ordeal. But I had always taken the advice of the Branch throughout my career and, as a consequence, I naturally decided to take their advice on this occasion.

All these thoughts were racing around my mind as we drew closer to Belfast. They just made me realize that I had to be fucking careful during my stay in the city, making sure I steered clear of both the IRA and any of the forces of law and order. I knew that no one in Britain knew of my secret trip, and if I was caught and held, the powers that be could do what they wanted with me. The thought sent a chill down my spine because I now believed the real intention was to have me killed.

Before making the final decision to undertake the fateful trip to Belfast I had spent sleepless nights trying to determine whether everything that Mike had told me was true. I could not find a single reason why Mike should travel to the mainland and inform me of the circumstances surrounding my abduction. At first I hadn't been convinced of the story but the more I thought of what happened to me, the more sense it made. In fact, I could find nothing to challenge his reasoning and the very fact that it seemed I had been sacrificed made me both angry and sad. I wasn't fearful but angry, a deep sense of injustice driving me onwards to prove that someone, either MI5, the RUC, the TCG or, heaven forbid, my friends at Special Branch, had been responsible for organizing my kidnap and probable death.

There was only one major problem. I could not work out the identity of the man MI5 feared I might accidentally betray to the IRA commanders and yet, according to Mike, I knew the man. I thought of all the likely people and then realized none of them appeared to fit the category of a vital intelligence source. Perhaps I would discover that during the time I planned to stay in Belfast.

Throughout my years working for the Branch I had only come across one man who had openly challenged my role as a Special Branch source – and that was a Chief Inspector whose first name was John, a Special Branch officer whom I had previously never met. In October, 1990, I was attending a Special Branch meeting at an SB safe house on the outskirts of Belfast which was attended by two of my handlers and three other senior Branch officers. Chief Inspector John was sitting in the room with one other officer when we arrived. Throughout the hour-long meeting the Chief Inspector seemed to spend most of the time closely watching me as he listened to our conversation. He hardly spoke a word and I was very suspicious as to why he was sitting in on the meeting.

I knew that room in the safe house had been wired so that senior intelligence officers could listen to conversations without being seen by the informants being debriefed by their handlers. As Inspector John had nothing or very little to offer to the discussion, I wondered why he was staying in the room throughout the meeting. His presence confused and worried me. His eyes hardly ever seemed to leave me, inspecting me up and down, watching my face, as if deliberately ensuring his presence was of real importance. He was making me feel uncomfortable.

At the end of the meeting I got up to leave as usual, intending to make my way to the back of the house where I knew a closed van was parked only inches from the back door. This was so that when I stepped from the house to the van I could not identify in which road or street or area the meeting had taken place. But as I walked towards the door of the meeting-room Chief Inspector John moved forward towards me, deliberately blocking my way.

He started joking, saying, 'Well, Marty, it's nice to meet you after hearing so much about you.'

I had no wish to prolong this conversation and mumbled 'Thanks' as I went to walk past him and out of the room.

Inspector John suddenly said, 'By the way, Marty,' and I turned towards him. As I did so he pulled a hand-gun – I'm sure it was a .38 Smith & Wesson revolver – from his jacket, which took me aback. No one had ever played such a trick on me in the dozens of times I had spent in various SB safe houses around Belfast.

In that instant I was convinced he was about to shoot me. I thought he was a madman and for some reason was about to kill me. It was just the way he had sat there throughout the meeting, watching my every movement. I looked at his face and I realized he was smiling. 'Fuck,' I thought, 'he's not a madman after all. I'm okay.'

'Here, Marty,' he said smiling, handing me the gun, giving me the pistol grip while he held the barrel.

I thought it was a friendly gesture; a light-hearted joke, knowing that I spent most of my life amongst IRA men. 'Thanks,' I said, a smile on my face as I went along with the joke, pretending to take the gun from him.

Though I am naturally right-handed I stretched out my left hand to take the gun. He snatched it away, a look of ferocity on his face, and rushed out of the room shouting to my SB handlers who had been in the room during the meeting, 'Come here, come quickly.'

'What's the matter?' I heard Felix shout as he ran back towards the room he had just left.

'He's that gunman, Marty's our man,' Inspector John shouted.

'What gunman?' Felix asked, unable to grasp what the hell was going on.

'You know, you know,' screamed Inspector John, seemingly in a state of frenzy. 'The fuckin' PIRA one, the baby-faced left-hand-ed one, the gunman with red hair who shot those boys in Belfast center.'

I recalled two appalling shootings in the center of Belfast in 1990; two officers shot in the back of the head as they passed through security gates near the Falls Road in broad daylight and another two RUC officers - dog-handlers - who were shot dead as they sat in an unmarked police van in High Street, Belfast, three months later. RUC investigations had led them to believe the same PIRA gunman had been responsible. I knew the Special Branch put a priority on tracing gunmen who shoot RUC officers in daylight in the center of Belfast.

'No, no, no,' shouted Felix, 'you've got it all wrong . . . calm down . . . for fuck's sake calm down . . . you're talking a load of fuckin' nonsense . . . have you taken leave of your senses . . . I know Marty . . . I know him well . . . he's no PIRA gunman.'

I was surprised to hear Felix talking to a Chief Inspector in that tone of voice for the Inspector was a higher rank. I had never seen Felix in such a rage but I admired him, and was very, very happy that he was sticking up for me.

But Inspector John kept interrupting Felix, telling him to shut up, screaming at him to listen to what he had to say. Raising his voice again, he kept shouting, 'I know he is . . . he took my gun with his left hand . . . and his hair . . . it's red . . . it's like that PIRA man. Jesus, don't you realize that we've been using a fuckin' PIRA gunman as an informer?'

As the Inspector continued to rant and rage, convinced that I was the left-handed PIRA gunman, Felix grabbed him roughly by the arm and pulled him away from the room and down the corridor, helped by other SB officers who had come running as the shouting match had raged on. Within seconds the Inspector was out of the house. I would never see him again. Felix came back into the room a couple of minutes later and apologized for what had happened.

'I'm sorry, Marty, I don't know what got into him,' he said. 'I honestly think the poor bastard's cracking up. He was more like a mad-man than the rational, sensible RUC officer I've known for years.'

I heard later that Chief Inspector John had been reprimanded by a senior SB officer and told never again to attend SB briefings with informants without permission. The extraordinary fracas had upset me more than I realized at the time. I could not believe that such a senior officer would react in that way towards me when I had been working for the SB for nearly three years. I took Felix's advice and put it down to stress but it still seemed crazy an officer of that rank should be permitted to continue his work in that frame of mind.

The nearer the Sea-Cat came towards Belfast the more tense I became until I saw the big office blocks and major buildings of Belfast fast approaching. Then, for some unknown reason, the view gave me a sense of safety, of returning home and seeing all the old familiar haunts and faces around West Belfast. As I saw the armed RUC officers with their black flak jackets standing on the quay, my former life came hurtling back to me, wiping the smile off my face. I wondered if I would have any difficulty disembarking because I knew the terminal was always guarded by RUC and SB personnel, only some of whom patrolled in uniform. I knew also that an array of security cameras were constantly watched by police inside the terminal building. I understood it was common practice for Special Branch officers to ask people to step aside to provide an ID or a current driving license to prove their real identity. On this occasion, however, it seemed that no one, including me, was stopped and asked to produce an ID. In any case I was confident that I would have passed any checks because the only identification I was carrying was my English driving license in the name of Martin David Ashe, the new identity given to me on my relocation to the mainland. Indeed, I would never have thought of returning to Belfast to undertake the task I was now facing if I had not had the protection of a new name and new ID. It would have been suicidal.

I walked off the ferry, holding the little baby once again, and handed the child to a woman who was waiting to greet her friend. I happily handed over the baby and the woman, who had a Belfast accent, thanked me. I walked to a car rental office less than ten minutes from the terminal and drove away in a nearly new red Vauxhall Vectra. I told the girl in the office that I expected to be in Northern Ireland for a few days but did not know the exact date I would return the vehicle.

'That's all right, sir,' she replied. 'Bring it back whenever. If you're going to keep it more than a week though, will you phone to let us know?'

'Aye, of course I will,' I replied, 'but I can't see me staying more than a week.'

I drove out of Belfast on the M2, past Antrim and on to the A6 heading towards Derry. I was driving towards a little farmhouse where I hoped and prayed a woman I knew still lived. Peggy was a dear friend, well past sixty years of age, a woman who lived alone off the beaten track with only two cats and a few chickens for company. She was small, even petite. Her hair was grey, going on white, and her face was lined. But she had a ready smile and the sweetest nature of any woman I had ever known. I had met her some years earlier, around 1990, when I was working for the SB and driving my IRA alleged 'mates' around Belfast trying to win their confidence. I had been driving from Derry back to Belfast when I saw Peggy standing at the side of the road by an ancient Ford Escort. She didn't flag me down or make any sign but I guessed she was in trouble and needed help and so I drove past, stopped, and walked back towards her.

'Are you okay?' I asked.

'My car's stopped,' she said, 'and I can't get it going again.'

'What happened?' I asked.

'I was driving along and suddenly the engine slowed and the car began chugging along until it finally cut out and I pulled into the side. I've tried starting it but nothing happens,' she said. 'Do you know anything about cars?'

'Aye, a little,' I said. 'I'll take a look but I can't promise.'

'Oh don't put yourself out,' she said. 'You must be far too busy.'

'Don't be silly,' I replied. 'I might get it to work enough for you to get to a garage.'

As I opened the bonnet to see what I could do she went on, 'Are you sure you don't mind? You're very kind.'

I tried to start the engine but to no avail. After looking under the bonnet for a couple of minutes I decided to take off the distributor cap. Inside I discovered moisture and presumed that was the problem. I told her it seemed the cap must have been cracked and moisture had seeped in, and advised her that I might be able to get the car started but that she must immediately take the car to a garage and get it checked. In the meantime, I took a cloth from the car and dried the inside of the distributor cap, placed it back on and turned over the engine. As it sparked to life I knew it would survive a short journey.

'That's very kind of you,' she said. 'It's not many people who stop to help old people nowadays.'

'Will you be all right now?' I asked, sensing that she still seemed a little uncertain whether my mechanical skills would survive for long.

'Would you like a cup of tea?' she asked.

'No, that's alright,' I said, 'I'm fine.'

'Could you spare a few more minutes?' she asked. 'I only live a few miles down the road but it's along a lane where no one goes. I wouldn't want the car to stop down there.'

'Do you want me to follow?' I asked.

'Well, if you've got the time,' she said, 'I would feel better. You know, just in case it stops again.'

'Aye, come on,' I said. 'You drive ahead and I'll follow.'

We drove in convoy-fashion a few miles further down the road towards Derry and turned off left, traveling down some country lanes until finally driving more than half-a-mile down a dirt track. At the bottom, almost hidden by trees and shrubs, was a small single-story cottage which had seen better days. In a small adjacent field sheltered by trees and broken down fences were a dozen or more chickens pecking around in the dirt, searching for food. As we parked and got out of the cars, two black and white cats came up to the old woman and rubbed themselves around her legs as she made a fuss of them, chatting away to them as if they were human.

'Now, you come in and have a cup of tea or a drink of water,' she said. 'I'm not having you drive away with nothing after helping me.'

I sensed she was feeling lonely and somewhat vulnerable, having lost some confidence when her faithful old Escort had let her down, so I decided to stay for a short while and have a cup of tea.

'Do you live alone?' I asked.

'Aye,' she replied, 'I've lived alone for more than ten years since my husband died. I live here with my cats and the chickens. It gives me something to keep me busy and my little cats keep me company. It can be very lonely out here.'

'Do you have any children or any other relatives who come and visit you?' I asked, trying to make polite conversation.

'I used to,' she said as she puttered about the kitchen merrily chatting away to her cats while making the tea, taking out her best china, milk and sugar and putting them on the kitchen table. 'But they moved away and I hardly ever see them. There's not enough room for them to stay here because my daughters have children of their own.'

She asked, 'Do you often come this way then?'

'Sometimes,' I said. 'I'm all over the place.'

We sat down in the kitchen and had a cup of tea and a few biscuits which she kept in an old multi-colored cake tin.

'What's your name?' she asked.

'Marty,' I replied. 'I live in Belfast; born and bred there.'

'I can tell that from your accent,' she said. 'Everyone who lives in Belfast has such a strong accent, so different from country people like me.'

'Do you think so?' I asked.

'Just listen to yourself,' she said. 'It's the life you all lead in Belfast. It's so fast and furious.'

'And what's your name?' I asked.

'Peggy, just call me Peggy,' she said. 'Everyone does.'

'How much room do you have here?' I asked, a thought crossing my mind.

'Just two bedrooms, a living-room, this kitchen and a bathroom,' she said. 'Come with me and I'll show you.'

The little house seemed in need of repair and more than a lick of paint both inside and out. It seemed that no redecoration could have taken place for nearly a generation and yet the rooms were clean and the furniture old but comfortable. I thought what a wonderful place this would make for me as a hideaway. While working for the SB I had often felt like escaping from the pressures that arose from living my life among Republican sympathizers and mixing most days with leading IRA activists. Leading a double life can drive a man half-mad remembering never to make a mistake, ever. Of course I had sometimes made the out-of-place remark, which could have betrayed my double life; but I usually managed to cover it up with a laugh, nervous laughs which I hoped and prayed had not been detected by the people I was with. And then there was the constant worry over Angie, who had no idea of the double life I was leading. My greatest fear was leaving her and our expected baby if the IRA were to discover my double life. But here, in this little tumble-down cottage, I had felt instantly safe away from the hurly-burly of Belfast, the SB, the IRA and the impossible life I was leading, deceiving everyone but myself.

'Do you ever take in lodgers?' I asked.

'No, never,' she said. 'I don't trust no one, especially since the Troubles began.'

'Do you trust me?' I asked cheekily.

'Aye, I trust you, Martin,' she said. 'I know you're a good lad at heart.'

'Sometimes, when I'm passing this way, could I pop in and say hello?' I asked.

'Of course you can,' she said. 'It would be nice to see you. You would be a friendly face. Come anytime you want; just drop in, we're always here.'

'We?' I asked, fearful that I had missed something.

'Yes,' she replied, 'me and my cats.'

'Oooohhhh,' I said laughing, 'I didn't understand. Well, I'll be away now. Should I phone you before I drop in?' I did not want to shock the dear old pensioner if I should just drop in unexpectedly.

'That's a good idea; perhaps that would be best,' she said as she wrote down the number on a small piece of paper and gave it to me. I asked to use her toilet and memorized her phone number before ripping it up and flushing it down the lavatory. It was one of the tricks of the trade that the SB had taught me; never tear up a bit of paper with information on it and throw it in a bin but always rip it up and flush it down the toilet— for in that way no one can ever find it.

During the following two years I had visited my pensioner friend on more than a dozen occasions and after my first couple of visits she had asked whether I wanted to stay over. I jumped at the offer for it gave me an ideal hideaway that even the Special Branch knew nothing about. At Peggy's place I would manage to get eight or nine hours' sleep, a pleasure I never managed in Belfast, where my sleep was always disturbed waiting for that dreaded knock at the door which I was convinced would come one day.

Peggy would make us cups of tea and cook a meal for me in winter. I would phone and say I was coming over and she would tell me to try and make it by a certain hour, usually 6 p.m., because that's when she would have her one meal of the day. In return, she would ask me to feed the chickens, mend a fence around her farm, and sometimes cut down overgrown trees that she believed could be dangerous. And she would always ask my advice about her car, and when to have the Escort serviced, for she had come to believe, mistakenly, that I was an expert car mechanic. Peggy became something of a surrogate mother to me and in the end she would offer to wash my clothes, darn my socks, and treat me like the son she never had. And the more I visited her the more generous she became, encouraging me to come and stay more often. I would usually arrive with a small box of chocolates for her. She appreciated not only the chocolates but, more importantly, loved the fact that I had arrived to see her with a small present. Undeniably, we did form quite a good mother–son relationship, yet all the while she never had the slightest idea that she was providing me with a sanctuary.

The pressures I was facing at that time were increasing almost daily. The SB were pushing me to get as close as I could to IRA activists like Harry Fitzsimmons, one of the IRA's most skillful bomb-makers, and other Republicans who were now constantly asking me to drive them to various places in and around Belfast almost on a daily basis. More importantly, my lovely Angie was pregnant and, understandably, fearful of bringing a baby into a world where people were getting blown up, shot or wounded nearly every day. And in the back of her mind she believed that in some way or another I was directly involved in the Troubles, though she kept all those fears and those thoughts to herself.

One night in October 1989, Angie's family became central characters in a desperate IRA attempt to free IRA remand prisoners from Belfast's Crumlin Road Jail. At the time, Angie and I were at our flat in Beechmount Pass, West Belfast, when a knock occurred at their front door in Norfolk Parade, 150 or so yards from the heavily guarded Andersonstown RUC station. At home that night were Angie's parents, along with five of their six children. One of their young sons answered the door to find a man standing with a gun outside. The man pushed past the lad and burst into the living-room where the family was sitting, watching TV. 'Provisional IRA,' he yelled. 'Everybody listen to me and nobody will get hurt.'

Angie's father, a tough, strong man in his forties, jumped to his feet and confronted the gunman, courageously shouting and remonstrating with him. But it was to no avail.

'If you don't shut the fuck up and sit down I'm going to blow your fuckin' head off. Now sit down,' he yelled.

Angie's mother pulled at her husband's trousers, urging him to sit down and keep quiet, fearing that the IRA gunman would have no qualms about blowing his head off. The young kids were scared out of their wits and some were crying for they knew full well what men with guns did to people in West Belfast. The gunman told everyone to sit quietly and say nothing while Angie's mother comforted the younger ones. For ten long hours the entire family, including the children, were made to stay in that room, never being permitted to leave for any reason whatsoever, not even to go to the toilet or fetch food or water. Meanwhile, they could hear a number of other men in their kitchen and people coming and going throughout the night. They could only guess the actions of their captors in the adjoining rooms — terrorists who were known on occasion to take over people's homes and spend the night making huge bombs. In this instance, the team put together a 500 lb. bomb which they packed into two wheelie-bins that had been stolen locally. During the night the family occasionally heard one of the intruders speaking on the phone, chatting to others, whom, it became apparent, were indulging in making more bombs in various other people's houses across Belfast. What they didn't then know was the bombers' target.

In fact, Angie's family were now inextricably involved in one of the most daring IRA jail-break plots ever planned. The bombs constructed in Angie's home were transported to Crumlin Road Jail in Angie's father's Transit van and from there placed in the bucket of a JCB digger which trundled along to the intended target. The IRA planned a mass breakout of the 300 prisoners then held at the jail. A 2 lb. Semtex bomb, which had been smuggled into the jail, had been placed by the prisoners at the yard door, ready to be exploded as the huge 500 lb. bomb was detonated near the perimeter wall. The prisoners planned to escape into nearby streets where hijacked getaway cars had been parked with keys already in the ignition. The breakout plot was foiled when police discovered the bomb in the

JCB digger. As a result, fifteen IRA men were accused of taking part in the planned mass escape, but in November 1992, three years after the plan, the men were acquitted.

Angie and I knew nothing whatsoever of the family's involvement until later the following day when we had arranged to go together with Angie's mother to buy a pram for our baby. Angie's mother told of the family's role in the bombing while they were walking around Park Center, a West Belfast shopping mall. When they came over to me I could see that Angie was upset and I so asked what was the matter.

Suddenly her mother said, 'Marty, I've got something to tell you. Last night the IRA came to our house and held us at gunpoint all through the night. They were treating us like animals, not letting us go to the toilet and damaging our new kitchen. We have no idea what they were doing because they locked us up - all of us - even the little ones.'

At the time I decided not to tell Felix what had happened to Angie's family for I feared that the RUC might come and interview them, searching their house for clues and maybe even doing more damage. I also feared that the family might put two-and-two together and realize that I had been responsible for informing the SB. And I couldn't risk that. However, what the IRA had done to Angie's family, a totally innocent family caught up in the Troubles, was inexcusable. It was yet another reason why I came to the conclusion that I should become more deeply involved in helping the SB stop the IRA's plan to achieve their aims, even though occasionally my involvement resulted in harming, injuring and sometimes killing decent, innocent Catholics whom the IRA were supposedly protecting.

All these memories flashed through my mind as I traveled north towards Peggy's home wondering if she was still living there or, indeed, whether she was still alive. It had been six years since I had last seen her and she had then been as strong as ever. I hoped she was there otherwise my plans for a 48-hour stay in Belfast would be in disarray. I knew that I should have had a secure back-up plan but, at that stage, I didn't, risking that my luck would hold. I turned off the A6 and held my breath as I dialed Peggy's number.

'Hello,' the voice answered. I realized in that instant that Peggy was alive and well.

'Hello, Peggy,' I all but shouted, 'it's Martin. Do you remember me? I used to come and stay with you way back in the early nineties.'

'Oh, Martin,' she said, sounding somewhat taken aback, 'it's lovely to hear your voice again after all these years. Are you coming to see me?'

'Aye, I am that,' I replied, 'if that's all right with you?'

'That will be very nice,' she said. 'When will you be here?'

'I'll be there under the hour,' I said.

'Shall I put the kettle on?' she asked, and in that moment my heart went out to the poor, lonely woman who had shown me nothing but kindness since the moment we met.

'That would be wonderful,' I replied. 'I'll see you soon.'

I climbed back into my rented car and drove on to Peggy's place. She wasn't standing by the door ready to welcome me, which caused me some alarm, and I wondered whether she was too ill to even come to greet me as she had always done in the past. I hurried inside to check, concerned that she was unwell and alone, and found her standing by the cooker watching the kettle boil. When she turned towards me, however, I could see that the years had finally taken their toll. Although I had no exact idea of her age, I guessed she must now be well over seventy.

'How have you been?' I asked.

'Not so well of late, Martin,' she replied and I could see the strain on her face. 'I've got terrible arthritis in my leg and in the winter when it's cold and wet I can't even get out of bed in the mornings. I've been suffering with my chest too. The doctor says it's living here that causes the trouble.'

'You don't look that bad,' I said, in an effort to cheer her up.

'Don't you think so?' she asked, trying to smile. 'That's good news.'

'And where are the chickens?' I asked.

'They had to go. They got to be too much for me. I had to get rid of them.'

'And there's only one cat,' I said.

'Aye,' she said, 'poor Suzy had to be put down, she got so old. I didn't like having to do it but the time came. I was just being kind.'

'I'm sure you were,' I said, trying to comfort her.

'Are you going to stay a while?' she asked.

'Aye, if that's okay by you.'

'It would be lovely to have you stay, just like the old times. I would like that very much, Martin. Then you could tell me all you've been up to.'

'I've been leading a very boring life, Peggy,' I replied. 'I haven't been to see you because I've been living on the mainland for some years now.'

Later Peggy would tell me that a friend from a few miles down the road would pop in to see her every other day, keeping an eye on her, making sure she was okay and taking away her washing which she would return on her next visit. 'She's a sweet young girl and she's married but I've never met her children.'

I made my own bed and went out to buy some fish and chips which I brought back and heated in the oven because they were almost cold by the time I returned. Peggy seemed to enjoy them however, and that's all that mattered to me. I went to bed that night knowing I would sleep soundly but realized that the next few days were likely to be far more dangerous. I knew I was taking my life in my hands but I also knew that I had no option. I had to discover the truth.

CHAPTER NINE

T he following morning I set off for West Belfast with the words of Peggy ringing in my ears. 'Take care of yourself,' she said. 'You never know what can happen these days. Don't trust anyone, Martin. There's all sorts of trouble about.'

I was searching for my old friend Pete, a lad a few years older than me, someone whom I knew I could trust absolutely. We had been to the same school, messed around the streets of Belfast together as young tearaways and always supported each other whenever trouble loomed. We had also fought some battles together on the streets of West Belfast against young hoodlums who wanted to cause trouble. It was a long-standing relationship based on trust. Indeed, we had never lost touch ever since I moved to England in the autumn of 1991. We would talk on the phone every few weeks and he would keep me up to date with the latest developments in Ballymurphy. Like me, Pete was from Catholic West Belfast. He had also come to hate the way in which the IRA controlled the lives of everyone in their district; they ruled the entire area with a rod of iron, handing out punishment beatings as though they had the power of life and death over young Catholic boys.

Indeed, three of Pete's young friends had been badly beaten by punishment squads, one dragged out of a Ballymurphy pub and smashed unconscious with baseball bats in front of his girlfriend because they claimed, incorrectly, that he was involved with crime. Another friend had his car taken away from him by some IRA thugs who beat him senseless when he refused to cooperate; and the third was beaten for taking the side of nine-year-old kids whom IRA thugs decided to beat up for allegedly stealing from parked cars. Sometimes when I spoke to Pete from the safety of Newcastle

I would feel guilty at having fled my native city, leaving others to face the thugs of the IRA punishment squads while I lived in peace across the water.

After leaving Belfast in August 1991 I spoke openly to Pete of the dangerous life I had led in an effort to help the people of Northern Ireland. I eventually arranged for him to meet my Branch handlers, knowing how much he also hated and despised the way the IRA thugs operated. Some months later I learned he was in fact working for the Branch but he never joined the IRA as I had done. Many IRA commanders did, however, trust him and would frequently ask him to help out in various ways.

A year later a worried Pete called me on my mobile phone number, something I instructed him to do only in an emergency if things were becoming really dangerous. On this occasion he called to tell me he was coming under increasing pressure from his SB handlers to join the IRA. I advised him strongly never to do it, as I had done, because such an action would place his very life at risk. I recalled telling him, 'Listen to what I have to say and listen very carefully. If you join, Pete, I guarantee you that within a couple of years you won't be around - the IRA will make sure of that. When you're inside the IRA there are only a few people who know what's going on and everyone is under suspicion, especially when operations start going wrong. You just can't win because the Special Branch is always pushing for results. That causes you to take risks, sometimes stupid risks. And, in truth, the Special Branch won't help you and often can't help you when the chips are down. Then you're on your own and no one will stick their neck out for you. And one last point: if the IRA discovers you're an informant, the Special Branch will have no further use for you. I can guarantee you, Pete, that if you do go ahead and infiltrate the IRA you will end up with a bullet in the back of your head.' Fortunately, Pete took my advice to heart and remains alive today.

Shortly after 9 a.m., when I was some miles from Belfast, I stopped and phoned Pete, greeting him as I usually did. 'How is it going, kid? What's happening?' I asked.

'Fine,' he replied. 'what do you want me for?'

'Can you do me a big favor?' I asked. 'Are you doing anything in the next hour or so?'

'No,' he said.

'Would you be able to go and meet a close friend of mine?'

'It depends,' he replied. 'But it should be okay.'

'I want you to take a private taxi down to Balmoral and my friend will be waiting outside the King's Hall,' I said, deliberately selecting a place Pete knew well.

'What's he look like?' Pete asked. 'Can you give me a description?'

'Yes, of course. He'll be on foot and he's going to give you some papers. He'll be wearing a beige sweatshirt and jeans. Have you got that?'

'Aye,' he replied.

'And Pete, listen to me. Make sure you get out of the taxi at the corner of Harberton Drive and walk back to King's Hall. And before you go, there's one more thing. Tell no one, not a soul. Okay?'

'Marty, you know me better than that,' he said.

'I'm sorry,' I said. 'But I'll talk to you later. Okay?'

'Okay, kid. Bye.'

Thirty minutes later I arrived at King's Hall and saw Pete standing as arranged. I saw him look at the car but he didn't recognize me. Then I gently tooted the horn and he came over, still not recognizing me. I threw open the passenger door as he walked up to the car.

'Jesus, Marty,' he said, turning pale at the sight of me back in Belfast, 'what the fuck are you doing here? Are you trying to get me stiffed or something?'

'Get in,' I said. 'It's good to see you. I'm sorry I couldn't tell you the truth on the phone but you know how it is.'

'Jesus, Marty, aren't you taking a terrible risk coming here like this?'

'Maybe, but I had no option. I've got a problem, Pete, and you might be able to help.'

'You know me, Marty. If there's anything I can do to help I will. Just say the word.'

'That's great, Pete,' I said. 'You're a real pal. We had better go somewhere else to talk. We might become a bit too conspicuous if we stay here chatting.'

And we both laughed. I put the car into gear and drove off down the Upper Lisburn Road to Derriaghy near Lisburn. We pulled into a shopping center and decided to stay in the car to talk.

'What's it all about?' he asked.

I explained to Pete how I had been visited by an SB officer in England who had told me that my abduction by the Provos had been no accident but appeared to be carefully planned by MI5.

'You're joking,' he said. 'Are you sure you're not going mental?'

'Pete, listen,' I said, 'I'm deadly serious. I promise you. I'm only speaking to you because you're the only person I can really trust. Do you understand?'

'Fuck me,' he said, 'I had better watch my arse because I'm working for the cunts.'

I explained in some detail exactly what had happened to me on the day of my kidnap, the way I had been closely watched by the SB on my way to the meeting at Connolly House; how I had walked out of the main entrance to the Sinn Fein headquarters in full view of any surveillance unit. I explained how minutes later the two IRA bastards had been able to drive away with me in the back of the car without anyone noticing; and that despite the SB and other surveillance units boasting the most sophisticated high-tech tracking equipment they had been unable to trace the car.

But I didn't tell him that MI5 had instructed the TCG to withdraw the Branch officers watching my back and leave me to my own devices.

'How can I help you?' he asked.

'I need to know anything you can tell me about any rumors or gossip concerning me and my kidnapping. Anything, anything at all.'

He burst out laughing and I looked at him wondering what the fuck was so funny.

'Jesus, Marty, you'll never know the shit you caused those two bastards who had you held in that flat. In fact I will go so far as to say that I nearly felt sorry for the two cunts.'

'Why, why, why?' I said. 'Spill the beans, for fuck sake.'

'After you escaped Chico and Jim fucked off across the border, shit scared that the RUC would get them. After the dust settled they returned to Belfast believing they would receive a heroes' welcome having kidnapped you, Marty McGartland, the traitor. In fact it was the opposite. Even now they're still getting abuse about it. For a while Chico and Jim were kicked out of the IRA because the leadership believed at first that one of them had actually helped you to escape. They couldn't believe that three men holding anyone at gunpoint in a third floor flat, whose hands and feet were bound together, could have let him escape. It sounded unbelievable. Some people were calling them 'Mr. Bean' after the TV character famous for making cock-ups.'

'Fuckin' brilliant,' I said. 'I love it.'

'And those two are still in shit,' Pete went on. 'There's stories going about how they're now involved with protecting drug dealers in return for money, saving them from getting beatings from the punishment squads. And both of them are still involved in punishment squads.'

After we had both had a good laugh at Chico Hamilton and Jim McCarthy's expense I again asked Pete whether he had heard any reliable information about my abduction.

'Listen, Marty,' he said, 'you know 'Spud' Murphy who is a commander in the IRA? Well, he told me and a few others that if he ever comes across you he will put a bullet in your head, no questions asked. Steve, who had been a good friend of yours when you were in the IRA, also told a few people that he would love to put a couple of bullets in you.'

'But, Pete,' I went on, 'did you not hear anything about my abduction?'

'People inside and outside the IRA were confused about the kidnap. They thought it odd that you were asked to go to the Sinn Fein headquarters and that Chico and Jim were sent to collect you. People in the Republican pubs and clubs were asking why Chico and Jim, two people who had nothing to do with the IRA's security team, were sent to abduct someone whom the IRA obviously knew was an informer. It's never done like that. Usually, senior members of the IRA will trick an individual, who they believe is working for the Branch, into a false sense of security, like asking them to go fishing, where they can be easily abducted. But trying to kidnap someone like you in the middle of Andersonstown where the Brits and RUC regularly patrol is suicidal. And I can tell you here and now that no one believes the IRA would invite you to go to a meeting at Connolly House and then kidnap you. They may as well have phoned the Special Branch and told them they were going to do it the following day. It just doesn't make any sense. Most people who knew you well believe there was something deeply suspicious about all the events surrounding your abduction and your escape.'

'So what's the general consensus of opinion then?', I asked.

'People just don't know what to believe,' Pete replied, 'but they know there was something really fishy about the whole affair. There had been no other kidnap like it.'

'Did you ever hear any rumors that the whole business was a set-up?' I asked.

'Most people thought there was something odd about it,' he replied.

'But did you pick up anything definite that I could use in evidence?' I asked.

'No, I'm afraid not,' he replied. 'Only the IRA leadership would know that, Marty.'

'I thought so,' I replied, somewhat disappointed. 'But thanks anyway. There's one more question you might be able to answer. Do you think the IRA have any idea where I'm living now, and if they did know, do you think they would take any action against me?'

'Funny you should say that, Marty,' he replied, 'because just before all this shit about you and your court case in England over the driving licenses I honestly couldn't believe half of the places you were meant to be living. There were rumors you were still staying in the south of Ireland and then some said you had been sighted in Scotland. Now, due to the recent press coverage, everyone knows that in reality you were living in Newcastle all the time. Jesus, Marty, those fuckin' cops over there are worse than the RUC and that's saying something. Did they go out of their way to drop you in the shit by revealing your name or was it an accident?'

'You don't know the half of it, Pete,' I told him. 'It took them almost two years to bring the case to court. The Crown Prosecution Service actually contacted several different agencies including MI5 and the RUC Special Branch, seeking advice on whether I should be taken to court. It was only after my so-called friends in MI5 or one of the other Crown agencies told the CPS to go ahead that the decision was finally taken to prosecute me. Only then was I charged. Now you see, Pete, that someone, somewhere was determined to take me to court and they knew, they must have known, that as a result of taking me to court my true identity, McGartland, as well as my new identity, Ashe, would be revealed.'

'You're kidding,' said Pete. 'That's going over the top. I didn't think the fuckers would go to those lengths to expose you, would they?'

'Don't you fucking believe it,' I replied.

'How do you know?' Pete said.

'Listen to me, Pete, listen carefully.'

'Fire away.'

'One day, months before the case came to court, another of my solicitors, Philip Hindson, held a meeting with Kingsley Hyland, a special case worker for the Crown Prosecution Service, and expressed concern that as a result of bringing this case to court the only outcome would be to reveal my true identity. My solicitor explained that was the only defense I had to offer otherwise I would have to lie in court. My solicitor also made Mr. Hyland aware that I would most certainly plead not guilty and he asked whether the CPS was aware that by taking me to court they would be putting my life at risk.

'Immediately after that meeting Philip Hindson phoned me and reported what had occurred during his meeting. He told me, 'Kingsley Hyland showed me a letter he had received from the Special Branch but I didn't catch the address at the top. The letter stated that the SB had consulted with another agency which Hyland assumed was either MI5 or MI6. As a result of those consultations and subsequent recommendations Kingsley Hyland was told there was no reason why he should not proceed with the prosecution.'

'My solicitor continued, 'I told Kingsley Hyland that you [Martin McGartland] would plead not guilty and a lot of shit would come out in court. Hyland replied that if it appeared things were getting very embarrassing for the Government he might back off. Hyland waved a letter in the air, telling me that he had been instructed to continue the prosecution with the words, 'Don't worry, just prosecute. Do him."

'My solicitor presumed that the letter must have been sent from MI5 or some other government agency because he was aware that the police are not permitted to interfere in a case once the file has been handed over to the CPS for consideration.

'What my solicitor didn't know, however, was that, as usual, I taped the conversation. Since my problems over my two identities had come to light I had taken the decision to tape each and every conversation I had about all these various matters. I would tape them not only during phone conversations but also during face-to-face meetings. As a result, I now have hundreds of hours of taped conversations with everyone involved. I have deposited these tapes in safe places.'

'Fuck,' said Pete, 'that's shit. I never thought the authorities would play that game. If they treat people who work for the Government like that, what would they do to ordinary fuckers?'

Then he changed tack, saying, 'Marty, what the fuck have you done to be treated like this? Is there something you haven't told me?'

'Hand on my heart, Pete, I've done nothing that you don't know about,' I replied. 'I thought all this aggro had occurred because I wrote a book about my experiences but now I think there's something more sinister going on, I really do.'

'Now that you've told me all this shit I agree with you,' he said. He went on, 'Marty, take some advice. You must watch your arse; you might be involved in something of real importance, something of which you are unaware, that you know nothing about.'

I replied, 'I've thought of everything, Pete, and I'm at a loss to know what the fuck I've done to deserve this treatment. What the fuck this is all about I just don't know. I'm nearly getting sick wondering why all these government agencies: the RUC, the SB, the Northumbria Police, and even the Home Secretary are getting involved in it. I don't know, I honestly don't know what hornets' nest I've disturbed.'

'We had better get out of here,' said Pete, 'we've been here too long already.'

'Before we go I must tell you two things. I know you now work for the SB but you must tell no one of this conversation. Pretend it never took place; that you haven't seen me since I moved to England in 1991. And then there's something else. You see what's happened to me; well, remember this shit could happen to anyone. Trust no one; not the RUC, not the Special Branch, no one. Nor any fucker in the IRA.'

After dropping Pete on the outskirts of Andersonstown from where he planned to take a taxi back home, I drove around Ballymurphy and Moyard, the places where I had lived. I knew it was crazy to take such a risk but I couldn't help myself. That was my home, where I had grown up, and all my memories were on view to me. Something inside made me determined to see them again and I thought: 'what the heck' and drove through the area. The traffic was quite heavy which was good for me because I had more time to take a look around. I spent much of my time looking out the car window to see if I recognized anyone, but I didn't. I wondered if my memory had gone or the people had just changed in the past six years, then I realized I was just being stupid. In the days that I had spent around West Belfast I thought I had grown to know hundreds of people but in reality, of course, it was hardly more than a handful. Despite the risk I was taking I felt a warm glow, a feeling of happiness and contentment at being back home. I realized how much I had missed everyone.

Ever since I had made the decision to return to Belfast I had tried to push to the back of my mind the possibility that here was a chance to see my boys, Martin, then seven, and Podraig, then six. I also wanted to see Angie, but I knew that was unfair even though she would always be precious to me. I had no intention of letting Martin or Podraig see me even though I wanted more than anything to grab hold of them and kiss and cuddle them and tell them that I was the Daddy they thought had been killed in a car crash. I knew I was torturing myself even trying to get a peek at them but I couldn't stop my impulses. I wondered whether one of the underlying reasons I had returned to Belfast was the fact that I had a desperate need to see them again. Everytime I was alone they would occupy my thoughts, and it pained me to realize that I had sacrificed two wonderful boys for the sake of a job with the fucking SB. I became aware everytime I thought of them how I had wasted my life. But here was a possibility, or at least a faint hope, that I could see them. I told myself that I must make no effort to talk to them or get too close because that would be grossly unfair of me. They had been told that their Daddy had died in a car accident, that I was no more, and to see them face to face would be nothing short of cruel and pernicious.

I also knew that I must make bloody sure that Angie didn't see me. Angie had been given a raw deal, not knowing whether to throw in her lot with me or stay at home near her family and bring up the kids on her own. She had also been visited by the IRA on her return from England and questioned closely about every detail she knew about me. And she had been warned that if I should ever contact her or, more importantly, visit her again in Belfast she was duty bound to tell the IRA immediately. To let Angie see me for even a split second would place her in jeopardy for if she did not tell the IRA she had seen me there was no doubt in her mind that she could face a beating. I had already been grossly unfair to Angie and I had no wish to cause her any more pain or trouble.

I knew they lived off the Springfield Road in the Falls, an area where many IRA members also lived as well. I didn't really care about myself for I had a fast car and a getaway would be quite easy. I decided to make only two runs down the road, for to continue driving up and down in a new Vauxhall would only attract attention from neighbors. I had no idea, of course, whether they were at home, staying with her parents or away with friends. There was a ten to one chance that I would see the lads in any case, maybe a fifty to one chance, but I had to try it. I assumed this was my last chance ever to see them and as I made a first attempt to drive down the road it was near deserted. I continued driving to the end and parked a mile away, waiting for five minutes in the hope that on my next run they might, just might, be out playing in the street or going off shopping somewhere with Angie. As I thought of them tears filled my eyes and I kept wiping them away. I had no control over my emotions and had never realized how powerful such affection for two little kids could be. I knew that at that moment I had the opportunity to just walk up to their house, knock on the door and see my two darling lads. But, thank God, I was able to stay in control because that one simple, selfish act could have put their future and Angie's life in danger.

I drove off again, returning down the road where they lived and saw three kids playing at the end. My heart leapt as I drove towards them, neglecting to look at the house where they lived, praying through my tears that two of the lads I might spot were Martin and Podraig. But as I grew nearer I realized they were neither of my boys and I cursed myself for letting my wishes become too unrealistic. I drove by and looked at them, wondering what I would have felt if either of had been my sons. And I knew I could have done absolutely nothing. I drove on, forcing myself away from the scene, telling myself over and over that even if I had been able to see them I could have done absolutely nothing. And in my heart I felt like shit.

But I wasn't finished yet. The emotions that had torn me apart that morning were still surging through my mind and body and I decided to go and see my Ma. It had been more than six years since we had met and I felt an urge to see her once more. Though our relationship had always been distant I felt a strong respect for her. I knew she was a good woman and always had been. We had never been terribly close or affectionate with each other, but I had always tried to take care of her even though I knew she often thought of me as a mad young tearaway who had been too difficult to calm or control.

I drove to Moyard Parade at a normal speed, determined not to draw attention to myself and parked immediately outside her garden gate, just twelve feet from her front door. I left the engine running and the driver's door open in case we should be interrupted by some unwelcome bastard who happened to be nearby. I ran to the front door and banged the letter-box. I looked through the window in the front door and saw my Ma walking towards the door. She saw me and stopped dead in her tracks. I could see her face go pale before me. For three or four seconds she paused, not knowing what she should do, and then briskly walked to the door and flung it open.

'Martin,' she shouted, before I had a chance to say a word, 'what the fuck are you doing here? Are you fucking mad or what? Now get the hell out of here at once.'

I was just about to tell her that all I wanted to do was to see her and chat for a few minutes when her lifelong friend Alfie came into the hall still dressed in his boxer shorts. 'Martin, you stupid cunt, what the fuck are you doing here? Do you want to get us stiffed or something? Just fuck off, will you, and don't come back.'

I stood and roared with laughter at their response to my appearance at their front door. Within a split second all the emotion that had built up in my heart that morning had disappeared like dust in a wind but as Alfie was saying his piece I looked at my mother and, though her words had been violent and unrelenting, her eyes had betrayed real fear. 'I'll call you sometime,' I shouted as I ran to the car, jumped inside and drove away. I realized we hadn't even touched.

But those few seconds of harsh reality with my Ma had brought me to my senses. I was once again my old, confident self, not worrying about anything in particular and ready to enjoy life. And for some unknown reason in that moment I didn't care a damn about the IRA, MI5, the RUC or the Special Branch. At the top of Moyard Parade, the street where I had played as a youngster, I stopped the car to take in the view of my old hunting grounds. For a few minutes I was mesmerized, knowing that this was the place where I really belonged and where people I could trust still lived. Of course I knew this didn't apply to everyone, yet in some ways I felt a lot safer here than at the mercy of government agencies that had tried to kill me and were now hounding me at every turn.

As I looked down the hill and across the estate, my attention was drawn to a young woman in her twenties as she passed by my car. I realized that I had known her quite well some years ago. Almost involuntarily, I wound down the window and called out to her. 'Arlene,' I shouted and she turned and looked at the car.

'Jesus, I know you; you're Marty McGartland,' she said. 'What are you doing here?'

'Just visiting,' I replied.

'So you're not stopping?'

'No, only a few hours, then I'm off,' I replied. 'Are you still going out with Bob?' I knew Arlene had been going with him and they had had a baby together.

'Ah, Marty, that was finished years ago; you're well out of touch.'

'Have you got a new boyfriend?' I asked.

'I have that, yes,' she replied. 'And what about you? I hear you and Angie are finished.'

'You know me, Arlene, I still keep myself to myself; there's no woman who will take me after Angie. She was a diamond.'

'Well, Marty, it's been nice speaking to you; take care of yourself now.' And she walked off down the road.

It was only after she had gone that I recalled that the person whom she had named as her new boyfriend was a staunch Republican who had close connections with senior members of the IRA. 'Fuck,' I thought to myself, 'I can't hang around here for long. I've only been here minutes and already my past has caught up with me.'

I slammed the car into first gear and began to drive off down the street when I saw a really familiar face, a young man named Sean who used to work with me in the scrap metal business, one of my covers when working for the Branch. Sean was always a cheerful lad, a few years younger than me, who seemed to have a permanent smile on his face. I liked him. I slowed down and shouted, 'Sean, Sean,' and he looked round and recognized me instantly.

'Fuck, Marty, are you back here again?' he asked.

'I'm not staying,' I replied.

'Jesus, that's a nice car, Marty. Is that yours?'

'No,' I replied, 'I stole it.' And he burst out laughing.

I wanted to stop and chat to Sean because we had always been friends but I also worried that Arlene may have already told people about the latest gossip; that she had just seen Marty McGartland at the top of Moyard Parade, though she would not have meant me any harm. I guessed my arrival back on the scene might have caused some tongues to wag. And if any Provo heard I was back they would be out looking for me within minutes. In that instant I realized I was putting my mission in jeopardy by indulging my emotions and driving around Ballymurphy and I cursed myself for not acting in a more professional way. I knew I had to get out of the area, and quick.

'Where are you going?' I asked Sean.

'Top of the Rock,' he replied, meaning the Whiterock shops near the Springfield Road.

'Jump in,' I said. 'I'll give you a lift.'

I dropped Sean near the traffic lights at the junction of Whiterock and Springfield roads and waved him goodbye. 'Goodbye and good luck,' he said.

'Same to you, too,' I shouted after him as he slammed the car door and walked off to the shops with a wave.

Seconds later, Sean was walking past a group of young jobless lads who were standing around chatting together when one asked him, 'Who owns that smart car you just got out of?'

'It's Marty's,' he replied, without thinking.

'Marty who?' another asked.

'Marty McGartland of course, who else?' he replied.

'Marty McGartland?' someone shouted and the call was taken up. The dozen or so lads hanging around all gathered together and began earnestly discussing the dramatic news as Sean walked off.

I would hear what happened after I returned to the safety of Newcastle and it made me realize, if I needed any further proof, that for my own safety I should never return to Belfast again. More importantly I also heard what happened to Sean and what upset me was that it had been my fault for taking such risks. Later that day as he was walking back home two IRA members, whom he recognized, came up to him. He sensed he was facing trouble, if not danger, from the way they came and stood looking at him, menacing him.

'We want you to come with us,' one said.

'Where to?' Sean asked.

'Mind your own fucking business and come with us,' the leader said.

'What do you want me for?' Sean asked.

'Did you see Marty McGartland today?' asked the other.

'Aye,' he replied.

'We want to talk to you, so shut the fuck up and come with us.'

He knew there was no way out and reluctantly turned and walked off with one man at either side of him. They took him to a house not far distant and he feared he was facing a beating. They asked how he had met me. Where was I going? Where was I living? Who else was with me? Was I asking any questions? Did I visit anyone in the area?

These barrage of questions were fired at poor Sean as he stood trembling, trying to answer them all quickly enough before more were fired at him. He was shaking with fright because he believed that if he did not give the answers the IRA members wanted they would try the rough treatment and he could be severely injured. He had seen how others had been given severe beatings before and it wasn't a pretty sight. But he had one asset. He knew nothing about me or my whereabouts. All he could tell them were details of the car I was driving with no idea of the registration number.

One important question that worried him was when they asked, 'Was Marty carrying a gun?'

Sean, of course, had no idea and he told them so, but that didn't mean they believed him. 'Listen,' Sean told them time and again, 'I was only in the car a few seconds, as long as it takes to drive the few hundred yards. He told me nothing, nothing.'

Finally, he convinced the IRA men that he knew nothing but before he was allowed to walk free he was given a warning. 'If you see Marty again don't talk to him and don't get into his car. You come and find us straight-away and tell us. Do you understand?'

'Aye,' he replied.

'Now fuck off,' one said.

I decided to get the hell out of Ballymurphy and West Belfast because it was obvious that I had already chanced my arm too often that day and to take further risks would be unprofessional, if not crazy. I hadn't returned to Northern Ireland to indulge my personal emotions but to try and determine the facts around my kidnap. I had permitted my personal life to interfere with the job in hand. I drove away determined to focus on my mission and fuck my emotions.

CHAPTER TEN

I drove back to Peggy's place very, very relieved to be away from West Belfast but knowing that my mission was only half - completed. As I approached her farm I realized that I needed to spend time alone, to sort out my mind and decide how I should tackle the final hurdle. I turned off the A6 towards Magherafelt and found the road all but deserted. I parked the car and decided to take a walk to collect my thoughts and check what I was about to do, making sure that I would take no further crazy chances, putting my balls on the line.

I now knew that my abduction and escape from the IRA had caused loads of trouble inside the Republican movement, making this so-called professional army look like a bunch of amateurs, unable to hold an unarmed man in a block of flats where the goalers were holding the guns. I was really pleased that Chico and Jim had been given such a hard time, having the piss taken out of them by their IRA mates. It was obvious that there was no love lost between other IRA members and the two men and, to my mind, they deserved all the shit they received. But they could be of no further use to me.

I realized that Chico and Jim had only been obeying orders and that it was their incompetence that had let them down. Indeed, when in 1994 I saw that Gerry Adams, President of Sinn Fein, had appointed them as his personal bodyguards, I was somewhat taken aback because I believed he would have wanted more professional men around him than those tough-talking tin-pots. I also knew that any would-be assassin would find it very easy to take out Gerry Adams with those two guarding him. But that was Gerry Adams' concern.

I wasn't sure how to tackle the SB. I knew that if I phoned my former handlers they would be bound to find some way to trace me, pick me up and put me on the next flight back to the mainland. I had to assume that I wasn't welcome in Northern Ireland, poking about, causing strife, trying to find out what really happened to me and what part the authorities had played in my kidnap. And in my heart I wasn't certain that the SB or the RUC hadn't been involved. It seemed extraordinary that MI5 would have planned my kidnap on their own without informing someone what was at hand. I believed it unlikely that my handlers knew of the plot because of the close relationship they had built with me during the four years we had been working together.

In his book, however, Ian Phoenix had pointed the finger of suspicion at the TCG (Tasking Coordination Group composed of MI5, Special Branch, SAS and military intelligence officers) suggesting that they had been involved, but to what degree I had no idea. After all, I told myself, no one, no official and no organization had to take any positive action against me on that fateful day. All that had been necessary was negative inaction, for all someone had to do was withdraw the surveillance unit watching me and leave the dirty work to the Provos' hitmen. It had been a neat plan, so neat in fact that it was difficult putting my finger on one single person who would have the vital piece of information necessary for me to challenge and nail whatever agency had been responsible for trying to get me killed.

I realized that, in all probability, there were two sets of people who had taken an active part in the plot—the planners and the operatives. I could easily imagine those high-minded snobs in MI5 planning my abduction from the safety of their offices behind the protection of well-guarded headquarters but I also recognized that they wouldn't have been directly involved in undertaking any of the dirty work, not when there were so many security agencies on hand in Belfast. I suspected that senior RUC officers might well have been kept informed of what was happening so that no one further down would have ensured my appropriate protection when I went to the meeting at Sinn Fein headquarters.

I recalled in as much detail as I could what I had seen and what I had not seen that morning. I had expected the SB to ensure that either some plainclothes SB officers were brought in to watch Connolly House or at least members of E4A, the surveillance department of the RUC Special Branch, who were experts at keeping people under close observation. But I couldn't recall seeing anyone around that morning and even at the time that had worried me. As I walked down the narrow country lane, with the hedges protecting me from the wind that was squalling quite hard, I recalled some of the extraordinary episodes when E4A had carried out long and difficult surveillance operations. One involved a stake-out over several days and nights in January, 1990 when a team from E4A had watched a house in West Belfast where they believed the IRA were holding Alexander 'Sandy' Lynch, an RUC informant. When the RUC finally raided the house and rescued Sandy they discovered the Sinn Fein publicity director, Danny Morrison, whose nickname was 'Lord Chief Executioner', in attendance along with eight other IRA men, all of whom were arrested and charged. Lynch had taken a terrible beating and he recounted later how he feared he would never leave that house alive. The RUC believed that Sandy was on the point of being murdered. The RUC also found a film of Lynch's wedding day which the IRA security team had shown him, telling him that if he did not confess to working for the Special Branch he would never see his wife again. That had been a highly professional surveillance task and yet, seemingly, it had been impossible to track me once I had left Connolly House even though I had walked out of the front door with two well-known IRA thugs!

Whenever I thought of that time I would get mad as hell, for the more I concentrated on what happened the more I realized I had been hung out to dry, deliberately. But now I had to nail the bastards once and for all.

Ideally, I knew that I needed to find someone who was aware of the details surrounding my abduction, someone involved with the Tasking Coordination Group, which included senior officers from the SAS, MI5, Special Branch and military intelligence. I needed to talk to just one person who worked with the TCG and whom I could trust from any of these agencies. I knew there must be some honorable people in TCG, as there were in the Special Branch, who would happily tell me what really happened that day. But how to find them and how to get to them? If I took too many risks as I had done earlier that day I could even find myself taken out, for I figured that if they were capable of arranging my funeral in August, 1991 when I was a well-known informant it would be a fucking sight easier for them to get rid of me now when I was meant to be living in England. All these thoughts weighed heavily on my mind as I considered how to proceed.

I decided to sleep on it and drove back to my secret hide-out at Peggy's place. As I walked through her open front door which was only held by a latch it seemed I had entered a different world. All seemed so peaceful and relaxed as my new-found little furry friend came up to me, pressing herself against my legs until I bent down and stroked her for a few seconds. 'It's only me,' I called, not wishing to frighten Peggy who I knew would be sitting on her bed resting her legs. It seemed extraordinary that life out here could be so calm and peaceful when, in reality, just a car ride away, devilish machinations occurred day and night, where even trusted friends were killed without a moment's thought.

I decided to phone Mike, my SB pal, and ask to meet him. I knew I would be giving him the shock of his life, visiting Northern Ireland with no protection while conducting my own one-man-band detective agency, but I believed he would be strong enough to understand and take the possible risk. I recognized that Mike had already broken RUC rules by informing me that a secret plot had been organized to have me killed. I went for a stroll and a mile or so from the cottage dialed the number he had given me on my mobile, which I had brought from England for just such an eventuality. I knew that there would be no hope of anyone tracing such a call if I made it from a mobile some distance away from where I was staying. I knew the SB and the other security agencies possessed the most sophisticated bugging and tracking devices but I had been led to understand that no one was yet capable of tracing a mobile phone call with any accuracy, especially if the call was made in the middle of the country.

I dialed and waited. A minute or so later the phone was answered. It was a woman who, I presumed, was his wife. I knew it would be crazy to ask for Mike's number so I left a message saying that his friend from Birmingham had called and would try back later that evening. I knew I was taking something of a risk but believed that Mike would understand that I was only phoning him because I needed his help. He had told me to phone him if ever I needed him. That time had now arrived and I only hoped he had meant what he said.

I cooked Peggy a light meal, scrambled eggs on toast, and at 9 p.m. went out for another stroll. I called Mike's number again and, as I expected, he answered the phone.

'Hi, Mike,' I said, 'it's your little friend calling. I hope you don't mind but you told me it was okay for me to contact you if I needed your help.'

'Yes, that's fine,' he replied. 'How can I help you?'

'I need to see you,' I said. 'It's urgent.'

'I know,' he replied. 'I was expecting a call from you. You've come across for a visit.'

'How the fuck did you know that?' I said, somewhat taken aback that news of my arrival in Belfast had reached the Special Branch.

'Marty, you should know it's our business to know everything that's going on in Belfast,' he said laughing.

'Do you know my whereabouts?' I asked, checking what he really knew of my movements.

'I know you've been back to your old territory, West Belfast,' he said, chuckling. 'Anything else you want to know?'

'Fuck off,' I said, 'you know nothing; you're just guessing. But can I see you tomorrow?' I asked.

'Aye, mucker,' he replied.

'On your own.'

'You cheeky cunt,' he said, 'do you think I would want anyone to see me talking to you? I'd be for the fucking high jump if anyone saw us together.'

'When do you want to meet?' I asked.

'Sometime early in the morning,' he said. 'There's a job I have to do at ten in the morning. Can you make it for eight-thirty?'

'Aye,' I replied. 'Where?'

'I'll see you at Victoria Park,' he said.

'Victoria Park?' I said with some surprise, for I had heard of it but had no idea exactly where it was.

'Oh, fuck me, Marty,' he said, 'you must remember Victoria Park; you know, off the Sydenham Bypass.'

'Ah, up there near Belfast City airport?' I said.

'That's it,' he said. 'I'll see you there.' And the phone went dead.

I was up bright and early and driving towards Sydenham shortly after six the next day, giving myself plenty of time to check out the area, making sure that Mike and I would be on our own. Now I was treating the whole mission with more determination and professionalism. I slowly toured the perimeter of the park. I assumed that Mike would arrive at Victoria Park station searching for me so, as eight-thirty approached, I drove round the area by the station.

We met as arranged. I saw him driving past the station and he saw me. I turned and followed him and he drove a few hundred yards away until he found a convenient place to stop in a road overlooking the playing fields. He got out of his car and walked over to me saying nothing until he got into the passenger seat. 'How are you doing, mucker?' he asked, shaking my hand.

'I can't answer that until we've had a talk,' I said with a laugh.

'What can I do for you?' he asked, sounding skeptical. 'To start with, what the fuck are you risking your neck coming over here for?'

'You know,' I said, 'it's what we talked about in Birmingham.'

'Oh that,' he said. 'I thought you would have forgotten all about that.'

'How could I?' I said, raising my voice. 'All that came as a real shock to me, you know, Mike. I couldn't sleep for days after that.'

'If I thought my news would have had that effect I would never have told you,' he said.

'If you knew the shit I've been put through since we last met, you would understand why I'm so concerned. Have you no idea what those bastards have put me through in England?'

'What are you talking about?' Mike asked.

'Did you not read in the newspapers about my trial in Newcastle?'

'Aye, of course I did,' he said. 'You were a smart-ass, Marty.'

'Balls,' I replied. 'Mike, you've no idea how those bastards hounded me, stopping me every fucking day, asking stupid questions like my identity. On one occasion I was driving a brand new car with the latest plates on it and the traffic cops stopped me demanding to see my MOT, demanding I get out while they examined the tires, the exhaust and all that shit. Mike, the car was brand fucking new.'

'Fuck,' he said, sounding concerned. 'Why were they playing that game with you?'

'Let me go on, Mike. When I asked why they had stopped me that day they had the fucking gall to tell me that it was just a routine check. After a while that treatment gets on your nerves. I knew they were just winding me up and I tried to stay calm but after weeks and months of that treatment you just lose your rag.'

'I understand,' he said.

'No, Mike, you couldn't understand because it's never happened to you. These bastards would stop me week in, week out asking for my ID, checking my driving license and insurance and sometimes arresting me just to confirm my identity. And yet they knew full well my identity because they had so frequently arrested me in the past. I thought they would stop that game after a while but they didn't. In a four-year period I must have been stopped more than fifty times and that's no exaggeration, I promise you. What concerned me, Mike, was why – why were they picking on me? I thought you might be able to help.'

'Shit, I didn't know that,' he said.

'It got so bad immediately after my trial that Northumbria Police officers, not just traffic cops, began arresting me, handcuffing me and taking me down to the station, leaving me in a room for hours on end and then letting me go with no charge. It was all a set-up, a game to get me to lose my rag so they could arrest me for a public order offense.'

'We heard nothing about this over here, nothing at all,' he said.

'Listen to what happened,' I continued. 'After my trial I couldn't go back home because my real name and my new ID had been read out in court along with my home address. For six years I had kept mum, no one knew that Martin Ashe and Martin McGartland were one and the same person. Now the world knew. As a result, I left home and spent weeks driving around northern England, living rough in my car. So when the traffic cops stopped me and asked for my address I would tell them, 'No fixed abode'. One day the Northumbria Police stopped me, asked to see my license and when they checked it with the police computer they found I was down as living at my Blyth address. But they refused to believe I was no longer living at Blyth. They knew who I was; they knew I had just been in court; they knew I had made the police look stupid by winning that case so, in retaliation, they would arrest me and keep me at the police station for a couple of hours while they allegedly checked me out. Every time, however, they would insist on arresting me at the roadside, handcuffing me and taking me away in their police car.

'That's tough,' he said, 'but how can I help?'

I sensed that I had been going on a little too long about my problems back in England.

'I wondered if the treatment I was receiving in Newcastle was linked to what you told me happened the day I was supposedly kidnapped?'

He thought for a while and I kept quiet, giving him time to turn things over in his mind. After a couple of minutes he said, 'I don't know, mucker, but I doubt it, I really do.'

'So why do you think they would pick on me for so long as though they were carrying out a vendetta against me?'

'I can't answer that,' he replied. 'You're asking me questions which I find impossible to answer.'

I thought it was time to stop that line of approach for it was obvious that Mike wanted no part of it. 'Can you help me with the abduction?' I asked, treading carefully.

'It depends on what you want to know,' he replied.

'Everything,' I replied. 'I need to know if there was anything that you forgot to tell me during our meeting in Birmingham. Have you heard anything more because, Mike, I'm desperate to know what really happened that day. It's been driving me crazy trying to understand why MI5 should attempt to have me killed.'

'I told you everything I know in Birmingham,' he said. 'There's nothing more I know; there's nothing more I can tell you.'

He must have seen the look of dejection on my face as I struggled to find the right question to ask him which would cause him to talk openly about my kidnapping. Now, it seemed to me, he wanted to walk away from the question as though I was embarrassing him.

'Answer me this, can you?' I said. 'Have you any further idea of the identity of the man MI5 were supposed to be protecting?'

'I've thought about that too, Marty,' he went on, 'and I just don't know, not for certain. All I know is that he was a very senior man doing the same job you were doing, but he was in deeper.'

'But why didn't they just ship me out, relocate me and let me be?' I almost pleaded.

'Sometimes, Marty, but only sometimes, the men who run these agencies believe that the only solution to such a problem is to remove the offending informant from the scene completely so that he can never cause an embarrassment or, as in your case, accidentally reveal a source's identity. But, Marty, don't ask me why because

I just don't know.'

'But have you no idea?' I asked again.

'First, Marty, you must accept what I know; that I promise you that I don't know the reasons behind their decision to get you picked up. But there is one question you must ask yourself. Was there anything you did in the four years with the Branch that made Box [the name RUC and SB officers gave MI5 officers working in Northern Ireland] act in the way they did? It may be that the only person who can answer that question is yourself. You must examine your mind to see if there was something that you were involved in which, at the time, you didn't realize was highly sensitive but which in fact may have been of tremendous importance. Maybe, just maybe, there was something you became involved in that they feared you might one day reveal. And that revelation could have caused the most terrible consequences for a number of other sources.'

His reply puzzled me and I wondered what Mike was driving at because I knew of nothing that I had done during my years with the Branch that could be of such extraordinary significance in intelligence terms.

'Mike, I think that's shit,' I said. 'But nothing has changed from what you told me in Birmingham?' I went on, wanting to get to the core of my investigation.

'Nothing,' he said. 'I told you everything when we had that chat, everything I knew.'

'Do you think they're still after me?' I asked.

'No,' he said, 'I really don't think so; in fact I'm sure they're not after you.'

'How can you be so sure then?' I asked.

'Because that's life in our business, Marty,' he said. 'They would only have another go if there was something of real importance. But you've been away from it all for six years now. I don't think they would touch you, honestly.'

It was good to hear such assurances but it didn't really help me. 'So there's nothing more you can tell me?' I said with some belligerence in my voice.

'You're right, mucker,' he said, 'I can't help you any further. You must understand that fucking coming over here is like putting your balls on the line. I came to see you because I thought you had been treated disgracefully but if you're starting to come over here, asking questions and walking around West Belfast you're simply asking for fucking trouble. You have to walk away from this, Marty, and forget it.'

'But why should I stop it? It was my fucking life they nearly took, Mike. Can't you understand that?'

'Of course I do and I admire you for having the balls to follow through, but you must understand, in our business, bygones are bygones. You can't keep looking back on what happened; you must only look forward. You survived and that's it, forget it, walk away and continue with your life.'

'Let me change the subject, let me ask you to answer some questions of a different nature,' I said.

'Fire away,' said Mike, 'if I can help, I will.'

'It's about Chico Hamilton and Jim McCarthy, the two IRA men who kidnapped and held me at gun-point for seven hours.'

'Go on,' he urged.

'I cannot understand why these two men were never questioned, never arrested or never charged over my kidnap. I was alive; I could have given evidence in a court case. From what the RUC and the Special Branch have said these two men were seen going into Connolly House and leaving with me. Then, mysteriously, I disappeared, but because I survived the ordeal I could have given evidence in court which would have led to their conviction. Why was no action taken against them?'

For a minute Mike looked down, obviously deep in thought, and he shifted his body nervously. 'Your guess is as good as mine, Marty, I just don't know.'

'But isn't that suspicious?' I asked.

'I agree. I agree absolutely,' said Mike. 'There was no reason at all why those two men should not have been questioned at the very least. And from what we know happened they should have been charged and probably convicted.'

'Doesn't that scream to you that my abduction was not simply an IRA attempt to see whether I was guilty of betraying the cause but some sort of inexplicable, devious plot?' I went on, now more determined than ever to drive home my point in an effort to persuade Mike to open up. 'From what I know, Mike, whenever the IRA wanted to interrogate one of their own members they would tell them to attend a meeting at someone's house. They were then grabbed, interrogated and usually tortured. But I was asked to see the head of the IRA discipline at the Sinn Fein headquarters which was always kept under surveillance by one or other of the security agencies. Don't you agree that that in itself seems an extraordinary place to kidnap someone?'

'Aye,' Mike replied. 'I agree.'

'And you may not know, Mike, but when I was interviewed by the RUC detectives following my plunge from the flat a Special Branch Superintendent told me that under no circumstances must I tell the investigating officers that Chico Hamilton and Jim McCarthy were the two men who had abducted me. At the time I thought I was given that order to protect myself. Now I can see that in fact they were protecting Chico and Jim and who knows who else. But why would the Special Branch want to protect two well-known IRA thugs who had kidnapped one of the Branch's loyal informants? It just doesn't make sense unless I was just some tiny cog in a much bigger MI5 plan of action of which I am still totally unaware.'

'The more we examine what occurred that day, Marty, the more complicated and impossible it is to unravel the reasons behind your kidnap,' said Mike.

'Tell me,' I asked, 'do you think I would have been killed if I hadn't jumped?'

'Aye,' he replied, 'there's no doubt about it.'

'Now you know why I can't let this pass. Now you know why I'm risking my neck once more coming over here to try and find out what the fuck really went on.'

'I understand, Marty, but you must look to the future. Right now there's a cease-fire in operation. Who knows whether it will last? That's what we're doing now, trying to keep the peace. We're working harder than ever, putting in more hours than at the height of the Troubles.'

'Bullocks,' I said. 'Don't give me that. Pull the other one, Mike.'

'I'm serious, Marty,' he said. 'After this chat I have a meeting on the other side of Belfast with someone who is now doing the job you did. The IRA is in fact up to more shit now than they've ever been but it's behind the scenes. The bombings and the shootings may have stopped but the IRA are working flat out, gathering intelligence, working the protection rackets, taking money from the drug dealers, making sure the money is coming in like never before. They believe they may only have a few more years of creaming in the money before the taps are turned off. They might even have to become respectable, but now, right now, they are controlling West Belfast with an iron fist, using every means available to them to keep control and bring in the money. That's why there are so many punishment beatings going on. Most of it is all about money. That's why we're working so hard. Just because there are no bombs the politicians in Westminster think everything is fine, but let me tell you it fucking isn't.'

'I understand,' I said. 'You'd better be on your way then.'

'Marty, I'm sorry I couldn't be of any more help to you but truly I don't know any more.'

'I understand,' I told him. 'If I do find out anything else can I phone you?'

'Yes, you can,' he said, 'but only if it's really essential. Is that a deal?'

'That's a deal, okay.' And we shook hands.

He opened the car door. 'I'll be seeing you then, mucker. Be good and keep your head down.'

'You told me there's no need now,' I replied.

'Don't you believe it,' he said. 'If the IRA got half a chance they would have your guts for garters tomorrow. And despite what I've told you today, trust no fucker.'

'I never do,' I replied, and he was gone.

As I drove away I wondered why Mike had been so reluctant to talk about the affair this time, having taken the trouble to come to England and relate in great detail what had happened. I wondered if there was a hidden agenda in his visit to Birmingham, something that I didn't fully understand. Then I thought that maybe his reluctance this time was his fear that I might have been taping our conversation. That would have made sense. Little did he know that in fact I had taped our first conversation when he had revealed everything quite happily. Now there was only one more person for me to press for information, someone very close to the IRA leadership in Belfast.

CHAPTER ELEVEN

I felt I had known Mary K... most of my life. I suppose we first met on the streets of West Belfast during a night of rioting when we were both teenagers. We often talked about those times, when we, along with scores of other young kids, felt we were taking on the might of the British Army and the batons of the RUC, who all seemed to take a delight in knocking the shit out of us. At that time we felt the nightly street battles were more like rough and ready games rather than a serious escalation of sectarian violence. In the heady atmosphere of teenage enthusiasm we didn't realize that on most nights we had been egged on by the men who stood some way behind the barricades cheering our efforts; those faceless IRA leaders who wanted us kids to cause as much mayhem as possible to the forces of law and order, though they took no part themselves in the street rioting.

I remember on one occasion all of us being given bricks and stones with which to pelt the British troops on the other side of the burning barricade we had built across the Springfield Road. This happened hundreds of times. We would be handed the stones by the older, more experienced IRA men who intentionally kept out of firing range while we youngsters kept up a barrage of stones in a deliberate effort to entice the soldiers to charge the barricades. Only then would the older men, who were in fact only in their twenties and early thirties, come from behind walls and cars and wait for the troops or the RUC to charge, scattering us as they ran through the burning barricades. Then those lying in wait would let fly, not with stones, but with petrol bombs and empty milk bottles which the troops hated, for they landed on their heads and in their faces, splintering into a thousand shards. As the rioting became more intense some IRA men would take up positions with rifles and hand-guns, firing off a dozen or more rounds before turning and running as the army and RUC tried to ascertain who had been responsible and give chase. I can hardly ever remember a single IRA gunman being captured in those circumstances.

Mary grew up faster than I did and for awhile we hardly ever saw each other, but I always enjoyed chatting with her even though I felt she was more sophisticated than me. I thought she didn't fully approve of my wild life, rioting at every possible opportunity and provoking the RUC into retaliation. Mary had told me that after a few months of almost nightly rioting she had grown tired of the constant action, fearful that by her behavior she was bringing problems to her family, friends and her neighbors. Of course I disagreed because I enjoyed the thrill and the action of taking on the might of the British Army and the hated RUC in a bid to help the downtrodden Catholic minority who had been given such a rough deal by the Protestant majority.

Whenever I did see Mary the talk would inevitably turn towards the Troubles and the problems caused all by the more drastic actions to which the IRA were resorting, such as indiscriminate bombings and shootings. Mary and many other Catholics didn't approve of such a policy. Slowly, I began to share that view and when the IRA punishment squads began their evil work I found myself in open conflict with such cruel treatment.

For a while I lost contact with Mary. When we met a couple of years later she told me that she had fallen in love and was living with a man whom she had later discovered was a fully fledged member of the IRA.

'When I discovered he was a member of the IRA I didn't know what to do,' she told me. 'For weeks and months the realization worried me that I was in love with someone capable of planting bombs and killing people and I didn't approve of that. I had a real problem coming to terms with that, Marty. I would go to bed at night and fear making love to him because everything that I had seen and heard about Ireland on the news would come rushing back to my mind. I realized I was making love to a man capable of killing people, all for politics.'

'Why didn't you leave him?' I asked her.

'Because I couldn't. Part of me loved him and I couldn't alter that. But I would have to push the other thoughts to the back of my mind and try to forget what he and his IRA mates were doing day in, day out; organizing bombings.'

'But you used to be so anti-IRA, Mary,' I went on. 'You would be really angry and upset whenever you heard young kids were being given terrible punishment beatings by the IRA for trivial matters.'

'I know, I know, I know,' Mary said in an agitated manner, putting her hands over her ears as if trying to block out what I was saying. 'Marty, you don't realize what this has done to me. I feel ashamed for living with such a man but part of me still loves him. I try to block out what he does because I never know any of the details. I never ask and he never speaks about it. But I know in my heart what's going on and I don't like it and I certainly don't condone it.'

As she recounted all this Mary looked at me quizzically, wondering how I would take the fact that she had turned her back on her anti-IRA views and had even thrown in her lot with the hardline Republicans to the degree that she was happily living with one. She knew from my questions and the disappointment in my voice that I didn't approve. And I could tell she was full of guilt, living with a man whose political activities she loathed but whom she found impossible to leave.

Mary had moved back into West Belfast and, despite our disagreement over her relationship, we began to see each other from time to time. I sensed that she needed to confide in me, to rationalize the life she was now leading and, as a result, our friendship became even closer. Mary would want to talk to me about every facet of the IRA's campaign of terror and violence saying, 'Marty, you're the only person I can confide in because all the other people I meet and mix with nowadays are committed Republicans who believe everything that they are doing is right, even when it involves the killing of innocent people.'

On one occasion in 1989 I had bumped into Mary in Castle

Street, Belfast, while she was out shopping. She seemed to lack her usual chirpy, happy personality and I sensed something was deeply wrong so I invited her for a bite to eat.

'What's the matter? I asked, coming straight to the point after we sat down.

'I'm worried, Marty,' she said. 'I'm scared out of my wits. I've recently moved out of the flat I've been sharing with Tom and I'm living with my Dad.'

'Did you have a row or something?' I asked, hoping to find the reason for her black mood.

'Not really,' she explained. 'What I'm going to tell you now I don't want you to repeat to anyone. Tom's been hiding arms and Semtex in our home and he now spends hardly any time in there. I'm left on my own most of the time and if the RUC were to ever raid the place I'd be in deep trouble. I'm worrying myself sick. I can't eat and I can't sleep at night but I know if I say anything he'll fly into a temper. I don't think I can last out much longer, Marty, but I don't know what to do.'

'Have you spoken to anyone else about this?' I asked.

'No, no one at all,' she said. 'Most of my old friends disapprove of me living with him and I can't talk to them; they wouldn't understand.'

'Is that it?' I asked.

'No,' she answered, looking more nervous and apprehensive, as though on the verge of tears. 'One or two of my girlfriends have told me that they've seen Tom at a number of clubs and local pubs drinking with his mates and flirting with some of the local girls. I'm sure he's seeing someone else.'

'What the fuck are you thinking about, Mary?' I told her. 'Just get rid of him. If you go on like this with him being an IRA member, the odds are that he will end up in jail and so might you.'

I advised Mary to stay out of the flat, at least until all the arms and Semtex had been removed. She said she would think about it but as I looked into her eyes it seemed to me that she had no intention of taking my advice. After I left her that day I realized that I had been put in a very difficult situation. I was working for the

Special Branch who spent most of their time searching for IRA arms and explosives and now here was Mary telling me she had arms and Semtex hidden in her flat. I knew that I could not and would not tell my handlers what I had just learned but I decided to keep in contact with Mary and try to persuade her to move out or, better still, to persuade her IRA man to move the arms cache out of their home.

Mary told me later that she had moved out of her flat for a few weeks but had then moved back again. She also told me that Tom was still a very active member of the IRA.

After I left Northern Ireland and Angie had decided to return to Belfast with the boys, I would occasionally phone Mary simply for a chat. There had never been any suggestion that the two of us were romantically involved but, nonetheless, there was a strong mutual relationship between us which had lasted for more than ten years. Whenever we had bumped into each other in the village that was Belfast we would always chat and exchange gossip and we both knew that we could turn to each other in times of trouble. I had enjoyed phoning Mary from my new home in England, asking her for all the latest gossip, and finding out what was happening back in West Belfast. I felt a need to keep in touch, my way of wanting to feel I was still a part of the community where I grew up. She understood that and was happy to talk despite the fact that her live-in lover Tom was still in the IRA. But we never discussed my role as a Special Branch source, nor the fact that I had infiltrated the IRA and fed information to the authorities.

Before returning from my flying visit to Belfast I had thought long and hard about calling Mary. But I needed to talk to her and hoped that it would be possible to find a way of meeting her without Tom finding out. I felt that the combination of our long friendship and my discretion about the arms that her lover had stored might elicit some information from Mary about my abduction. I just knew that if ever my name came up in conversation Mary would automatically have taken a mental note simply because of the friendship we had shared over so many years. I felt she could have been, in fact had been, my eyes and ears over the time I had been away and would know more than most of the tittle-tattle that members of the IRA spoke about me and my time with the Branch.

I decided not to phone her home but call her at work, something I had never done before. This time, however, contacting her created a far greater risk than ever before. I looked up the number of the shop where she worked as a sales assistant in Belfast city center and called her on my mobile. Eventually she came to the phone.

'Mary,' I asked tentatively, 'can you talk?'

'Who's that?' she asked, obviously not recognizing my voice.

'It's Marty, your old friend,' I said.

'Oh Marty,' she said, somewhat relieved. 'What are you doing phoning me here at work?'

'I need to talk to you,' I said.

'What about?' she asked.

'I can't tell you over the phone. I just need some advice.'

'When are you coming over?' she asked.

'I'm here now,' I replied.

'Jesus Christ, Marty, are you fucking mad?' she said.

'No, I'm not. Are you still living with Tom?'

'Aye, of course; what makes you ask?' she said.

'I'll tell you everything when I see you,' I replied. Can you get away from work a little early?'

'Aye, I think I could,' she said. 'Why can't you meet me on my lunch break?'

'Mary, are you crazy?' I said. 'I can't just walk around that area. Could you come to Belfast Central Station and meet me there? It's not so open. How about 4:30 at the entrance, is that okay?'

'That's fine,' she said.

'Mary, not a word to a soul.'

'Don't be daft,' she said. 'See you later.'

I drove into Belfast, my heart in my mouth, hoping that Mary was still the same trustworthy girl I had known all my life. I was glad I was driving a reliable and quite fast car, just in case I needed to make a quick getaway. I drove around the area for ten minutes checking if I could see any suspicious characters hanging around. I saw nothing to arouse my fears. Mary was standing just inside the entrance and at first I didn't recognize her. As soon as I did see her I drove over and she jumped in, throwing her arms around me and giving me a hug and a friendly kiss on the cheek.

'It's lovely to see you, Marty,' she said and my fears subsided. Instinctively I knew this was the old Mary, the girl I could trust.

As I drove away from the station Mary began bombarding me with questions, wondering why I was risking my life returning to Belfast and why I needed to talk to her so urgently. I drove to Castlereagh, to one of the places where I had frequently met and talked to Felix during my four years working for the Branch. I thought we might be safe there though I conceded that I might bump into Branch officers debriefing one of their sources. But I reckoned I had less chance of being recognized by SB officers than by old muckers in West Belfast who had known me all my life. It was a chance I had to take.

'I've probably no need to say this, Mary, but I must ask you to keep secret everything I'm about to discuss with you. I must be able to trust you.'

'You know you can, Marty,' she replied, 'we've always been able to trust each other.'

'Good. Well, listen: you remember my kidnapping and all that back in August 1991?' I began.

'Sure,' she replied, 'it was the talk of Belfast especially since Chico and Jim were made to look such fools.'

'Well, I need to know whether you heard anything suspicious about the abduction. Whether anyone found anything odd about it,' I asked, speaking slowly and deliberately.

'You must be joking,' she said, 'we were all talking about how it was possible for Chico and Jim to walk you out of Connolly House and abduct you in broad daylight. I had no idea you were working as a double agent for both the IRA and the Branch, Marty; you must enjoy danger.'

'Did you hear anything else?' I asked, ignoring her remarks about my reasons for working with the Branch.

'Marty, I could talk to you for hours about what everyone was saying but I don't think it would help. I listened whenever the subject came up because of our friendship but I couldn't even attempt to defend you because of Tom. He's never had any idea, thank God, that we've ever met, let alone been good friends.'

She went on. 'There was one night when I was with Tom and two of his IRA mates in a club and they were talking about you. They thought that Chico and Jim had thrown you out of the window because they had become increasingly nervous as the day wore on and the IRA security team had still not arrived. Another theory put forward was that the Branch had dumped you because you had outlived your usefulness.'

As I was digesting what she had told me, Mary asked, out of the blue: 'Did you know many secrets then, Marty?'

'No, not really,' I replied, laughing at such a direct question about such a highly secretive subject. 'Nothing that wasn't everyday work. All I did was tell the SB what the IRA were planning so they could step in and stop the killings.'

'I thought that's what you were doing,' she said, 'but I could never say so because your name was shit after everything came out about you.'

'So you didn't hear anything that surprised you?'

'Not really,' she said, 'but there was one point which people kept bringing up about you. They all said you were a hard man who would knock the shit out of anyone who got in your way. They wondered if the Branch became scared of you losing your temper if anything went wrong and you over reacted. Some even jokingly suggested that the reason Chico and Jim were sent to pick you up was because someone at the top wanted you to give the two big-headed bastards a good thumping.'

'And what did everyone think?'

'They were all confused,' she said. 'No one was able to work out what really went on and why. It was because everything seemed so mysterious and bizarre that people talked about it for so long.'

'Can you think of nothing else?' I asked, a little disappointed that she had not been able to give me a more concrete lead that might help me find out what really happened.

'Wait a minute,' she said excitedly. 'There was one more thing which I could not get out of my mind for a long time and which I thought was odd, even extraordinary at the time.'

'What was that?' I asked.

'When Chico and Jim returned from the South some weeks after you jumped from the window, the IRA sat back for a few days wondering if the Branch would come and pick them up. But nothing happened. Neither the RUC nor the Branch even bothered to question them and that aroused real suspicion in IRA circles. Everyone was talking about it, for it seemed so strange. After a few days Chico and Jim were picked up by the IRA security team on suspicion that they were working for the Branch. Some IRA people apparently believed that you hadn't jumped out of the window but either Chico or Jim had let you go and concocted the story to make it seem dramatic. They were held and questioned for at least a day. Remember, Marty, Jim McCarthy had been kneecapped by the IRA for helping prison officers while he was in jail when all the other IRA prisoners were involved with the dirty protests. From the IRA's point of view Chico also had a suspicious past because when questioned by police over a charge of attempted murder involving a British soldier he had admitted to being a member of the IRA. You know an IRA man could commit no worse sin than telling the RUC they are a member of the IRA. Everyone was saying that neither man was considered trustworthy by the IRA leadership.'

'So have you any idea why they were sent to kidnap me?' I asked her.

'No, Marty,' she replied, 'no idea at all. It seems so extraordinary, unless of course Chico and Jim were really working for the Special Branch.'

I said nothing to that line of argument but it was probably one of the most important pieces of information Mary was going to give me that day.

'But you're not going to stay around here are you, Marty?' she said, sounding concerned.

'No, I'll be away in a few days.'

I dropped Mary back at the train station and she gave me some warm hugs and a couple of kisses on the cheek, telling me to look after myself. Her last words to me were, 'Don't worry, Marty; I'll tell no one we've met. Take care.'

As I was driving away from the station I came to some lights that were red. When the lights changed I was about to drive away when I caught the eye of a taxi driver who was traveling in the opposite direction. The man was looking intently at me. As he looked at me I saw his mouth drop open and then he shouted, 'Marty, Marty McGartland . . .' Fortunately the lights had changed and I drove away convinced the man was a member of the IRA, a man whom I had known when working with Davy Adams, Gerry Adams' nephew, in IRA intelligence. At first I couldn't recall his name and then I realized it was a man named 'Billy' who had known me quite well. 'Fuck,' I thought to myself, 'he's recognized me.'

I had first met Billy when he was working as a driver with one of the many taxi firms which owed allegiance to the IRA. These taxis would sometimes be used to ferry men and weapons across the city. For many years the taxi firms had been a wonderful courier service for the IRA and the Branch believed that some of the firms were funded and run by the IRA hierarchy, frequently employing well-known IRA men who had been jailed for IRA activities and had been released. Understandably, these men found it very difficult, if not impossible, to find work or get a regular job because of their backgrounds. The IRA would give them jobs as taxi drivers so they could earn some money. They could also be trusted.

I was annoyed with myself for permitting someone to recognize me yet it hadn't really been my fault. I told myself to keep calm and act accordingly. There was no direct threat to my security and the man Billy obviously had no idea where I was staying. Nevertheless, there was now an IRA man who knew I was in Belfast and driving around in a red Vauxhall Vectra. I had no idea whether or not he had managed to note the registration number but I was doubtful as there had been so many vehicles blocking his view of the number plate. Now I knew that I had to dump my hire car, and quickly.

I drove back to the car rental depot as calmly as possible, checking my rear-view mirror every other second. As I drove I put on the baseball cap that I carried in the car and took off my bomber jacket so that anyone driving past would see a man in a sweatshirt and cap. It may not have worked but, on the other hand, I knew it might put off anyone searching for me. I had to accept that Billy would have swung round his taxi and done his damnedest to trace me and I would take no chances. I also wondered if he had been in radio contact with his base. If he had, and had raised the alarm of my return to Belfast, I knew I could really be in the shit.

When I arrived at the garage I parked the car out of harm's way in the middle of a line of other hire vehicles, some of them Vauxhall Vectras. I walked into the office, keeping a wary eye open for Billy and his taxi but throughout the ten minutes or so I was in there I saw no taxis whatsoever in the area. Now I had to decide my plan of action. The necessity was to get out of the city, out of Northern Ireland and back to the mainland as quickly as possible. I knew it could be risky waiting around the Belfast ferry terminal as it would have been so easy for the IRA to send a few men to search the place. I decided it would be safer to make my way to Larne and take the ferry from there. I made my way on foot through the back streets the few hundred yards to the Belfast City Hall from where the buses depart. I had to wait around for half an hour or so before the next bus left for Larne. I stood behind the shelters, not wanting to sit on the bus waiting because I knew I would feel exposed. As more people gathered I stood amongst them, trying to make myself inconspicuous.

The journey to Larne was long and tedious and seemed to go on for hours. I bought a copy of *The Belfast Telegraph* and spent most of the journey reading, concealing my face from anyone who could be checking me out. I must have read the paper from cover to cover during the hour-long express coach service. For the final ten minutes or so I worried about what I would do once I reached the terminal, for I realized that the Larne terminal was always stuffed with SB officers checking everyone coming and going. There was also the small matter of the CCTV cameras which were constantly checked by the RUC looking out for suspected terrorists. I also had to take into account that the SB now knew that I was back home in Belfast and would be asking questions. I judged that if Mike had heard I was back in Northern Ireland then nearly every other SB man in Belfast would have been made aware of my arrival.

More importantly, although I believed my arrival in Belfast would not trigger any major interest in me from the RUC or the Branch, I had to assume that 'Box' and their surveillance units might still have a residual interest in me which I would ignore at my peril. I wanted to believe what Mike had told me, that it was very unlikely that 'Box' was still interested in taking action against me, but I couldn't take that risk. As far as I was concerned MI5 were nearly as much of a danger to me as the IRA. And the thought made me chuckle. What I did know from conversations held with my SB handlers over the years was that MI5 was a ruthless organization which would stop at nothing, and was prepared to go to any length if they believed the so-called 'national security' was at stake. It had also been explained to me that on many occasions what MI5 deemed the 'national security' was more often than not an excuse to carry out whatever devious activities they wished, including taking the law into their own hands.

"Never trust 'Box'" was the maxim that the Special Branch in Belfast lived by, for they believed MI5 officers worked to a different agenda from any of the other intelligence and security services in the fight against the IRA and the Protestant paramilitaries.

"'Box' is a law unto itself,' I was told by more than one SB handler in Belfast. 'They are happy to ride roughshod over anyone, including those they are meant to be working with. They treat us as second-class citizens to be ignored until we are wanted to carry out some task or other that they don't want to do. We never trust them further than we can throw them because they're so secretive. We are meant to be working together combating terrorist activities and yet they keep everything to themselves, never sharing information which, sometimes, could be of real importance to us. As a result, some Branch officers are loath to keep 'Box' informed of all the intelligence they gather. It's a mad way to go about combating terrorism but it's all the fault of 'Box'. They believe they are superior and think we are here just to follow their orders and carry out their demands.'

Of course, I had no idea whether the attitude of Special Branch officers was deserved or simply petty internal jealousies among competing intelligence agencies, but I did have every reason to be wary of 'Box' and make fucking sure I kept out of their grasp. I had not wanted to believe what Mike had said about the 'Box' plot to get me killed but there was no other logical conclusion I could arrive at. I was not going to trust them one inch.

As we all trooped off the bus at the Larne terminal I tried to make myself as inconspicuous as possible. Most of those on board seemed to be families so I looked, in vain, for some person or group of people that I could latch onto in an effort to draw attention away from me. I needed to buy a ticket and as I walked into the booking area I noticed a few RUC officers, wearing black flak jackets and carrying sub-machine-guns, slowly patrolling the area as a deterrent to any would-be bombers. I realized that they would also have been looking out for any suspicious characters who might have been working for the IRA or indeed any of the paramilitaries.

'Afternoon sir,' the voice behind me said, hitting me like a thunderbolt for I had not been aware I was even being watched. I spun round and there must have been astonishment on my face as I looked into the eyes of two RUC men standing stock still only a matter of feet from me.

Desperately trying to regain my composure, I replied, 'Afternoon,' and forced myself to smile. I feared that the two officers would want to question me because I realized I must have looked very nervous, and I tried to relax, telling myself to stop being stupid.

I walked over to the ticket office and queued for my one-way ticket. Then I immediately made my way to the café for a cup of tea and a chance to escape the prying eyes and possible questioning of patrolling RUC men. I realized that as a youthful man in his mid-twenties traveling alone with an obvious Belfast accent, I was an ideal suspect for peelers bored from hours of pacing up and down the departure areas.

As I sat drinking tea my attention was drawn to a man I judged to be in his late twenties. I had heard him asking for a cup of coffee in a Belfast accent, one which sounded remarkably like a West Belfast tone of voice. Instantly, I recognized the man but I couldn't for the life of me put a name to his face. Yet he worried me. I felt he was a young man I had met during my two years inside the IRA. I recalled the times, the hours I had spent poring over Special Branch photographic files trying to remember the faces of people, mostly young men, whom my handlers asked me to keep a sharp lookout for. I believed that this young man was one of those IRA suspects the Branch had asked me to watch out for.

And then he noticed that I was looking at him. Our eyes met and I was more convinced than ever that I knew him, not only from a photograph file, but on a more personal basis, and that worried the shit out of me. I looked away and when I managed to look at him again, via a mirror in the café, I realized that he had recognized me also but was similarly confused about my identity.

I decided to sit still and pretend to keep sipping my tea, though in reality I had finished it some time ago. Occasionally I would glance over towards the young man, but every time I looked across the café he would all but stare back at me as if trying to confuse or frighten me. I wondered whether I should go over to him, engage him in conversation, try to find out if I did in fact know him or whether my fears of detection were playing on my nerves. In retrospect I was glad that the RUC officers had nodded to me and said 'good afternoon', treating me in the same way as many other travelers that day. That was an indication to me that all was well and that the suspicious man was probably not armed and that in fact, if push came to shove, I would have a fair chance of making a escape.

The man was quite well built but I noticed that, despite his youthful appearance, he carried a bit of a beer belly. I figured that if he challenged me I would be quite capable of giving him a good thumping. That thought gave me some confidence, for I realized that the palms of my hands had been sweating as though I suspected my cover would soon be blown.

He finished his cup of tea and came across to my table. 'Don't

I know you?' he asked in a strong Belfast accent, looking intently at me in what seemed to be a friendly manner.

'Don't think so,' I lied. 'Where do you think you know me from?'

'I can't place you,' he said, 'but I'm still sure we've met some time.'

'Maybe,' I lied again, 'but I don't think so.'

'Do you visit any of the clubs in West Belfast?' he asked, suggesting to me that this was his way of informing me that he was an IRA sympathizer if not an activist, trying to find some common ground between us.

'I doubt it,' I replied, 'because I live in England now. I was just visiting my folks.'

'Do you fancy a drink?' he asked.

'No thanks,' I said, not saying anymore because I was keen to end this conversation.

'Well, I'll be away,' he said, 'but I'm still sure I know you. It'll probably come to me later.'

As he walked away I decided to go and buy another cup of tea. I realized my mouth was dry and my palms were sweating. I was convinced now that he was an IRA member and I wondered why the peelers hadn't paid any attention to him.

Ten minutes later my new-found friend reappeared and walked up to my table. 'You're Marty McGartland,' he said.

CHAPTER TWELVE

The IRA man turned on his heel and walked out of the café. I knew instinctively that he would go to a phone to call someone. Whom, I did not know but I'm sure my guess would have been pretty accurate. I realized it was his duty to arrest me, kidnap me or arrange for some of his IRA mates to pick me up and deliver me once again to the Civil Administration Team for interrogation. I also suspected that because of all that had occurred since my last abduction by the IRA, word would probably have gone out to all members to kill me if they ever came across me. Sixty seconds after he left the café I followed, keeping him in sight, hoping that he hadn't any of his mates on site at the Larne terminal. I thought it highly unlikely but I couldn't be sure.

I saw him walk to a telephone and begin to dial. I wondered whether I should try and stop him making that call but thought better of it. I couldn't approach an RUC patrol, reveal my identity and suggest they arrest the man on the phone because I had no reason to give. I also had no idea of his identity though now I was convinced the man was IRA. As soon as he began to speak I disappeared, walking quickly away from where the ferries dock at Larne, as far away as possible from my IRA suspect.

I guessed that he would never think I would return to Belfast but would be more than anxious to get the hell out of Northern Ireland back to the safety of the mainland. After using the phone I guessed that he would spend the time searching the departure area for me, angry at letting me out of his sight and, more than likely, waiting for one or more of his mates to join him. I realized that there was very little possibility they would try to abduct me at the Larne ferry terminal but I guessed that if I had been on board the next ferry to Scotland they would have a crack at me either on board the ferry or after landing at Stranraer.

As soon as I reached the other side of the terminal I went immediately to the bus departure point and bought a ticket for Belfast. This time luck was in my favor for after an agonizing ten minutes the bus set off again for the city. I was sure that my IRA friend had not seen me and had no idea that I was at that moment heading back towards Belfast. About two miles down the road I asked the driver to stop and let me off; I alighted as if he was dropping me near my home. After the bus had disappeared from sight I walked across the road and began walking back towards the ferry terminal once more. But I had no intention of completing the journey to the mainland that night.

As I walked along I wondered where I could sleep that night; I didn't relish sleeping rough on a cold, damp, overcast night. I heard the wailing of police sirens and remembered not to look back as two RUC cars sped past me, seemingly en route to the ferry terminal. I wondered whether they were searching for me or the lad who had interrupted my return to the mainland. It seemed so strange not knowing what was going on and not knowing whom I could trust. Having spent four years in the protective, all-embracing security of the RUC Special Branch it seemed strange to feel so vulnerable, so lonely in the same country where I had once felt so safe and unassailable. There was even a certain fear that the world had been turned upside down and I was now on the run; my friends and comrades had now become my antagonists, my feared enemies. The siren noise had made me feel uneasy and at that moment I wondered why the hell I had taken such a risk returning back home. And for what?

I vowed to myself that if I managed to escape from this predicament I would never return to Belfast again, not even if there was a peace settlement. As more RUC cars raced past me I began to concentrate on my immediate worries rather than think a load of nonsense. Where was I to sleep the night?

Finally, as I realized I was getting closer to the ferry terminal and to possible danger I decided I had little option but to creep into a field and lie doggo till morning. Having checked the road was clear I nipped over a five-barred gate and, stooping below the level of the hedge, made my way along the side of the field looking for a reasonable place to lay my head. No place looked particularly inviting but I knew I had to grit my teeth and stop pussy-footing about. I found a reasonable patch of bare ground beneath the hawthorn hedge and settled down for what I knew would be an unpleasant, cold and damp night. But I knew it would be a fucking sight more comfortable than lying bound hand and foot on the sofa in an IRA flat being guarded by armed men while awaiting interrogation and torture.

I had never appreciated the effect those seven hours of waiting for interrogation and torture had on me until shortly after my acquittal at Newcastle Crown Court when I overheard an interview with my neighbor who lived in the flat below me. She said, 'I had no idea of Martin Ashe's background; I had no idea that he had been working as an undercover agent inside the IRA and yet I had worried about him because I heard him suffering terrible nightmares. And it was always the same one, shouting, 'please don't do it, please don't do it'. The first couple of times I heard him yelling like that I thought, 'God, that young man must be very disturbed' and I wondered what his past life must have been like. But the nightmares still continue to this day and it's always the same one, the same screams, the same pleas.'

As the hours rolled by, darkness fell and the cold of the night penetrated my very soul. I was still wide awake, unable to sleep in such an uncomfortable, damp hole. I thought how ironic it was that when I left Belfast for the first time I had been escorted by two armed SB officers, taken to the port in an RUC car and treated with kindness and, more importantly, respect. Now, six years later, I was holed up in a cold, damp field with no cover and no protection, waiting for daylight so that I could make my escape like a fugitive running from justice. It brought a smile to my lips thinking how the cards fall, sometimes riding high, at other times caught in a web of deceit and lies while trying to battle for justice. And I thought of the work that I had done in the past, work which usually resulted in praise, compliments and a pat on the back.

Only a few had ever known the information I had gathered while working inside the IRA. Those whose lives I had saved had never even been aware that they had been targeted by the IRA or that their lives had been saved by a lad from Ballymurphy who had been raised a staunch Republican and whose teenage years had been spent baiting the RUC and the British Army. I'm glad those who had cheated death had no idea of what had really happened.

As I lay curled up in a ball trying to keep warm my mind went back to those heady days when I would live cheek by jowl with active service members of the IRA, drinking in Republican bars and clubs, rubbing shoulders with those IRA commanders who decided which targets should be bombed and which targets should be left alone. During my early days working with Davy Adams, before I had been officially recruited into the IRA, I would learn most of my information from driving him around Belfast and listening to his conversations with the people he was visiting. It was, in retrospect, the perfect job for the task I had been recruited to tackle, feeding everything I heard back to the Special Branch, for as intelligence officer for the Belfast Brigade of the IRA, most of the planned operations passed through his hands. Later, when I became a fully fledged member, I would be permitted to hang around the clubs and bars where IRA members would spend most evenings discussing ideas and possible targets, planning their next bombing or attack on some poor, unsuspecting individual.

The conversations I overheard and joined in would sometimes make me shudder for they would discuss the cold-blooded murders of police officers, prison warders or British soldiers as if they were of no consequence whatsoever, with never a thought as to whether the men had wives, families or dependents. And the easier and more simple the selected target the more the IRA killers would gloat, even laughing at what they were about to carry out.

After such an attack the yelps of joy could be heard in the club where the gunman had decided to celebrate his 'hit' with his mates. They would take a certain pride and triumph in their achievement, describing in detail exactly what had happened and how the wretched man had reacted when confronted by a man with a gun. As I listened to these sickening tales, pretending to show enthusiasm, I would on occasions feel my stomach churn with nausea that young men could have such negative feelings towards a total stranger whom they had targeted and killed in cold blood. Though I had been brought up as a good Catholic boy and learned at my mother's knee the treatment that the RUC, the Army and the Protestants had meted out to the Catholic minority for generations, I never for one moment believed I was betraying my fellow Catholics. I considered such horrific murders to be a stain on the reputation of the great majority of good Catholic people who wanted nothing to do with shootings and bombings of innocent people, killed solely because of their religious differences.

During the summer of 1990 I heard from one of my PIRA pals with whom I was becoming increasingly friendly that his unit intended to go ahead and plant one-and-a-half pounds of Semtex under an RUC car attending the Radio One Road Show at Bangor in Northern Ireland. At the time he was chatting to a mate, another PIRA member, and saying that they had targeted the Radio One show the previous summer and intended to carry out the bombing this year. The plan was to build a bomb, the size of a video cassette, and stuff it with one-and-a-half pounds of Semtex, enough to wreck an RUC car and kill the occupants. Anyone else caught in the immediate vicinity of the explosion might also be killed or receive serious injuries.

'Might you not kill a load of kids?' I asked him.

'That's nothing to do with us,' he replied, 'we're just after the peelers. If they get caught in the blast that's their bad luck.'

As I warmed to the plan I asked him, 'How do you plan to put a UCBT on an RUC vehicle?'

'Easy,' he replied, 'we rehearsed it last year. We went and watched how the RUC patrolled the show. The peelers parked their car not far from the stage and then got out of the vehicle and patrolled the area, searching for any troublemakers. The point is not only that the peelers left the vehicle for maybe ten to fifteen minutes, giving us plenty of time to plant the UCBT, but they never bothered to check for any bombs underneath the vehicle when they returned.'

'How will you set it off with the car parked near hundreds of people?' I asked, as though totally innocent in the ways of PIRA bomber techniques.

'Easy,' he replied, 'we'll use a mercury tilt switch. When the peelers drive away the bomb will explode whenever the car goes uphill or downhill. One-and-a-half pounds can cause terrible damage, I promise you. They won't stand a chance.'

'But how will you get the bomb into the area?' I asked. 'I thought everyone was searched before they were allowed to enter the area where the Road Show was being held?'

'No,' he said, 'and this is where we're clever. We noticed that nearly everyone turns up at the Radio Show with their ghetto blasters. Well, we're going to buy a radio, strip it clean and put the booby trap inside. In that way we will walk in and no questions asked. Once inside we take out the bomb and attach it under the RUC car. Couldn't be easier.'

As my friend spoke I conjured up in my mind the devastation that such a bomb could cause in an area crowded by hundreds of teenagers enjoying the sun and the music. I couldn't imagine how young PIRA members could even contemplate such a bombing, with total disregard for the young people who would be killed or injured in the blast. The one fortunate piece of information was that the bombing could only take place when the Radio Show was touring Northern Ireland, which meant that the RUC could be forewarned precisely.

As always in such a case I contacted Felix as soon as possible and told him every detail of the planned bombing. I recall him shaking his head, as if unable to grasp that there were young people perfectly happy to let off a large explosion which would not only kill two RUC officers but also kill, maim or wound a number of carefree teenagers. Sometime later Felix told me that an order had gone out from RUC headquarters telling all officers never to leave their vehicles unattended, even for minutes at a time, for fear of UCBTs being attached. Whenever Radio One Road Shows were taking place that year I would make a point of listening to the news but I was thankful that I never heard of one being bombed. Such little pieces of information which I supplied and which helped save the skin of innocent people always gave me a warm feeling.

It was in fact the only warmth I felt that night, lying under the hedge waiting for sleep to overcome me and thinking of a few of the escapades I had been involved in during my years inside the IRA. I recalled one of the most daring PIRA spectaculars which I heard about when a team of PIRA gunmen planned to use an RPG 7 – a rocket launcher – two AK47s and a Semtex coffee-jar bomb to attack a convoy of two RUC Land Rovers and an army jeep as they drove from the heavily guarded New Barnsley RUC station along the Springfield Road to the joint RUC–Army base at Springfield Parade a few miles down the road.

The vehicles were taking RUC officers back to their cars which they left each morning behind the perimeter walls of the RUC base because it was considered far too risky for the RUC personnel to drive their own cars along the Springfield Road in the heart of IRA-controlled West Belfast. Most evenings at around 10:30, about fifteen officers were taken at a time in the Land Rovers and jeeps. The PIRA planned to attack the convoy at the top of Springhill Avenue on the Ballymurphy Estate from where the attackers could make a quick escape back to their homes. Springhill was known among the Republicans of West Belfast as 'Beirut' because of its fearsome reputation and the number of attacks on the security forces through the years.

I heard of the plans while chatting to a number of PIRA members in a local Republican club where they gathered most evenings for a few pints. I often called in because I found they would chat more openly after a few drinks and I could learn what was being planned.

'We know exactly what time they pass by,' one older PIRA man said as he explained the plan of attack in front of half-a-dozen of us eagerly listening youngsters. 'We will first hit them with the RPG to immobilize the jeep then throw the Semtex coffee-jar bomb and pour in 120 rounds from two AK47s with double magazines. That lot should give the black bastards something to cry about; they won't know what's hit them. If we don't get a good result out of this one I'll be quite surprised.'

'How many men will we need?' someone asked.

'We're planning the operation now,' he said. 'But what we do know is that this attack will be one of the most spectacular ever seen in Belfast. We'll show that we can take on the might of the British Army and the RUC and knock the shit out of them. It'll be great. If we can kill the fuckin' lot, all the better.'

'Do you know when the attack will take place?' someone asked.

'Aye,' he replied, making a cardinal mistake in showing off in front of a group of young enthusiasts when he should have kept quiet. 'A week tonight. It's all planned.'

As a result of the PIRA man shooting his mouth off I was able to give Felix precise details, dates and the exact time the attack would take place. British Army commanders and RUC chiefs were immediately informed and the area of the proposed attack was swamped by police and army personnel, blotting out any chance the PIRA gunmen had of launching any armed offensive.

And there were many other PIRA plans I was able to thwart, though none of such a grand scale. In the spring of 1991, some four months before I was led to my entrapment, I was attending a meeting of my IRA cell in the commander's home when someone mentioned that he had a possible target.

'I've been watching this peeler,' he said. 'I noticed one day that he was riding a motor-bike through the grounds of the City Hospital, taking a short-cut to work. I've been watching him every morning for the past five days and he's as regular as clockwork. You could almost set your watch by his timing. I think he would be so easy to take out. He's always on his own and I think we could take him either when he slows down to enter the hospital grounds or at the exit, when he drives across the footpath and on to the main road again. If someone waited at either end it would be so easy; a cinch.'

There was general approval among the eight or so members present and the commander said that he would pass the idea to the 'OO' (Operations Officer), the man who took all the decisions of whether IRA operations went ahead or not. If given the go-ahead, plans would be drawn up for an early hit, maybe within the next few days. The IRA liked to act as quickly as possible when such targets were selected, for various reasons, and one of the principal reasons was that on so many occasions selected targets would simply vanish into thin air within days of being targeted by PIRA active service units. They didn't like to think that, more often than not, the targets moved because someone tipped off the RUC that an attack had been planned. They preferred to think that it was simply 'bad luck,' that the target had come to their notice too late, just when the quarry had decided to change his pattern of operation.

Within an hour of the meeting's conclusion I was sitting in a car talking to Felix, telling him everything I had heard. 'They seem really keen on this one,' I told him.

'Why this one?' he asked.

'Because they think it's going to be easy, a simple job they called it.'

'Is there anything else you learned?' Felix asked, looking perturbed.

'Only that they want to carry out the operation within the next few days.'

'Do you know how they plan to murder him?'

'Aye,' I replied, 'they're going to use a hand-gun.'

'And the getaway?' he asked.

'Not decided yet. Either a car or maybe the back of a motorbike. They're going to discuss that later after someone has carried out a recce.'

'So they seem confident?' he asked.

'Confident?' I replied, with some surprise in my voice. 'They think it's a done deed already, they're so confident.'

Felix said, 'Leave it to me' and he dropped me somewhere discreetly so that no one would see me getting out of his unmarked car. I didn't hear another word about the operation until Felix told me the following week that the RUC man had been tipped off and told to find another way to work. But he was never told how the intelligence had been gathered or by whom.

Weeks later, I was giving Paul Lynch, a well-known IRA gunman, a lift across Belfast when he began talking about an operation he was planning in Bangor, the Protestant seaside town on the north-east coast of Ireland. He had received a tip-off from one of his IRA moles who worked in a bar in Bangor that there was a potential target that might interest him.

As we drove out of Belfast and headed north Lynch said, 'Our man has told us that these two peelers walk down the High Street every afternoon around 2 p.m., and then stroll along the quay for a few hundred yards before returning the same way back to the town. They're dressed in flak jackets and carry revolvers in hip holsters but that should be no problem.'

'Would you go it alone?' I asked.

'No, impossible,' replied Lynch. 'I would probably take Skin Bennett, he's game for anything.'

I knew that if Lynch and Bennett were planning the shooting then there was a real probability that the attack would take place no matter how difficult the logistics were. I had always been told by my SB handlers to listen intently to anything Lynch said because he was a highly professional gunman. Both Lynch and Bennett had fearless reputations and were prepared to tackle any operation, taking the greatest risks. I knew that the SB had been on their trail for months because of their reputations for ruthlessness.

'How would you do it?' I asked.

'By bike,' he said. 'Too difficult to use a car because the High Street is often full of traffic. I think we would take a bike. And if we found we had to take them on the quay we would be too conspicuous driving along in a car; hardly anyone takes a car along there. Skin would drive and I would ride pillion . . . ride up behind them as they walked down the steep High Street or along the sea front and blast them in the head from behind . . . they wouldn't stand a chance . . . a piece of cake.'

'But wouldn't you be too exposed in Bangor?' I asked.

'Our mole would provide a safe house,' he went on. 'We would stay there for forty-eight hours or until the hoo-hah had died down then we'd leg it back to Belfast. Easy. I'm quite looking forward to it.'

That day Paul Lynch and I parked our car in Bangor and took a walk around the town, checking the traffic flow, the No Entry streets and examining the best way to make a quick escape if it became necessary. We stopped for a bite to eat at the Kentucky Fried Chicken shop so we could have a grandstand view of the two peelers walking down the High Street and on to the sea front. The two peelers appeared so nonchalant, so laid back, that I too realized how easy it would be for two determined gunmen to shoot down their men in broad daylight and make a successful getaway. I looked at the two peelers, thinking how close they could be to death if I didn't remember every clue and tell Felix all the details I could remember.

Within the hour after returning to Belfast I had checked in to the SB and arranged a meeting with Felix.

'Do you know when they're going to strike?' he asked when I had completed my briefing.

'Not exactly,' I said. 'I didn't want to ask too many questions for fear of sounding too suspicious but I guessed from the conversation that Lynch anticipated having a go within the next few days.'

As usual, Felix said, 'Leave it to me; we'll have to nip this one in the bud and pretty quick too.'

Much to my relief I heard nothing on the radio nor the TV, and read nothing in the papers about any attempted murder of police officers in Bangor and a few weeks later I asked Felix what had happened. 'We suggested a constant change of operational duties for patrolling peelers,' he said, with a knowing smile. 'We've doubled the officers on the beat as well as having a mobile patrol as back-up so that the IRA won't be able to move a muscle. It seems to have done the trick.'

All these memories returned so vividly to my mind as I lay shivering in the cold night air. I had become so uncomfortable and sleep seemed so far away that shortly after dark I decided I had to move and stretch my legs. I had heard no RUC or Army patrols about and felt and prayed that if the TCG had been told to search for me they would have presumed I had made good my escape and was now safely back on the mainland. But of course I couldn't be sure. As I walked along the road once again, this time away from the ferry terminal, I tried to reason once more why it had been so necessary for MI5, or whoever, to arrange for my kidnap. It still didn't make any sense and so, as a consequence, I knew it was crazy to risk falling into the hands of the RUC, the Branch or any of the security forces.

The thought of being delivered once more into the hands of the Provisional IRA scared the shit out of me and I immediately turned around and retraced my steps to the hide beneath the hawthorn hedge. But the walk had done me a power of good, allowing my muscles to get some feeling back in them and making me feel more relaxed and in control of myself. I had seen no patrols around and hardly any vehicles for I presumed the last ferry had arrived and there would be no others until early the next day. Somehow I must have fallen asleep, tired out by the anxiety and the nervous tension which I was no longer used to. But I had to face the following day not knowing what it might bring.

I shall never forget those last few hours in Northern Ireland for my nerves were on edge and, as I made my way from my hideout to the ferry, I feared that at any moment someone would approach me, catch me off guard and take me away. I looked at everyone with suspicion that morning, anxious, sweating, even praying that I would make my escape back to England without being recognized either by the plain-clothes SB men who patrolled the terminal or some Provo given the job of checking passengers. Throughout the journey across the Irish Sea not for one moment did I relax my guard but as I saw Stranraer emerging through the sea mist I felt my pulse race, knowing I was within an ace of reaching safety. I walked off with a group of other people not wanting to attract attention to myself and walked slowly as I left the terminal and made my way through the streets to where I had parked my car. It was still there and, remembering everything I had been taught, I bent down and checked beneath the vehicle, just in case some bastard had planted a UCBT. It was clean. I opened the door and sat down but, before I could start the engine, I felt a wave of relief and emotion wash over me. My body began to shake and the tears to flow as I realized my mission was over. I sat there for a few minutes giving way to my pent-up emotions, coming to terms for the first time the strain I had been under during those forty-eight hours back home. I vowed then that I would never return home again. As I drove back to Newcastle, memories of Angie and the boys only added to my feeling of isolation and despair but I knew my fight with the authorities was far from over. It was the anger I felt towards those bastards ranged against me that revived my spirit of determination.

Back in Newcastle I wondered what trouble I had caused during my flying trip to Belfast and, more importantly, wondered whether the Provisional IRA or the Crown authorities were the more concerned by my visit. I knew the IRA gauleiters would have been angry that they had missed another chance to abduct, interrogate and shoot me. As far as they were concerned there was no question that I was as guilty as sin for I had confessed all in my book. But I smiled to myself as I realized that MI5, or whatever other government agency wanted me dead, would be holding meetings, demanding reports and, hopefully, worrying about what I had discovered about my abduction during my forty-eight hours in Belfast.

I realized that the security services may have heard of my arrival in Belfast within a day of my setting foot on Irish soil. Though they probably knew of my return I hoped few would know the purpose of my trip and, hopefully, none of them would have information identifying the people I had seen and spoken to. I hoped my visit had made the guilty ones feel nervous for they must have learned during the past two years that I was probing ever more deeply into the manner of my kidnap. They would also have been made aware of the questions I was asking through my solicitors as to the reasons why I had been treated in such a bizarre way by the Crown agencies, that group of faceless men whose identity neither I nor my solicitor were permitted to know.

But why, I kept asking myself, were we not permitted to know who was advising the Crown law firm Burton & Burton? It seemed extraordinary that the agency pulling the strings was too embarrassed to own up and inform either me or my solicitor. The more I thought about the preposterous and stupid way the mystery agency was hiding behind a law firm, the more I realized that it was likely to be MI5. And why? It seemed the only solution was that MI5 had been the agency responsible for organizing my kidnap by the Provisional IRA.

On my return to Newcastle I was confronted with two further discreditable turns of events. After months of haggling between my solicitor and the mysterious Crown agents, Burton & Burton the solicitors representing the government, decided to try and force me into accepting a disgraceful offer. They wrote to my solicitor in April 1998, stating, 'Following your client's rejection of all offers made to him, there is no agreement between us [concerning paying my legal fees] and under these circumstances no payment can be made towards his fees.' I knew my solicitor's fees would amount to thousands of pounds which I had not received. From evidence that I had gathered, it simply showed how low the government would sink in their attempt to force me to comply with their wishes.

While probing the various legal problems that were surfacing every other month, my solicitor, Nigel Dodds, discovered that there was a major discrepancy in the amount of money that the RUC had paid me for my resettlement on the mainland back in 1991. When he checked the figures he discovered that, according to the Command Secretariat of the RUC, a total of only £82,000 had been paid to me. Later, however, I would hear from a senior civil servant in the Northern Ireland Office that, after checking, he had been informed that I had been paid a total of £120,000! I was amazed, staggered by the statement. That meant that somewhere, somehow, a total of £36,000 had mysteriously gone missing. When someone such as a government agent or an RUC informant needs to be resettled and given a new identity, account has to be taken that he, or she, will have major problems. They will be in a strange place, without a home, a career, a job, friends, relations or a way of earning money to live on or save for a pension. All this – the basics of a good, decent life – the agent has sacrificed working on behalf of the government. As a result the government takes care of those men and women. Other agents, of course, have sacrificed much more including, quite often, their very lives. Former agents are given grants to resettle but never enough to compensate – because they have to be given a new identity, a new social security number, new passport, new bank account, new driving license and yet he, or she, has no record of ever having worked in a responsible job. The agent has no past, no history, no references.

Like anyone, former agents want, above all else, to settle down and live a normal, ordinary life: forget the past, live in a decent home, secure a good, well-paying job, build a pension and, hopefully, find a new circle of friends. Such grants were intended to take into consideration some reward for the dangerous tasks undertaken on behalf of the government and of society in general. RUC informants, in particular, risked their lives every day they mingled with PIRA activists, often taking extraordinary chances to gather information which they passed to their handlers and which often saved the lives of innocent people.

When I was resettled on the mainland a house was purchased for me for £52,500, a Ford Fiesta for £4,500 and I was given a further £6,000 to buy furniture and to cover other expenses to start a new life from scratch. I also received £21,000 – a resettlement allowance – which I understood was an RUC grant for the dangers I had faced during my four years working as an RUC informant. In all, this money amounted to £84,000. I was more than happy with this sum because I then had a three-bedroom, semi-detached house with a garden of my own, a small car as well as money to survive on for a year or two while I searched for a job. I also had some money to put towards a pension.

As a result of correspondence between the Command Secretariat of the RUC and my solicitor, however, the discrepancy of £36,000 came to light. The mystery of the missing money was enthusiastically taken up by Robert McCartney, the MP for North Down, who is also a Queen's Counsel. He asked the Northern Ireland Secretary of State to list the sums of money paid to me since August 1991 and to state which agencies paid the money and under what powers. The Secretary of State was also asked how much was paid to me by the Criminal Injuries Compensation Agency.

Probing the money paid to me arose after my solicitor had applied for a hearing to the Criminal Injuries Compensation Agency for the serious injuries I had received as a result of throwing myself out of the third-floor window. To this day, seven years after the event, I still suffer from splitting headaches, for my head had been severely lacerated in the plunge. Neurological consultants have told me that I still have scar tissue on my brain and am suffering minor brain damage.

Kevin Ham, a senior case worker for the Compensation Agency, informed me that another anonymous Crown servant had told the Agency that a house costing £80,000 had been purchased for me and that I had been given a further £40,000, in cash, which took fully into account compensation for injuries caused when jumping out of the window. As a result, of course, the Agency wanted to know why I was making an application for further compensation.

What horrified and enraged me, however, was a note which had been sent to the Compensation Agency from the RUC Special Branch which stated, 'Martin McGartland was known to be an IRA sympathizer and had never worked for the Special Branch.'

The statement– a direct, unquestionable lie – puzzled me and I wondered why such misinformation could have been sent to the Agency by the Special Branch who knew I had worked for them for four years. I didn't immediately condemn the SB for sending that note because I just found it totally inexplicable. But it made me realize I not only needed to write a book telling of my career as an undercover agent, but I also needed help from the most influential people in the land.

As a consequence, I wrote to the then Prime Minister John Major, Opposition Leader Tony Blair, Lord Tebbit, former Northern Ireland Secretaries Tom King and Michael Mates as well as the Unionist leader David Trimble. All wrote letters of support to me as well as correspondence to Sir Patrick Mayhew, then Secretary of State for Northern Ireland, demanding that my case be looked into as a matter of urgency.

But those I saw as the forces of evil seemed to be doing their damnedest to refuse me justice. Sir John Wheeler, Minister of State, wrote to MP Robert McCartney telling him that I could not claim compensation because there were no medical records covering my injuries and I had not served notice of my claim for compensation within twenty-eight days as required by legislation. The Minister's argument was totally spurious. The reason there were no medical records submitted was because after I had been moved from the Musgrave Park military hospital to safety in an army barracks the Special Branch took away all my hospital records and burned them. The reason why I had not put forward my claim within twenty-eight days was because I was only semi-conscious and under police guard in protective custody throughout that time. It seemed extraordinary that a minister of state would go to such lengths to deny me natural justice. But the minister's fallacious arguments would go further in an effort to blacken my name.

In one letter Sir John Wheeler wrote to Robert McCartney, it is stated: 'Mr. McGartland applied for compensation to the Compensation Agency in 1992 in respect of an incident in August

1991 in which he alleges he had been injured when he jumped from a third-floor flat having been kidnapped'. It continued, 'Mr. McGartland then appealed to the County Court against the Agency's decision but before his case came to hearing, information came to light which suggested that he had been a member of the Provisional IRA and involved in terrorism including the murder of an off-duty soldier. His case was heard at Lisburn County Court where the judge dismissed his appeal primarily on the grounds of his membership.'

When I read that reprehensible, even wicked accusation I saw red. The Northern Ireland Minister Sir John Wheeler must have known that I had been recruited by the Special Branch; that I had been urged by my Branch handlers to join the Provisional IRA and work as an undercover agent supplying information to the Special Branch. Sir John must have been made aware by his advisers that I had been responsible for reporting activities of PIRA members and their plans to bomb strategic targets as well as their evil plots to kill individuals, usually members of the security forces, the RUC and prison officers. For four years I had risked my life trying to save people's lives and this was the way I was being treated by the British government. I felt Sir John Wheeler's disingenuous letter was a disgrace, an insult, a calculated attempt to deny all I had done.

But was it more? Did Sir John Wheeler know more? Was he trying to engineer a cover-up because he knew there was a serious discrepancy of £36,000 due to me and which the Command Secretariat was trying to hide? Or, I wondered, had he taken advice from MI5?

I was determined to establish the truth, not solely because the money would have been very useful but also because this revelation seemed to be part of the overall pattern to undermine my credibility, to spread false rumors, to instruct the police to harass me, to bring me before a Crown Court on flawed charges. And all because I had escaped a bid to have me murdered, probably organized by that most secretive Crown agency, MI5. But why?

And then silence. I presume the Northern Ireland Office and

RUC senior officers hoped the accusations would go away. For more than twelve months I heard nothing whatsoever and as the months passed by I became even more angry and determined. I believed the very fact that no reply was sent to my solicitor meant that the authorities realized they were guilty and were too ashamed to own up to lying and stealing. Some newspaper friends of mine believed that they saw the hand of official chicanery behind my court case. They argued that if the Crown had been able to convict me on charges of perverting the course of justice I would have been jailed and my good name tarnished to such a degree that no one would believe any accusations I might make against MI5, the RUC, the Home Office or the Command Secretariat.

In May 1998 my solicitor wrote to Ronnie Flanagan, Chief Constable of the RUC, demanding a substantive reply to the questions that had been asked over the previous two years, adding, 'This matter is beginning to acquire the flavor of a 'cover-up'. Seven days later a reply was finally received from the Chief Constable stating that, according to their records, I had been paid – surprise, surprise – a total of £82,000 including an amount of £12,500 for the purchase of a 'milk round' for me to run as a business following my resettlement. The letter came as a considerable shock because it was the first time ever that I had heard anything about the purchase of a milk round!

My solicitor immediately wrote back asking for full details and the records of money paid to me and by whom, where and when. He also asked for full details about the alleged milk round, asking particulars about the business, from whom it had been purchased, and where and when. There was no reply to any of those questions. More than six months later the Chief Constable has still not produced any records to me or my solicitor, no details whatsoever have been supplied and nothing has been heard of the mysterious milk round. It seems someone has been economical with the truth.

Unhappy with the extraordinary course of events, I phoned Kevin Ham at the Northern Ireland Compensation Agency, the civil servant responsible for authorizing payments to people injured in attacks and beatings by the IRA and the Protestant para-militaries. He knew of my case and produced the answers to my questions. I taped the phone call.

I asked him how much my house had cost.

Kevin Ham: 'I was told the figure paid for your house was £80,000.'

Me: 'But I have the letter from the solicitor that the RUC used and it states that the house only cost £52,500.'

Kevin Ham: 'Well, as I understand it, and what they have told me . . . I have to accept from a fellow Crown servant what they have stated.'

Me: 'Did they definitely say £80,000, are you sure that they said £80,000?'

Kevin Ham: 'I can't depart from that figure of £80,000. I mean, what I am saying is that the total figure was £120,000 including £80,000 for the house.'

It appeared that the Chief Constable himself had been given false information, unless, of course, he was being deliberately dishonest. But after talking to Kevin Ham, an honest civil servant, I was convinced that someone in the system had cheated me, though not for one minute did I believe the Chief Constable was involved in such deception. And yet it seemed unbelievable both to me and my solicitor, that someone, or some organization, would want to steal from an agent who had risked everything. I wondered how many other agents and informants had been treated in the same way, receiving less money than had been authorized. I knew there would have been dozens of agents who needed to be resettled during the Troubles and I wondered if they too had been ripped off.

Menacingly, however, and more troublesome, I wondered how many other agents who had worked undercover inside the IRA had been betrayed by MI5 or any other British security or intelligence agencies, kidnaps arranged in secret deals between the Provos and MI5 officers, which ended in the most appalling beatings, tortures and deaths. I knew the Provos loved to capture British agents and informants because their torture and killing would be seen as a warning to other Catholics and Republicans who were thinking of working for the RUC, MI5 or any other of the government security services. That was why whenever an informant was captured by the Provos and subsequently shot dead, statements were always issued by the IRA propaganda machine. Every killing of every informant instilled fear in the hearts and minds of any Republican who might have been thinking of working for the British government or the RUC.

I also understood only too well that if agents or informants had been betrayed by the British government's security services, in the same way that I had been betrayed, there was no possibility that the Provos could make a mistake, accidentally interrogating and killing an innocent person. They were certain the men and women they interrogated and tortured – tape recording their traumatic confessions – were guilty. Thus, no matter how long it took for the punishment squads to tear a confession from the wretched victim, the squads never gave up demanding the answers they required. One can only wonder how many have been betrayed by the security services during the Troubles. About fifty men and women were executed by the Provos and Loyalists for giving information – 'betraying the cause' as they called it. And there were apparently only a couple who were innocent of the accusations made against them by the IRA. It led me to believe that with such an extraordinary success rate – ninety-five per cent accurate – the Provos must have been either brilliant detectives or they had been receiving impeccable information from the forces of law and order and the intelligence agencies.

Each and every time I thought through what I had been told by my SB friend Mick, that I had been set up by MI5 or some other intelligence agency, I shuddered not only at the thought that I only just managed to escape but more so for those poor bastards who hadn't managed to elude the Provos, who had taken terrible beatings and torture 'til their spirit had eventually been broken. They knew the consequences. Every informant and agent in Northern Ireland knew the penalty if they were ever caught. What those brave men and women never bargained for, what they never knew, was that when the powers that be decided that an informant had passed his sell-by date, when his usefulness was at an end, he wouldn't be handed a pension and put out to grass but, instead, would be sacrificed, treated like a pawn in a game of chess.

Now that it appears peace has finally come to Northern Ireland, however briefly, I hope those who infiltrated the IRA, risking their lives to save other people, will be handsomely rewarded. They should be honored by the authorities, not treated like nuisances. Those men and women fully realize that even today, there are those amongst the Provos, including some hard men released from jail, who are hell-bent on seeking revenge, determined to teach the 'touts' a lesson. In today's political climate that penalty might not be death but would likely be a severe punishment beating that might maim them for life. I only hope that those agents and informants who are now seeking a new life won't be betrayed as I was. But I wouldn't bet on it.

Autumn 1998

Chapter Thirteen

For some months I had come to believe that I was finally a free man–free from the constant attentions of Northumbria Police and all the government agencies which had given me shit over the past few years. Unfortunately, I was being too optimistic, for in the autumn of 1998 they began to target me once again. And, even more troubling, the Provisional IRA had once more directly targeted and intimidated my family in West Belfast in their customary cowardly way.

On the morning of Friday, October 2, 1998, I was driving along a main road in Tyne and Wear when I heard the siren of a marked police car behind me, the blue lights flashing. I slowed and stopped. I wondered why they were targeting me.

Constable 5999 walked to my car and told me had pulled me over because one of my brake lights wasn't working. He asked me for my name and address and I told him my name, 'Martin David Ashe', and, as I always did on such occasions, gave him the address of my solicitor instead of my home address. I had previously given my solicitor's address, not wishing to give my home address to every police officer who stopped me. In the past the police had always accepted the solicitor's address. But not this day.

Ironically, on this occasion, the police officer knew me, knew my identity and, I presumed, my background. It made no difference. Constable 5999 accused me of refusing to give my home address and called for assistance. Within minutes I heard another police siren and watched as the car came flying down the main shopping street weaving at speed through the traffic, the siren blaring, the blue lights flashing. People came out of the shops and the bank wondering what all the commotion was about, and a crowd gathered. The police car came to a sudden halt and PC 2630 walked over, leaving the car's blue lights flashing. He, too, knew me well. He asked his colleague why assistance had been called for and was told that I had refused to give my address.

I showed the two officers an old 'HORT/1' form, which motorists are given when requested to produce their driving documents at a police station. That form, written out by another police officer, gave my solicitor's address instead of my home address. On that occasion, that officer had accepted my solicitor's address. I knew I was perfectly within my rights giving my solicitor's address instead of my own.

'Nick him,' said PC 2630 to his colleague. 'Section 25, refusing to give his details.'

I was searched in front of the crowd of more than fifty who had encircled us. Then I was handcuffed before being arrested and led away. The actions of the police that day seemed extraordinary, designed to make me appear to be a dangerous criminal rather than someone who had been stopped for having a defective brake light. I knew that meant I was being arrested for failing to give my home address. As if to embarrass me further in front of so many people, PC 2630 then lifted the bonnet of the car and checked chassis and engine numbers suggesting to everyone watching that the car I had been driving was a stolen vehicle. As I was put into the back of the police car and taken to the station I knew that I had been deliberately targeted once again by the Northumbria Police. I could not believe that all this palaver had taken place simply because I had a defective brake light. I knew that in the great majority of such cases police would simply advise a motorist to replace the bulb and leave it at that. But worse would follow. At the station I was, as is customary, taken before the custody officer and details of the offense were read out.

'Put him in a cell,' said the custody officer.

'What?' I asked, a note of startled surprise in my voice.

'Put him in a cell,' repeated the officer.

I couldn't believe it, shaking my head in disbelief as I was led away. For one hour I was detained in the cell, treated like a common criminal and made to feel I had no rights under the law. And yet I had done nothing wrong. In law, I was perfectly entitled to give my solicitor's address and those two officers had no right to arrest me. Fortunately, someone called a superintendent for advice and I was ordered to be released after receiving a verbal caution. The following morning I returned to the police station and asked Inspector Bray to check and retain the video from the council's CCTV that monitored the area where the police stopped me. I told him the videotape would provide full evidence of what occurred at the scene. He readily agreed to do so. What he didn't know was that I had deliberately stopped my car under the CCTV camera so that it would record the actions of the police officers. My solicitor also wrote to the officer in charge of the station asking him to retain the videotape as evidence. Two weeks later I received a phone call from a police inspector saying that, unfortunately, the videotape had been recycled by accident a week after the incident and, as a result, the recording had been lost. Not for one minute did I believe that cock-and-bull story, but there was nothing I could do. As I drove home I wondered whether this would be the start of another 'Get Marty' campaign. I didn't have to wait long.

The following week I had to appear at Newcastle Magistrates Court to answer a charge – another trumped-up charge – of 'using threatening, abusive or insulting words' under Section 5 (1) during an incident which had taken place six months earlier at 1:55 in the morning in the center of Newcastle-upon-Tyne in April 1998. During the day-long court hearing, both police officers gave evidence as well as my friend Usher, who had been driving the vehicle when we were stopped. But in court the police officers gave conflicting evidence, made to look like fools or liars as they told stories contradicting each other.

Giving evidence on oath, PC 3586 Milne said the car was stopped because it was being driven 'erratically', and yet PC 335 Webster who knew me very well later told the court that the car was being driven 'normally' but had been stopped because he thought it was strange for two young men to be driving around the center of Newcastle at that time in the morning. I had never heard anything so daft. On a Friday night the center of Newcastle is crowded with young people, the streets busy with traffic. Then PC Webster came to the nub of the charge, claiming I shouted, 'Don't get into the car with those fucking pigs.' As a result of that police allegation I was arrested for using abusive language.

The two officers were made to look rather foolish once more when they were asked how I was taken to the police station. PC Webster said that I was taken away in the back of a police van; PC Milne said I had been taken back to the station handcuffed to him and sitting in the back of the police car while PC Webster drove the car. The prosecution solicitor looked highly embarrassed.

In evidence, I told the court that I would never use the words 'pigs' in relation to the police for one very good reason. In Northern Ireland we always called the police 'peelers'; a 'pig' in Belfast is a vehicle called an APC – an armored personnel carrier. I knew that on that occasion I had been arrested for no valid reason whatsoever and yet I was taken to Pilgrim Street Police Station and left in the cells for three hours. But, I won the day. After retiring for thirty minutes the magistrates found me 'not guilty'. I had no doubt that the two officers had committed perjury that day.

Even more disturbing was the action taken by the Crown Prosecution Service one week before that case came to court. In late September 1998, the CPS wrote to my solicitors advising them that they were laying a further charge against me which they would raise at the start of the hearing. No such suggestion had been made to my solicitor at any time during those previous five months. The CPS had suddenly decided to accuse me of 'violent behavior in a police station' contrary to Section 29 of the Town Police Clauses

Act of 1847. My solicitor was taken aback by this extraordinary news for hardly anyone has been prosecuted under that particular Act for decades!

The CPS were being both devious and shameless for throwing that charge at me, for this is a charge which a defendant finds almost impossible to win. A single police officer has only to state what he saw or believes and his evidence will automatically be accepted against the defendant's word. No witnesses or corroborative evidence are required to support the police officer's evidence. It seemed obvious the CPS believed they had found a way of winning a conviction against me and, thereby, blackening my name. Once again the magistrates proved their honesty and independence, refusing to give permission for the case to go ahead at such short notice. What seemed extraordinary and disturbing however, was the fact that the Crown Prosecution Service, or their advisers, would go to such lengths to win a conviction against me. I knew that I had never used violent language or behavior in the police station and yet, someone of authority had gone to the trouble to persuade a police officer to give evidence on oath and perjure himself, in a rash, ill-advised attempt to gain a conviction against me. I felt the whole idea of such a prosecution stank, the entire CPS plan a corruption of the legal system. A question always remained at the back of my mind: who were the guilty men prepared to go to such lengths to get me? I had my suspicions but no proof. I knew whoever was ultimately responsible needed to have extraordinary power if they could tamper so outrageously with the justice system, persuading, or perhaps ordering, the Crown Prosecution Service to take whatever action they requested or demanded. I would sometimes lie awake at night convinced I had become paranoid though my solicitor reassured me that my concerns were not groundless.

My endless stream of legal problems was nothing compared to those I had unintentionally inflicted upon my family back in Belfast. Of course I had been ridden by guilt when I heard how my courageous brother Joseph had been taken from his home by a PIRA punishment team, tied up and bundled in the back of a van;

taken to a lonely spot; tied to a fence and mercilessly beaten with iron bars and baseball bats. The reason: he was my brother. According to the twisted thinking of PIRA discipline bosses, that was sufficient reason for these sick people to vent their anger on him, simply because they couldn't find me and kill me. The night I heard what happened to my brother I cried like a small boy, feeling so helpless and so very, very guilty.

On the night of Wednesday, October 7, 1998, my sister, Elizabeth, was at her home in Moyard Crescent, West Belfast, with three of her six children asleep upstairs when a noise began outside her house. She heard the chant 'Drug Dealers Out', and went to investigate. Outside her home she found a group of about 200 men and women, some holding placards demanding 'Drug Dealers Out', and she asked them what they were doing, waking her children. The crowd also chanted 'McGartland Out', using her maiden name, my name.

The demonstrators claimed they were holding a peaceful demonstration on the estate demanding that everyone involved in drug dealing must leave the area or take the consequences. No one, however, explained what those consequences might be. And yet Elizabeth recognized only one or two people from her estate; the rest were PIRA members or well-known Republicans. Fortunately, Elizabeth, who is 34, is a strong no-nonsense woman, so she castigated the crowd, yelling back at them that she had never taken a drug in her life nor had anything to do with buying or selling drugs. She told them all to go away and stop their trouble-making. Hearing of the commotion, our mother Kate, now in her fifties and a grandmother ten times over, left her home and pushed her way to the front of the crowd, shielding her daughter from the mob. My mother has an awesome reputation in West Belfast, known for speaking her mind with authority and, if necessary, giving abuse to those who dare challenge her. Indeed, in her younger days, Kate had been known more than once to fell a man with a right cross for daring to challenge her.

'Go to hell,' Kate yelled at the crowd as soon as she arrived on the scene. 'Leave my Liz alone,' she shouted, 'and fuck off back to your homes.'

It was only after Elizabeth told the mob that she would move out the following day that they stopped their chanting and moved away. Later, Elizabeth told me how she had sat up all night fearing an attack from a PIRA punishment squad, scared that PIRA might deal with her or her children in the same way as they had smashed the legs and ribs of our brother Joseph. The following day, Elizabeth and her children were escorted to a hostel where they stayed until alternative housing could be arranged. Her new address would never be revealed.

I knew that Elizabeth, who had recently separated from her husband, had never had anything whatsoever to do with drugs. The RUC also issued a statement saying they had never received any intelligence that Mrs. Elizabeth Lindsay had any drug connection. She had enough on her hands caring for six children, especially since splitting with her husband. I knew the cowardly Provisional IRA were behind the so-called demonstration. I was convinced, and so were the Special Branch, that poor Elizabeth and her family had been targeted only because of me, and I wondered when the IRA and its supporters would cease to target my defenseless family.

Six months after the Good Friday agreement had been signed by all parties complete with the Mitchell principles of no attacks and no intimidation against any members of the community, the violent men continued their cowardly attacks with impunity. To many people in Republican areas of Belfast and Derry it seemed that nothing had changed, the hard men behaved in the way they had for decades, policing and disciplining their communities with rods of iron and baseball bats. And their political leaders did nothing whatsoever to stop their wicked behavior. Nor, it seemed, were those government departments responsible for implementing the Good Friday agreement prepared to take any action to ensure that men of violence finally stopped their punishment beatings. Indeed, it seemed that all the British government really wanted was a political settlement, leaving the families of those people living and suffering under the paramilitary organizations on both sides of the sectarian divide helpless and adrift. To many ordinary people living on the housing estates of Belfast and Derry, the Good Friday agreement was nothing more than a sick political joke, leaving them the hapless victims.

My battles to unravel the truth about the treatment and harassment I have experienced have continued unabated. Various government authorities and their agencies appear to be doing their damnedest to conceal the facts and obstruct my legitimate demands. Even today, seven years after my alleged abduction, no one has the honesty or the courage to tell me why I have been singled out for such treatment when all I tried to do for four years was to save people's lives on behalf of the British government.

And today the various government agencies, in particular the RUC and the Northumbria Police, probably orchestrated by MI5, are keeping up their war of attrition against me. I know I am still 'at risk' from certain elements inside the Provisional IRA who want revenge, but I also realize that I am at risk from those forces advising the British government, and their various agencies, who want to plague my life. I want both the Provos and the British government to realize one simple fact – that while I have even one breath in my body I will fight them at every turn.

June 18, 1999

EPILOGUE

Two years, and just over two months after the Northumbria Police revealed my real name and secret address in open court, an IRA active unit struck. I walked out of my current address in Whitley Bay during the early morning hours and checked the lane for strangers, but saw no one. I opened the up-and-over garage door and looked under the car checking for UCBTs (under car booby traps). But there were none. I had carried out this routine every morning since moving to the mainland from Northern Ireland in October 1991. I never got into the car without first checking for UCBTs; I never walked outside my front door without first checking to see if any strangers were about. I knew in my heart that one day the Provos would try to kill me, that it was just a matter of when. I hadn't believed the Northumbria Police when they said I was in no danger of attack. I hadn't believed Home Secretary Jack Straw who considered that I was at 'minimal risk', nor did I believe the Crown Prosecution Service who revealed in open court that I was in little danger. I had lived and worked with the Provos for two years. I knew and understood their way of thinking and their determination to kill anyone who dared to infiltrate their organization and feed information to the Special Branch in efforts to thwart the assassinations and bombing of innocent people.

That Thursday morning in June I unlocked the car door, got

inside and started the engine. But before I could close the door I sensed someone was nearby. I looked up and saw a man with a green coat pointing a gun at me. Instinctively, I raised my right arm to protect myself. A split second later, I felt two thuds hit my right side, the shock reverberating throughout my body. I knew in that instant that this gunman was a Provo assassin and from the impact the bullets made on my body, I guessed he was using a heavy caliber round, probably a 9 mm fired from an automatic. But thank God, my brain was still working and I remained aware that I had to stop him from shooting me again. I knew he would go for my head; I knew he would have been told where to target and what to do. I knew the Provo orders - always shoot people in the head because then you know they are dead men. And dead men can't talk.

The power of the shots had thrown my body across the seat to the passenger side and the assassin stretched out his arm so that his gun was close to my head. Before he could pull the trigger, I somehow managed to grab the barrel of the gun with my left hand and it went off, the bullet ripping through my hand and lodging in my stomach. I tried to keep hold of the gun. Something inside my head told me that I had to keep hold of it if I was to survive. I wanted to turn the gun so that if he pulled the trigger he would shoot himself. But my strength was fading fast. I felt suddenly powerless, almost at his mercy. I tried to hang onto the gun but I couldn't. With a concerted tug he managed to wrench the weapon from my hand. At that instant I believed I was a dead man. But the will to survive, to live another day, took over and something stirred deep inside me. I wasn't finished yet. I tried to lunge towards him again, to grab the gun, but I simply didn't have the strength. He stepped back a pace and fired four more times hitting me twice in the chest, in the stomach and in the top of the leg. I heard the 'tap-tap' of the automatic and two bullets thudded into my chest with real force. The pain surged throughout my body and the power of those bullets sent me sprawling backwards across the car seats. I thought he had shot me in the heart and I knew that would be curtains. Before

I could sit up I heard the sound of two more 'tap-taps' and I felt pain in my stomach and in the top of my leg. I could do nothing to protect myself. I couldn't move. I was now at his mercy. This was the end. I thought in that split second that I didn't want to die, sprawled on the front seat of a car, my body punctured with bullets from a Provo gunman. My mind flashed to the number of times I had seen others killed this way in Northern Ireland over the years - their dead, broken bodies sprawled grotesquely in the cars they were driving. Something told me that I had to survive.

For what seemed like minutes I waited for more bullets, but there were none. I looked up and he had gone, disappeared from sight. Convinced that he had carried out his mission, certain that I was dead, the bastard had fled. I realized that grabbing the gun had so disoriented the Provo gunman that he had panicked. It took me a couple of seconds to collect my thoughts. I guessed he wouldn't return for he must have thought with seven rounds inside me from something like a 9 mm automatic I hadn't a hope in hell of surviving. I wasn't too sure myself at that stage. Now the pain began to take over, wracking my chest, my side, my stomach and my leg. I looked at my thumb hanging by a thread and repeated over and over: 'fuck, fuck, fuck, fuck.' Somehow, swearing like that helped me get my head together. I told myself that I was alive and if I could stay alive until I got to hospital I would be okay. But how the hell could I get to hospital like this? I thought of trying to drive and then told myself I was being stupid. I hoped to hell someone had heard the sound of shots. As I struggled to get out of the car, to get help, I felt again the thudding impact of the bullets each time they hit my body, knocking me backwards, knocking the stuffing out of me, preventing me from lunging at him and getting the gun. I managed to pull myself out of the car and then I collapsed onto the ground. I knew I had been shot six or seven times, but I was still breathing, although blood was pumping from my chest, side, and stomach and my thumb looked as though it had been shot away. My only fear was that I would lie in that garage and bleed to death. I put my arm across my chest to stop the blood from gushing out but it was everywhere. I wondered if the Provo bastard had hit my heart or a main artery and realized that above all I had to stay conscious. I tried to feel my heart to see if it was okay and it was pumping away. But I worried as I feared all the blood was being pumped out of my body instead of around my arteries. I kept telling myself that no matter what happened I must not fall asleep although I felt like closing my eyes and drifting off into oblivion. I kept talking to myself, saying over and over again, 'if you fall asleep you will never wake again. If you fall unconscious you will simply die. Now, for fuck's sake, keep awake.' And then I felt pain. A minute or so must have passed since the Provo bastard had run off, and, until that moment there had been little pain. Now the pain wracked my body, my chest, my side, my stomach, my arm and my hand. Shit, it hurt. I grit my teeth to try and stop the pain from getting to me so much but I couldn't. I kept talking to myself, telling myself that I could handle the pain as long as I lived. I kept repeating these words to myself, but the pain was getting to me. I just wanted to curl up and sleep. I also knew that if I didn't get to hospital quickly I would die. I tried to shout for help but the words wouldn't come, only moans came from my throat. Alone in that garage, with the blood pouring out of my chest, side, and stomach, I felt my life was over. The bastard Provos had got their revenge.

Then I heard voices shouting 'Marty' and it was the most glorious sound in my life. Now there was hope. I managed to open my eyes and through blurred vision I recognized my neighbors, the Connon family, bending over me and asking if I was all right. Jesus, it was good to see them; I could have cried when I realized they had come to the rescue, had come to help me. I knew the whole family. They were good, honest people and I knew in that instant they would help and save me. Somewhere in my mind I recalled that their elder son Adam, aged around eighteen, had studied first aid and that his mother was something to do with a hospital. I heard them asking questions and I can't recall if I replied or not. My memory was going and so was my brain. I think I murmured 'fucking Provos'. 'Keep quiet, stay still,' Adam said. 'An ambulance is on the way. Just lie still and you'll be okay.' Adam took off my T-shirt and someone ran off and returned with cling film which he wrapped around my chest and my side in an effort to stop the bleeding. I remember him stuffing socks into my wounds trying to stop the flow of blood that was everywhere. I recall his mother Andrea cradling my head in her arms, talking to me, soothing me, keeping me conscious as we awaited the ambulance. I owe my life to that family, particularly Adam. If it hadn't been for his quick thinking I probably would be dead. The next thing I remember was waking up in the hospital some two days later, drifting in and out of consciousness. My mother Kate, sister Lizzie and brother Joseph were standing around my bed and I wondered why they were there as though this was all part of a dream. I couldn't understand what they were doing there, standing at the end of my bed, looking at me. I asked if I was going to live. They gave me the answer I wanted to hear and I drifted once more into unconsciousness. Five days after the shooting I was still in intensive care guarded around the clock by seven armed police officers, all wearing body armor. Ten days later I was moved from the hospital to a safe-house but I was still under armed guard.

For two years I had pleaded with the Northumbria Police and Home Secretary Jack Straw to give me some protection but they had always refused, saying I was in no danger from the IRA. They even refused to give me any CCTV system (closed circuit television system) to check outside my house for suspicious strangers. And yet my former friends in Northern Ireland's Special Branch knew differently. They knew my life was under threat even though there was a so-called cease-fire, even though peace talks were due to start within days, attended by both Prime Minister Tony Blair and the Irish Prime Minister Bertie Aherne. The Belfast SB knew I was still high on the IRA's death list. But the Northumbria Police and the Home Secretary chose to ignore their advice. If they had listened to those senior officers who know the minds of those hard-line IRA activists, the protection I would have been awarded would have prevented me from being shot. I was never cavalier about my security. I always knew that sometime, somewhere, the IRA would have another go at me. And I was determined to make sure they didn't get me. After the Good Friday Peace Agreement was signed in 1998 I had high hopes that one day I would be able to lead a normal, ordinary life: get a proper job, enjoy my life a little without the constant worry of waiting for the unexpected, the knock at the door, a bullet in the back or a gunman waiting by the garage to kill me. The longer the peace deal was intact the more my hopes rose. Then Eamonn Collins, a self-confessed IRA killer who turned against the terrorist movement, was murdered by the Provos. At the time of his shooting I made a statement saying, 'Now I feel like I am waiting for someone to come to my house and shoot me.' I tackled Sinn Fein President Gerry Adams during a radio talk show earlier this year asking him when Sinn Fein/IRA were going to allow people like me to return to safety in Northern Ireland without fear of reprisals. His answer was evasive. That too made me realize that I had to keep my wits about me. I also heard in May that MI5 had warned senior politicians, including several Northern Ireland Home Secretaries, to exercise extra care over security for they feared the Provos were intent on launching a new wave of violence. But no one warned me. My Ma told me when she saw me lying in hospital with bullet wounds all over my body, 'Marty, you can't go on like this. You've got to get away. You know the Provos will never give up trying to kill you, peace or no peace.' I know she's right, my Ma was always right. Now I must persuade the Home Secretary and the Northumbria Police to listen, take note, and give me some protection.